BREAKDOWN *and* RECOVERY

THE INEFFECTIVE SOLDIER

Lessons for Management and the Nation

THE LOST DIVISIONS

BREAKDOWN AND RECOVERY

PATTERNS OF PERFORMANCE

BREAKDOWN
and RECOVERY

by Eli Ginzberg

John B. Miner, James K. Anderson,

Sol W. Ginsburg, M.D., John L. Herma

With a Foreword by
Howard McC. Snyder, Major General, MC, USA

GREENWOOD PRESS, PUBLISHERS
WESTPORT, CONNECTICUT

Library of Congress Cataloging in Publication Data

Ginzberg, Eli, 1911-
        The ineffective soldier.

        Reprint of the ed. published by Columbia University
Press, New York.
        "Investigation ... undertaken by the staff of the
Conservation of Human Resources Project."
        Includes bibliographies and indexes.
        CONTENTS: [1] The lost divisions.--[2] Breakdown and
recovery.--[3] Patterns of performance.
        1. United States. Army--Recruiting, enlistment, etc.
--World War, 1939-1945. 2. United States. Army--
Personnel management. 3. Psychiatry, Military--Cases,
clinical reports, statistics. 4. Soldiers--United

States. 5. Manpower--United States. I. Columbia Uni-
versity. Conservation of Human Resources Project.
II. Title.
[UB323.G5 1975]   355.2'2   75-29042
ISBN 0-8371-7812-6

Reprinted in 1975 by Greenwood Press,
a division of Williamhouse-Regency Inc.

Library of Congress Catalog Card Number 75-29042

ISBN 0-8371-7812-6 (Set)
ISBN 0-8371-8468-1 (Vol. II-Breakdown and Recovery)

Printed in the United States of America

To

Dwight David Eisenhower

CONSERVATION OF HUMAN RESOURCES

The Conservation of Human Resources Project was established at Columbia University by General Eisenhower in 1950. It is a cooperative research undertaking involving the University, the business community, foundations, trade unions, and the Federal Government. Since 1955 the Project has been under the administrative supervision of Dr. John A. Krout, Vice President of the University.

SPONSORING ORGANIZATIONS

American Can Company
Bigelow-Sanford Carpet Company
Cities Service Company
Cluett, Peabody and Company
Columbia Broadcasting System
Consolidated Edison Company of New York
Continental Can Company
E. I. du Pont de Nemours and Company
General Dynamics Corporation
General Electric Company
General Foods Corporation
Radio Corporation of America
Standard Oil Company (New Jersey)
The Coca Cola Company
The New York Community Trust

In addition to the foregoing, the Ford Foundation has also contributed toward the financing of the Conservation of Human Resources.

STAFF

ACKNOWLEDGMENTS

THE CASE MATERIALS presented in this volume were derived from four sources: the personnel and medical records of men who had served in the Army; their claims, medical, and training records in the Veterans Administration; official and unofficial histories of the military units with which these men served during the war; and the replies of these men to our questionnaire. This volume could never have been prepared without the wholehearted co-operation of all concerned, in particular the Department of the Army and the Veterans Administration.

At all levels the assistance provided by the Department of the Army was outstanding. The then Chief of Staff, General J. Lawton Collins, authorized an exception to existing regulations and granted designated representatives of the Conservation Project access to individual medical and personnel records and directed that they be given every assistance practicable. The then Adjutant General, Major General Edward F. Witsell, made available the full resources of his Office, including specifically the Army Personnel Records Center in St. Louis. His successors, Major Generals William E. Bergin, John A. Klein, and H. M. Jones likewise rendered the Project's staff every possible assistance.

We wish to acknowledge specifically the help received from the Statistics and Accounting Branch of the Adjutant General's Office and its Machine Records Unit which prepared the extensive rosters of names from which our samples were subsequently drawn. The Personnel Records Center not only located records of men included in the sample but assigned personnel to abstract the information which we required. The Chief Clerk of the Demobilized Personnel Records Branch, Mr. Joseph Maley, and his successor,

Miss Melva Mae Doyle, provided technical advice in setting up the processing operation, supervised during the two-year period the abstracting of the case materials, and assumed responsibility for clarifying obscure and verifying questionable data.

The assistance and cooperation which we received from the Veterans Administration was likewise outstanding. The Administrator of Veterans Affairs, Carl R. Gray, Jr. and his successor, H. V. Higley, authorized our access to the veterans' records and provided for the temporary transfer of relevant files to New York City to facilitate our review of them. H. L. Peck, then Acting Chief of the Procedures Division, coordinated our roster requests in Washington, D.C. C. J. Reichert, Manager of the New York Regional Office, and members of his staff helped in a great many ways to speed our abstracting and evaluating the materials contained in the voluminous records.

We also wish to express our appreciation to C. E. Dornbusch, of the staff of the New York Public Library, not only for his personal assistance in helping us to use the military unit histories but for his foresight and imagination over the years in establishing such an outstanding collection in New York City. And we are deeply indebted to the many veterans who answered our questionnaire. Their detailed replies and comments were most helpful.

Douglas W. Bray, now Personnel Research Supervisor of the American Telephone and Telegraph Company, was a member of the Conservation Project for five years, during which he assisted in designing the framework and methodology used in the present volume.

Ruth Szold Ginzberg edited the entire manuscript and added substantially to its readability. Jeanne Tomblen typed the successive copies of the manuscript.

CONTENTS

FOREWORD

BACKGROUND INFORMATION regarding the origin of the Conservation of Human Resources Project, the research objectives, and working methods were set forth briefly in the foreword to the first of this three-volume series reporting the investigations into personality and performance by the staff of the Project.

In introducing this second volume, it may be helpful for me to recall that one of the reasons which led General Eisenhower to establish the Conservation of Human Resources Project at Columbia University in 1950 was his belief that the opportunity to make use of the large repository of military personnel records of World War II should not be ignored.

General Eisenhower believed that the Project could uncover the causes of the major deficiencies in the nation's human resources that World War II revealed. It was his hope that as new knowledge was acquired, constructive social action would follow.

A major concern, therefore, of the Conservation of Human Resources Project has been to discover why during World War II about 2.5 million men were rejected for military service or, after having been accepted, were prematurely separated because they were suffering from a mental or emotional disorder.

In my early discussions with the staff it seemed wise to all of us to call upon a number of distinguished psychiatrists who had served in responsible positions during World War II for a reappraisal of their experiences. The results of this inquiry were published in 1953 under the title *Psychiatry and Military Manpower Policy: A Reappraisal of the Experience in World War II*. This work threw a new light upon many problems which up until then had been erroneously assessed.

The Project has earlier published two studies in which specific use has been made of the personnel records of the Armed Services during that war. The first, *The Uneducated,* reviewed the important relations found to exist between a man's education and his ability to perform effectively in military and civilian life. *The Negro Potential* dealt with a related theme—the way in which a man's racial status affects his performance in both civilian and military life, and the changes required in the behavior of both the white and Negro populations before the potentialities of our 17 million Negro citizens can be fully realized. I have been pleased and encouraged with the response to these studies, each soundly grounded in the facts, constructive, and yet free of sentimentality.

Research into many other facets of human behavior uncovered a wealth of material which was pertinent to an overall analysis of the causes for the lack of effectiveness of millions of young Americans for military service. It is only now, nine years after the inauguration of the Project, that the staff is able to present the results of this comprehensive investigation in three separate yet related volumes under the overall title of *The Ineffective Soldier: Lessons for Management and the Nation.* The first volume, *The Lost Divisions,* presents the mass of statistical data where a careful and thorough study is made of the reasons why so many broke down in service and the impact of Army personnel policies and procedures on the performance of soldiers.

The third volume in the series, *Patterns of Performance,* makes use of both statistical and case materials to illuminate not only the breakdown of men in military service but also their performance after their return to civilian life. In addition, it contains the major recommendations for policy growing out of the entire investigation.

This helps me to set out briefly the purpose and limits of the present volume, *Breakdown and Recovery.* The staff early reached

the conclusion that the unraveling of so complex a phenomenon—
that during World War II about 1 out of every 7 young men between the ages of eighteen and thirty-seven was adjudged to be ineffective because of an emotional or educational disability could not
be adequately illuminated by relying solely on a statistical or a
clinical analysis. From the start, General Eisenhower had stressed
the value of studying soldiers who had encountered difficulties in
the Army in an attempt to discover what lay behind their ineffective performance. The staff seized the opportunity to make
systematic use of the extensive biographical materials contained in
the case records of ineffective soldiers to illuminate crucial aspects
of a man's performance in military and civilian life.

The Conservation staff has not been primarily interested in studying the war episode for itself—important as it is—or even to contribute what it could to the improvement of military manpower
policy—important as that would be. It has had a broader objective—
to advance the frontiers of knowledge about human resources by
making use of the unique materials which accumulated during
World War II by the screening of 20 million men and the calling
to active duty of 14 million.

This volume is a direct outgrowth of this central objective to
contribute to the advancement of basic understanding about the
development and utilization of human resources. In each of its
studies the Conservation Project has investigated from different
vantage points the factors that advance or retard the ability of persons to meet the performance demands which they encounter, particularly in their work. The more the staff has studied the problem
of performance, the more it has come to realize its complexity. As
all of us know who have had to struggle with ineffective performance in large organizations, military or civilian, the major challenge
is first to identify the wide range of factors that are operative and
secondly to determine how they can be constructively controlled.

It may be of interest to the reader to know the origin of the
case materials which form the core of this volume. The Army keeps

on permanent file the basic medical and personnel records of all soldiers. The Adjutant General of the Army retained a five percent sample of the separation cards of men discharged during World War II. These cards, totaling more than half a million, gave the staff a key to the sampling of the detailed records. The staff limited its basic investigation to individuals who entered the Army during the last four months of 1942 and who were separated prior to demobilization because of psychoneurosis, psychosis, inaptness, or undesirability.

One of the more striking aspects of the study is the care which the Conservation staff took to assemble as comprehensive a record as possible. In building up each case, information was abstracted from the soldier's service record, his hospital records, and from the proceedings of the board which acted on his separation as well as from other relevant sources. These military data have been supplemented for the postwar period by information obtained from the Veterans Administration, where the medical, claims, counseling, educational and training records of these men were abstracted through 1953. Since a considerable number failed to make much use of the Veterans Administration, the staff sent a questionnaire in 1954 to all about whom it lacked adequate information.

The life histories presented in this volume do not pretend to be representative of the controlled sample, and still less of the ineffective soldiers of World War II. They have been selected specifically to illuminate one or another of the strategic factors in effective or ineffective performance. Hence the primary criterion governing the inclusion of a case has been the fullness and adequacy of the materials to contribute to a deeper understanding of performance.

While the case material has been assembled from objective records, the staff could not test directly the validity of the original entries. But I have no reason to question their basic soundness. Wherever serious doubts arose about the accuracy of the information, the case was eliminated. I hope that the reader will appreciate, as I am sure that he will, the care that the staff has taken to avoid inflicting technical terms on him while keeping as close as possible to the language in the original records. Not the least of the merits of this volume is its readability.

HOWARD McC. SNYDER
Major General, MC, USA
Personal Physician
to the President

The White House
Washington, D.C.
February 1959

BREAKDOWN *and* RECOVERY

Chapter One: THE DETERMINANTS
OF PERFORMANCE

MAN HAS ALWAYS speculated about exceptional performance on the part of his fellow men. The ancients ascribed a man's unusual powers to a special dispensation from the gods, and thus explained both the genius and the insane. In the Middle Ages the artist as well as the mentally unbalanced were assumed to have lost their souls to the devil.

In each generation, fascination with the superior performer has continued, though the explanations have varied in accordance with the changing styles of thought. The contemporary world is no exception, but we have been more concerned with ineffective performers—juvenile delinquents, criminals, alcoholics, the mentally ill—than we have been with superior performers.

With the development of the scientific method, the old explanations, which relied on the intervention of supernatural forces, gave way to naturalistic social theories. Emphasis came to be placed on hereditary or environmental influences. The first treated superior or ineffective performance primarily in terms of unusual genetic endowment; the second centered on the influence of the environment in facilitating or handicapping an individual's development. More recently the proponents of either heredity or environment as explanations of performance have begun to modify their extreme positions and now believe that a better understanding of unusual performance can probably be achieved only by ascribing a causative role to both factors simultaneously.

As part of the new approach the concept of genetic endowment has been replaced by that of predisposition, which emphasizes the sum total of the individual's formative experiences. This broadening has resulted in subsuming under the concept of "personality" such diverse facets as the individual's intellectual and other potentials, his acquired skills and competences, the strength of his motivation, his emotional stability, including his tolerance for stress, and his values and other internal forces that condition and guide his behavior.

The concept of environment now covers the wide range of reality factors that broaden or limit the opportunities of the individual to develop and utilize his potentialities effectively. For instance, had it not been for the turmoil and confusion that characterized France in the first decades after the Revolution, Napoleon would not have reached the pinnacle of power and certainly would not have been able to stay there so long. A concatenation of environmental circumstances also gave Hitler his chance—the weakness of the Weimar Republic, Hindenburg's senility, Von Papen's recklessness, and the miscalculation of the industrialists. Hitler could not have acquired the power that he did had these factors not been present. This does not deny that Hitler, despite his psychopathy, possessed personality strengths—his demagogic powers —without which he could not have succeeded no matter how favorable the environment.

A less dramatic example of the influence of the environment on performance is the contrast between a business executive who took over the presidency of a corporation in 1930 and one who assumed office in 1950. The former had to find his way through the worst depression in the country's history; the latter moved in when the economy was at the beginning of eight years of substantially uninterrupted prosperity.

This reference to the business world suggests that we add a third category to the psychological and environmental in our study of performance. So much of a man's life takes place within structured organizations—schools, the Armed Services, the corporation, political parties, clubs, churches—that what he accomplishes or fails to accomplish will depend in considerable measure on the leadership and policies that characterize these organizations. The study of performance must make specific allowance for this managerial factor.

The study of performance even within such a simplified schema as the one outlined above, which relies on the analysis of personality, environmental, and managerial factors, is extremely complex. It is usually very difficult to identify the strategic factors in the performance of a particular individual or group of individuals. And the difficulty of evaluating their performance is compounded by the necessity of tracing the interaction among the strategic factors.

The Army presented a unique laboratory for the study of performance. Its controlled environment characterized by extensive record keeping made it relatively easy to obtain information about a great many men and how they performed under widely different situations. Some readers may feel that the unique demands of a military organization in times of war will preclude applying the findings of military performance to conditions prevailing in civilian life.

Clearly, no democracy can long survive unless its citizens are able to respond to the call of arms when their country is in danger. Meeting the performance demands of war is an obligation of every man. The fact that millions failed to meet these demands during World War II warrants investigation both for what it might contribute to a broader understanding of the qualities of the citizenry and the steps that might be taken to increase their effective performance in military and civilian life.

We must begin, however, by noting the unique aspects of an Army at war. First is the presence of compulsion. Men are not asked whether they want to fight; they are told that they must. The freedom of choice to determine the pattern of one's life—the hallmark of a democracy—is suspended during a war. While injury or death may strike the unsuspecting citizen in peacetime, in war the threat of death and injury can never be banished from a soldier's life. No man, not even the most hardened veteran, ever reconciles himself to them. At best, he can steel himself to endure the danger. But most men, from the day of their induction until their separation, are anxious about the possibility of being injured or killed.

Still another unique aspect of war is the fact that men who have always been encouraged to restrain their aggression are suddenly required to do the opposite—they are trained to kill. Finally, war tears men from their conventional surroundings—from their homes, their families, their jobs, and their friends—and transports them to faraway places where they frequently must live and fight under very adverse conditions.

Such uprooting fortunately has few counterparts in civilian life. Yet there are continuities in a man's life before and after his entrance into military service. His ability to meet the strenuous requirements of Army life will be determined by his physical stamina, technical skill, and emotional stability—factors that helped to determine his adjustment in civilian life. Although separated from his family and friends, he does not live alone in the Army but is a member of a small group from which he frequently derives much support. Then, too, he soon discovers that the Army is formally structured, with rules and regulations, rewards and punishments, much like the company and the community where he formerly worked and lived.

A man's performance in the military will also be influenced by the depth of his convictions. If he is patriotic and has a sense of responsibility towards others, he will do his best to meet the demands made on him, even to the point of sacrificing his life. But if he has been brought up to believe that killing under any circumstances is a sin, he may find himself in such deep conflict that he will be unable to perform effectively.

The biographical materials which have been assembled provide information on the performance of the soldier prior to his induction and his level of adjustment after his return to civilian life. These life histories emphasize that performance is not a stable entity but will vary as changes occur in a man's personality, in the environmental pressures to which he is exposed, and in the organization and leadership to which he must respond.

Although the case materials contain sufficient detail to permit the delineation of a man's performance in different periods of his life, they cannot be used for an exhaustive clinical analysis of the specific factors in the breakdown or recovery of the individual, such as would be of interest to psychiatrists and psychologists. Our aim is at once broader and less deep. We believe that the proper understanding of performance requires a broader framework than that used by psychiatrists when they seek to unravel the source of difficulties in the emotional life of a patient in the hope of contributing to his recovery. Since they are searching for leads which will help them to bring about therapeutic improvement they must concentrate more on psychological factors within the patient himself and relatively less on the environmental and managerial ones.

In presenting our cases we have found it necessary to enlarge the conceptual framework so as to include forces in the larger environment or within the specific organization that help to determine the level of a man's performance. This broadening of the matrix is essential for the social scientist who seeks to understand the strategic factors in breakdown and recovery of large numbers of people.

To facilitate identification of the strategic factors in performance we have developed a schema that is an elaboration and specification of the three major sets of determinants—the psychological, the organizational, and the situational. In placing a case in one or another section of the schema we aim to call the reader's attention to what we believe to be an important factor in performance, without suggesting for a moment that other factors were either absent or unimportant in the specific instance. We are using the case materials to develop a systematic and general framework for the study of performance, not to add to the clinical literature. An illustration may help to make this clear. In one case a soldier with a lifelong phobia of water is torpedoed. Ship is abandoned but he is unable to jump into the ocean until an officer threatens to shoot him. He remains in the water for many hours before being rescued. For many months thereafter he is seriously disturbed.

We present this case to illustrate the influence of a situational factor in the precipitation of ineffective performance. In so doing we do not overlook or minimize the long-standing predisposing emotional difficulties that found expression in the soldier's water phobia.

Our enlarged schema seeks to deal with the problem of performance in its full complexity. A more restrictive approach is likely to lead to faulty policy. As we sought to make clear in the companion volume, *The Lost Divisions*, as long as the Army proceeded on the assumption that only men who were emotionally unstable would break down in service it concentrated on rejecting them at induction. As the war progressed the Army had to acknowledge the fact that even the emotionally stable soldiers could become ineffective if forced to fight under very adverse conditions or even to serve in situations that were particularly upsetting to the individual.

The specific cases which comprise this book have not been selected as a representative sample of soldiers who broke down in service or who after breakdown succeeded in reaching a satisfactory level of performance after their return to civilian life. This is the objective of the companion volume, *Patterns of Performance*, where the materials have been developed with appropriate sampling and control to provide a sound base for policy recommendations aimed at more effective utilization of the nation's manpower. The cases in the present volume have been selected primarily from the viewpoint of their suitability to illuminate a particular facet of the category schema which we have developed to facilitate the systematic study of performance. One guiding consideration in selection has been the fullness of the materials, particularly the follow-up data outlining the soldier's readjustment to civilian life. We believe that the reader will gain a better understanding of the complex nature of performance if he has an opportunity to view it through the life cycle of a man, even if the story cannot be carried to the end. As they are, these life histories are sufficiently unusual to represent a valuable record for all who are interested in the social history of the country.

Our cases illustrate ineffective performance in the military and effective performances in civilian life. An all-inclusive scheme would have necessitated presenting two additional sets of cases—those reflecting successful performance in the military and those reflecting unsuccessful performance in civilian life. It was not practical to do this in this volume. Such cases have been analyzed in *Patterns of Performance*. Among the cases included here, however, are many men who performed successfully in the Army before they broke down; and many veterans who eventually made a good adjustment were unsuccessful in the first years after discharge. Hence some insight into these other situations can be gained from the materials which are presented.

While it was possible to develop a basic schema for the analysis of both ineffective performance in military life and effective performance in civilian life, some variations had to be introduced in the respective categories to reflect differences in the two environments. In studying ineffective performance in military life allowance had to be made for the impact of the Army as such, just as in studying effective performance in civilian life allowance had to be made for the contribution of the veterans organizations to the readjustment of the former serviceman.

In delineating personality factors the category schema makes provision for a consideration of the way in which the strengths and weaknesses of an individual are likely to affect his performance. Every organization has some kind of selection criteria which it hopes will enable it to avoid hiring people who will later prove incapable of effective performance because they lack the physical requirements for the job, the educational or intellectual background that will enable them to master the skills and disciplines required, or because they lack the emotional stability or motivation to perform effectively. The Armed Services, because of their mission, had to pay particular attention to a man's physical stamina.

Of the 18 million younger men who were screened for service, over 3 million were rejected on physical grounds—over 1 in 6. There remain relatively few jobs in industry where the question of a man's physical condition and stamina are of primary importance in determining his ability to meet minimum performance standards.

The Armed Services also have different requirements from most civilian employers with regard to a man's emotional stability or motivation. The danger of being injured or killed in war inevitably heightened the anxiety of those predisposed to worry about themselves. While industry is continually confronted with men who are emotionally unstable, it does not force its employees to work in a situation as disturbing as combat duty. Moreover, men who appear at the factory gate want work. Many who passed through the induction station had little or no motivation to turn themselves into good soldiers. But neither the Armed Services nor civilian employers, no matter how thorough a screening job they do, can effectively exclude all those who are likely to break down; one reason is that men become incapacitated as a result of conditions that they encounter only after they begin to work. A study of performance must therefore make allowance for the ways in which the individual's personal qualities can facilitate or retard his adjustment.

Our second major category refers to the influence of a man's family, parental or connubial, on his ability to perform effectively. Civilian employers have long been aware that many employee problems do not reflect specific work difficulties but are carried from the home into the work place. On the other hand, most employers overlook the contrasting situation where a worker manages to keep going only because of the support that he receives at home.

Military service always alters the relationship of the recruit to his family. Until they were drafted, many young men had never spent a night away from home. Homesickness was a major problem particularly during their basic training. Many married men, especially those who depended heavily on their families for emotional support and encouragement, also found their separation hard to take. Soldiers became seriously upset when they received news from home that things were going badly; some were unable to perform effectively until their home situation began to right itself. While difficulties at home contributed substantially to ineffective performance, most men found military service easier to endure because of the knowledge that their parents, their wives, or their fiancees were deeply concerned about them and were eagerly looking forward to their return. Many who returned to civilian life in an emotionally disturbed state were assisted in their recovery by the loving care and supportive assistance which they received from their families.

Many men in civilian life derive considerable satisfaction from the immediate work group with whom they are in daily association. If they run into conflict with their superiors or fellow workers, they can seek a more congenial job. The immediate group in the Army usually assumed a still more prominent place in the soldier's life. At best, it provided him with meaningful relations that compensated at least partially for his separation from his family. The buddy system is proof of this. But on occasion the immediate group might prove an obstacle rather than a support for the soldier. A recruit assigned to a unit composed of men from a different section of the country, with a noticeably different educational and social background, might find it difficult to be accepted as a part of the group. Or if a man's buddy were injured or killed, he might suddenly find himself alone. The dissolution of a close relationship was often so unsettling that some soldiers avoided entering upon another close relationship. But in general most soldiers required support from their immediate group in order to function effectively. And when their close ties were suddenly severed, many broke down.

We have noted earlier that the adjustment of men is greatly affected by their leaders. Nowhere is this more important than in the Army where a man is under surveillance not for eight hours during five days of the week, but for twenty-four hours, seven days in the week.

Confronted with the need to mobilize and train troops as quickly as possible, the Army adopted policies which would achieve its major objective even if it had to lose many individuals along the way. During the first two years of mobilization it would not adjust its training cycle so as to carry the slow learners. It preferred to separate those who fell behind and to get new men in their place. Frequently there was no opportunity to evaluate recruits carefully before sending them out to fill urgent personnel requisitions. It seemed better to give a commander 1,000 men immediately, even if he eventually had to get rid of 100 or even 200 because they proved ineffective. Pressure of time and shortages of skilled personnel made it very difficult to administer the personnel and medical policies which had such a potent influence on the utilization of manpower. Some men broke down because they were not given a second chance; others would have made the grade had the Army been stricter. Some were forced to stay in the line until they were emotionally exhausted.

In civilian life employees frequently object to the rules and regulations promulgated by management. In unionized and even in nonunionized plants they can make their objections known and often secure a change. If a change is not effected an employee who finds the situation too burdensome can usually leave. If he is an older man or if jobs in his field are scarce, he will have to endure what he finds objectionable. In the Army there was little chance, if any, of escaping from management's decisions. A man could complain about them, but that was all. Although most work even in the civilian sector is formally structured, there are many jobs where the individual who finds it abhorrent to take direct orders can work for himself—in farming, retailing, the professions, and in many service industries. In the Army there was no escape from the hierachial system. Every man had to accept it. There was no place for the individualist.

In civilian life many men who find their jobs unsatisfying continue to perform effectively because they obtain satisfaction in other areas—through membership in a church, political or voluntary organization, through sports, or in other ways. Such outlets were generally not available to the soldier.

The major differences between the civilian and military environments are reflected in our category schema by emphasizing the organizational determinants (the Army) in the study of ineffective performance, and the occupational determinants and the rehabilitative agencies which helped many veterans to readjust to civilian life.

All men live by a scale of values. Even the criminal adheres to a code. Few individuals grow up without some conflict with the values that their parents, their teachers, and the leaders of their community have sought to instill in them. But as the turmoil of adolescence recedes, most men distill for themselves the standards which henceforth will guide their behavior. Their values are central to their lives and if their actions should later conflict with their values, they will become unsettled.

Military service forced men into unusual situations and in the process made great demands on them. The man who was not able to identify with his country's need, who was not able to feel a deep bond with his fellow men, was likely to shirk his responsibilities and become ineffective. Some became ineffective when they found the Army life conflicted with values that were of paramount importance to them; this happened, for instance, when the Northern Negro could not accept the hostile segregation practices to which he was forcibly exposed in the South.

A special order of difficulty was encountered by those with aberrant sexual behavior. As civilians they were usually able to circumvent the negative attitudes towards homosexuality by acting discreetly and keeping their personal lives separate and distinct from their occupational and public lives. But this was much more difficult in an Army which assumed total control over men in uniform. Many homosexuals who became ineffective in the Army were able to make a good recovery once they were discharged to civilian life where they had more scope for working out a tolerable adjustment for themselves.

The final set of determinants relates to the influence of situational stress on the performance of the individual. If submitted to enough pressure even the strongest man will break. The Nazis and the Communists have proved repeatedly the effectiveness of extreme pressure in breaking men. Men who are forced to engage in prolonged combat, especially under unfavorable climatic conditions and difficult terrain, such as confronted the Fifth Army in its fight up the Italian peninsula, will be worn down to a point where they become ineffective. Their inability to escape from a situation where the odds are constantly rising that they will be injured or killed speeds their collapse. Time and again observers were startled by the rapidity with which men who had broken down completely in the midst of a battle recovered their stability as soon as they were removed from danger. Once freed from the dangers inherent in continued military service many men were quickly able to knit themselves together and once again to function effectively.

Situational factors can facilitate as well as impair the ability of an individual to perform effectively. The fact that in the immediate postwar years the economy was expanding rapidly and jobs were easy to obtain undoubtedly eased the readjustment of many veterans.

The category scheme which represents an elaboration of the individual, the organizational, and the situational factors in performance has guided the selection of case materials which will be presented and analyzed. The scope and details of the category scheme are presented in summary form in the analytical Table of Contents.

Chapter Two: THE PERSONALITY

OF THE SOLDIER

BECAUSE of the very wide range of ability among the members of a society, every organization must be selective in hiring individuals. This is true even for a voluntary organization whose aim is to contribute to the social good rather than to make a profit. For unless it is selective, it may find itself dealing with individuals who have such liabilities that they will detract rather than add to its effectiveness. Even a local political club, the ladies' auxiliary of a hospital, or a fresh air fund for poor children, all of which depend primarily on volunteer effort, will do some screening in order to exclude at least the obviously unfit.

Although in World War II the Armed Services had to expand as rapidly as possible, they still had to find time to screen all recruits. There was no profit to their accepting a man who would be unable to meet the strenuous demands that he would encounter once he donned a uniform.

The Army, like a corporation or voluntary organization, was unable to solve all of its personnel problems by screening. Certain facts bearing on a man's future performance are relatively easy to ascertain. But many others are so elusive as to raise serious questions whether the effort to identify them is worthwhile. It was relatively easy for the Army to put a man through a series of physical tests to determine whether he had any obviously disqualifying conditions, such as inadequate eyesight or hearing, heart trouble, or other major defects. It was also relatively easy for the Army to ascertain the level of a man's educational achievement, though somewhat more difficult to appraise his capacity to learn.

But in seeking to predict how a man would respond to military service in general, and to severe stress such as combat in particular, the Army was faced with a major difficulty. If the Army had had ample time and ample personnel to carry out careful psychological evaluations on each selectee it could undoubtedly have done a better job. But both time and personnel were very short.

As business has learned, a willingness to invest heavily in screening does not guarantee that all selected will prove satisfactory. In the first place the market sets limits on how selective a company can be. If it seeks to expand rapidly during a period of full employment, it will have to accept many who are marginal, or not much better. By late 1942 and early 1943 the Army had discovered that if it expected to reach its manpower goals, it had to adjust its selection criteria so as to avoid rejecting too many. The manpower pool was not bottomless.

There is a further reason why screening, no matter how elaborately it is carried out, will not yield completely satisfactory results. Men change with time. They may be well at the time of the examination and take seriously ill the next day, week, month, or year. In assessing the efficiency of a selection procedure allowance must always be made for this eventuality. Moreover, the environment in which he is to operate also changes, and it frequently contains within it assignments of vastly different difficulty. The limitations of screening, because of changes within the man and within the environment, have been dealt with extensively in *The Lost Divisions*.

PHYSICAL CONDITION

It is increasingly clear to all who deal with the sick and injured that no sharp line can be drawn between physical and emotional factors, for each interacts on the other. This interaction was the more pronounced in the Army during the war where all were under heightened orders of stress and many were forced to contend with poor environmental conditions.

The Army sought to reject not only all men with a serious physical condition but also all those who were likely to suffer an aggravation of a minor condition. For if such aggravation occurred the soldier would most probably become ineffective and would further be in a position to claim a pension—possibly for life. This fear of the potential financial liability helps to explain the careful physical screening that some companies continue to engage in, especially for jobs which are hazardous.

In adopting high physical standards the Army also reflected a sense of obligation to the individual citizen. It did not want to force him into uniform if service was likely to result in his physical or emotional breakdown. Further, it did not want to devote time and effort to rehabilitating those below an acceptable level. It finally did so—but reluctantly—in the case of men with venereal disease because the numbers who could be salvaged were large and the treatment relatively simple.

As we have explained in *Patterns of Performance*, our sample was not drawn to include cases of men who were separated from the Army for ineffectiveness growing out of a physical disability. However, we do have case material which shows how a man's physical disability contributed to his ineffectiveness. Two such cases are presented below.

One of nine children, R.D.G. was born and raised in a fairly large urban community in the Ohio Valley. Except for the usual childhood diseases, his early years were uneventful. He completed high school, entered college in the fall of 1929, but had to drop out a year and a half later. He worked at whatever jobs he could get during the depression years and got married. He finally found steady employment with a credit and finance company, working as a clerk, as a cashier, and finally as a credit investigator and collector.

He was drafted late in 1942 and immediately assigned to an ordnance unit. Upon completing his basic training, Private G. was trained as a munitions worker and, later, as a stock records clerk. While a trainee he was hospitalized for a month with a severe throat infection which was diagnosed as tonsillitis; however, his symptoms included severe headaches, high fever, inability to move his jaw, and a ringing in the ears. After returning to duty he was quite weak for a while, had occasional dizzy spells, and once fell to the ground. This condition seemed to clear up and in any event it was not serious enough to affect his work. He proved to be quite a good worker and was soon promoted to corporal; by the time his unit left for duty in the Southwest Pacific in the late spring of 1944 he had been promoted to technical sergeant. Just prior to going overseas he and his wife were divorced.

Overseas, Sergeant G. continued to perform his clerical duties ably, received a "superior" efficiency rating, and after about three months was promoted to first sergeant. Shortly thereafter he began to be bothered with sinus trouble and both his ears became stopped up; in addition, there was a recurrence of his dizzy spells. They became more frequent and he seemed unable to keep his balance. When he noticed that his hearing was also becoming impaired he went to the hospital. The hearing in his left ear grew progressively worse and within a few weeks he was completely deaf in that ear. Because of the inflammation of his inner ear (labyrinthitis), Sergeant G. was evacuated back to the States. Several months of hospitalization followed during which no improvement was noted.

He was released from the hospital for limited service duty in January 1945. Two months later he was back with a low fever, rapid pulse, palpitations, and pains in his chest. Within two weeks he was feeling well again. But since the soldier had mentioned that he had had similar symptoms after exertion for the past seven or eight years and since his blood pressure had remained normal during the course of his hospital stay, the doctors diagnosed his condition as neurocirculatory asthenia and he was discharged as having psychoneurosis in April 1945.

R.D.G. went back to work with his old firm. For several months he could not work steadily because he tired easily and tended to have pains in the chest after a full day's work. He worried about his growing deafness and how it would affect his work. Had it not destroyed his effectiveness as a soldier? Now, would it make him lose his civilian job as well? However, R.D.G. worked hard, encouraged by the fact that his dizzy spells were becoming less frequent. Within two years he was promoted to district manager.

In 1948 he was given an extensive examination by V.A. doctors to see if his disability compensation should be continued. This examination revealed that R.D.G. had total deafness in the left ear and a moderate perceptive deafness in the right ear. The doctors did not believe he had any psychiatric disturbance at this time. In view of his progressive deafness the Veterans Administration increased his compensation to 20 percent. Two years later he was again examined. He was still deaf in his left ear and his right ear now showed a fairly advanced nerve deafness, so that his disability rating was again increased, this time to 40 percent. He does not know how much longer he will be able to work at his job in the face of this physical disability. Already making plans in case he must give it up, he recently purchased a small farm in the valley.

J.E.S. had a difficult childhood. When less than a year old he nearly died of diphtheria. At the age of six he was hit by a car, which fractured his skull and left him unconscious for three days. For almost a year thereafter he was bothered by "double vision" and headaches. When he was nine, his father, a pool room operator and part-time farmer, committed suicide.

The oldest of three boys, J.E.S. had to help support the family, which he did by working as a farm hand. He thereby missed a lot of school and he failed a few courses. One day during high-school football practice he was hit by an older boy and knocked unconscious for two hours. For the next several days he was weak and dizzy, and he again began to be bothered by severe headaches whenever he had a cold or was anxious.

When he was eighteen years old he married a girl of the same age, dropped out of his senior class in high school, and moved to a nearby city. There he got a job as a mechanic's helper with a company which built trailers and tractor bodies. After three years with this firm J.E.S. was well on his way to becoming a skilled mechanic, but he felt that he would have a better opportunity to develop his trade in the Army. Leaving his wife and eighteen-month-old child with his mother and younger brothers, he enlisted in the fall of 1942.

Private S. was assigned to the Air Corps and was stationed at an airbase in the Southwest near his family. Even though he was quite disappointed that he did not get an assignment as a mechanic, he did his work as airfield gasoline truck operator very well. His efficiency during his first year of service was rated as excellent and he appeared to be fairly well satisfied with his assignment. Then one day, while refueling one of the base aircraft, he was struck on the head by the nozzle of the gasoline hose at the same spot which had been fractured in his childhood. Momentarily dazed but not unconscious, he was hospitalized for about a week and returned to duty. During the next month his headaches, which had subsided in the hospital, became more constant and severe. At times he became so dizzy he had to sit down. He again went to the hospital and this time stayed six weeks before he was returned to duty. The doctors considered his concussion mild and believed a large part of his symptoms to be due to anxiety hysteria.

For the next two years, J.E.S., by then a private first class, was never free of a constant dull ache in his head. Exertion or heat sharpened the pain. It became more and more difficult for him to perform his duties, but since he did his job and did not report to the dispensary, his superiors continued to rate his efficiency as excellent but did not promote him. In the summer of 1945, shortly after being reassigned for the first time, his headaches seemed to grow worse. He was tense, suffered from nightmares, and began to walk in his sleep as he had as a child. He reported to the dispensary and was finally hospitalized for observation. After six weeks in the hospital, during which no organic basis for his headaches could be found, he was released for limited service duty. However, he was unable to perform even light duty because of his constant headaches. He was again hospitalized and this time he was discharged a month after V-J Day with a diagnosis of psychoneurosis, severe anxiety state.

After his discharge J.E.S. returned to farming, taking the advice of an Army doctor who felt that he would better be able to handle his blackout attacks in such a situation. He was not particularly happy in farming; he wanted to work as a mechanic. The next fall, after having farmed for about eight months, he went back to his old job as a mechanic with the same truck body company for which he had worked before the war. But he was unable to work at his old trade. The noise made his headaches worse and his dizzy spells made it dangerous for him to work around machinery. So J.E.S. had to return to farming. Even this work was difficult for him. Most of the time he could work only a few hours a day because when he became overheated his dizzy spells came back. Nevertheless, he continued to do his best. He completed a basic farm management program in 1949 and later entered and completed satisfactorily an advanced farm management program. With the vocational assistance and guidance he was receiving under Public Law 16 he built his dairy farm up to 100 acres and acquired tractors and other necessary farm equipment. He is now making a satisfactory living from his farm and adequately supporting his wife and three children. But even today he is not able to work long periods at a time and must rest every few hours to keep from fainting.

The Veterans Administration, which has provided him 30 percent disability compensation ever since his discharge from the Army, considers his condition due to traumatic encephalopathy. However, J.E.S. is not bitter about his injury or about how it has affected his work and his occupational plans. As he put it, "The thing that happened was something I couldn't help or the Army couldn't either. I think it was a grand Army."

Both of these cases underscore how physical defects of a recurrent or progressively chronic nature can interfere seriously with the performance of men with a previously excellent record. They further illustrate the difficulties which physicians sometimes experience in arriving at diagnoses of illnesses where emotional and physical symptoms are commingled.

INTELLIGENCE

Every employer needs men who have skills which will enable them to perform their assignments effectively or who have the capacity to learn rapidly what is required of them. An employee to be successful must be able not only to perform his specific tasks but also to adjust to the rules and regulations that are part of every large organization.

One of the difficulties that the Army encountered in assessing whether a man had the ability to become an effective soldier was to distinguish between those whose intellectual deficiencies were the result of their failure to attend school and those who failed to learn because they were actually mentally deficient. By making a special investment the Army might bring the former to a satisfactory level but special efforts would be of no avail for men who were incapable of learning. As the war progressed, the Army refined its testing instruments to a point where it was able to distinguish more sharply between these two groups. Moreover, by the middle of 1943 it had moved to establish an effective system of special training units for remedial work with the more promising of the educationally deprived inductees.

The recruit was under considerable pressure to learn many new things quickly. If he came from a rural background and had had no prior experience with large organizations, he might be unnerved during his early weeks in the Army. It was often difficult to distinguish between the intellectually dull and those who were emotionally upset. The more limited a man's intelligence, the more likely that he would feel swamped by the multiple demands that he encountered immediately upon entrance into military service. The more intelligent the man, other things being equal, the easier his adjustment.

Although T.W.P. attended the local schools in a Midwestern town until the age of fifteen, he was never able to get beyond the second grade. He seemed completely unable to master even the simplest subject matter. After leaving school, he took a job in a lumber yard shoveling coal and stacking lumber. Since he did not even have sufficient knowledge of arithmetic to handle money, his weekly wage of $16 was turned over to his mother and all necessary purchases were made for him by other members of the family. His brother-in-law frequently took him to see western movies, and this was his major source of enjoyment.

In spite of this rather unpromising background the Army accepted him as an enlistee and Private P., at the age of twenty-one, was shipped to the South for infantry training. He joined an Organized Reserve division which had just been activated and started his training in military drill, rifle care and marksmanship, procedures for standing guard, and all the other skills essential for an infantryman.

However, he soon ran into difficulties. When Private P. was ordered to bring his bedding back inside the barracks after it had been put out for sunning, he did not know which was his. On the drill field he could not execute orders until he had seen the other men in the squad make the appropriate movements. Consequently he was always one step behind the rest. On the range he could not understand the reasons for keeping his rifle aimed toward the targets and finally, after he was observed on one occasion pointing his rifle at the battalion commander, all attempts at training him in marksmanship were discontinued. When he received his first pay, some $50, he became extremely excited and asked the first sergeant to keep his money for him until he could go to town and get two billfolds, since he had too much money for one. Later he asked the first sergeant to take charge of his money just as his mother had prior to his induction.

There were many other situations which were beyond Private P.'s comprehension. Although he had been shown several times how to make his bed, he would still place his comforter on top of the mattress and proceed to make his bed on top of the com-forter. He did not keep himself clean and even when he was placed in the shower by a detail of his barracks mates, he did not know how to use soap. When placed on special details he had to be supervised closely at every step of the task. On one occasion he was told to put toilet paper in holders which were empty. When the sergeant looked in to see how the job was coming, he found that all the paper had been removed from every rack in the latrine. Another time, when ordered to shovel coal into a bin, Private P., calling upon his civilian experience, performed the job success-fully. When he finished, however, he demanded the overtime pay which he felt was due him.

After about a month of such behavior, the company commander referred him to the station hospital for psychological examination. The results indicated that he was functioning at about the intel-lectual level of a seven-year-old child. Accordingly a board of of-ficers was assembled, and, after the presentation of evidence, a dis-charge for inaptness was agreed upon.

Thus, just four months after his induction, T.W.P. returned to his home. Since his discharge he has changed jobs a number of times, and when employed at all, he has worked as a common laborer either on the farm or in the city. During a few months he has earned as much as $40, but usually it has been less. He has never married and would probably be unable to keep going with-out the assistance of his family.

L.R. spent all of his life prior to his induction into the Army in small towns along the southern Mississippi River. Like many of the children in the Negro communities in that region, his schooling was spasmodic and for practical purposes almost nonexistent. His mother died when he was quite young and shortly thereafter the family broke up. He worked at a variety of unskilled jobs, but most frequently as a farm laborer, until drafted into the Army in late 1942 at the age of twenty-nine.

Although held at the induction station for an extra week because of suspected venereal disease, Private R. arrived at his first assignment in time to start training with a newly organized Negro infantry division. Much of his time was spent, however, helping in the company kitchen. His training was further disrupted by a brief, unauthorized trip home which resulted in a summary court-martial with a sentence of thirty days at hard labor. Then, after five months of service and just before his outfit was to move to a camp in the Far West for further training, Private R. disappeared completely from the military scene.

He first traveled almost a thousand miles to Houston, Texas to see a relative who, as he discovered when he arrived, was no longer living there. Bewildered and almost out of funds, he tried to turn himself in to the Military Police at the bus station, but for some reason the MP on duty would not take him into custody. Later he returned to his former environs along the Mississippi, walking most of the way, but occasionally hitchhiking. There he settled down, got married, and worked intermittently picking cotton and in restaurants until March 1946. At that time he was picked up by the Military Police and returned to military control.

The Army's initial intention was to try Private R. for desertion in time of war. However, while in the guardhouse prior to being brought to trial he seemed so bewildered and confused that the prison officer felt a psychiatric consultation was necessary. The psychiatric conclusions follow:

Pvt. R. has adjusted on a very borderline level throughout his life. He is an inadequate, dull, inept, defective, resentful individual, who has a very meager store of cultural and general knowledge. All of his ideas and productions were childish and it was my impression that he was a mental defective. As a result of this I requested that psychometric evaluation be obtained. The result of this examination cannot be given in terms of a specific mental age or intelligence quotient because his mental level is too low to be measured accurately by existing Army methods. Hence I am only able to supply on estimated clinical impression and I place this individual in the mental range of six to seven years.

The doctor's statement went on to suggest that Private R. was in all probability not aware of the consequences of his act of desertion and that accordingly he should be given an honorable discharge for inaptness. Later, while testifying before a board of officers which had been called together for his case, the prisoner seemed to corroborate this medical opinion. His earlier court-martial for being absent without leave had apparently made no impression on him. He appeared to know nothing of the Articles of War and said that at the time of his departure from military control he did not know that it was wrong to leave. The general impression one gets of this man is that he is too unintelligent to understand the nature of military rules and regulations.

The disposition board faced with the alternatives of a dishonorable discharge for desertion and an honorable discharge for inaptness decided on a middle course. Accordingly, slightly over a month after his apprehension, L.R. returned to his home discharged "without honor" from military service. At this time he would have much preferred to stay in the Army since his wife had left him and prospects of steady employment were dim.

The next, and last, report we have on L.R. comes from Chicago in late 1953. He had been fatally stabbed with a knife by his common-law wife at the door of her hotel room. The death was considered by the coroner as justifiable homicide. The certificate of death listed the deceased's usual occupation as "none."

Both men were mentally deficient but both had been able to make a minimal adjustment in civilian life prior to induction, T.W.P. because of the support which he received from his family, L.R. because of the very low demands made on him by his environment. The fact that the former's record showed that he had completed the sixth grade and that L.R. was not apparently different from many other Southern Negroes who became effective soldiers explains why the Army accepted them. But neither man could have made the grade no matter how much of an investment the Army might have made in them.

EMOTIONAL STABILITY

We cannot conclude that a man in good physical condition with adequate intelligence will function effectively in the Army. Whether he will or not depends on his emotional stability. Some men were clearly disqualified for service because of the severity of their emotional disability. The mentally unbalanced were frequently rejected by their local Selective Service Board without even being forwarded to the induction station for assessment. Others suffering from a severe neurosis such as an inability to tolerate crowds or loud noises had to be rejected once their condition was noted.

The major challenge that the Army faced was to identify those who gave evidence of overt or latent emotional difficulties which suggested that they might break under the stress of military life. On the basis of only a few minutes' evaluation, the psychiatrist had to estimate the individual's reserve powers and his ability to cope with the demands that the Army would make on him.

In the Army a soldier has no respite from the demands of his commander except if he is under the care of the medical department. One is in full-duty status or sick; there is seldom anything in between. Hence, many men sought to escape from mounting pressures by seeking medical help.

G.B.B. was born and raised in a small Midwestern town. He went to school there, graduated from high school, and worked for several years on a wheat farm. His father, a successful farmer, was nervous and quick-tempered. He suffered from severe headaches and traveled all over the country to consult various physicians and visit various hospitals for treatment. The headaches continued, however. The mother was highly emotional, also, although more prone to crying spells and periods of self-pity than to anger. She, too, had intense headaches. In this emotional environment, the children frequently found themselves blamed for things they did not understand. It was almost impossible to predict how their parents would react to a situation and frequently the safest procedure was to keep out of the way. The children soon learned that there was no room for expressing their own emotions at home.

At the age of fifteen, G.B.B. also began to develop headaches. When the headaches came on, he would first feel pain over the left eye. The pain would then spread over the whole left side of his head and neck becoming more and more intense. He would become anxious and tremulous, but had no idea what made him feel so afraid. Sometimes there would be continuous vomiting, but this did not afford any relief. Aspirin was no help. The only thing that gave him any relief was lying down in a dark room. Like his father he visited many physicians to no avail. The headaches always lasted for at least a day and sometimes as long as a week. Since he frequently had to quit work on the farm and go into the house to lie down, he would miss one or two days of work almost every week. He was much less anxious when alone and consequently began to avoid dances, movies and other social activities as he grew up.

At the age of twenty-two he married a local girl and about a year later moved to a neighboring city to work in a defense industry as an airplane sheet metal worker. Shortly after taking the defense job, an induction notice arrived and Mr. B. became Private B. of the Army Air Corps. He was sent to school as a sheet-metal worker and then joined a service group repairing damaged airplanes. Throughout his military career, his wife lived near him and on many assignments he lived off the post. His work was satisfactory, but the headaches continued and often necessitated a trip to the barracks to lie down and rest. By July 1943, these trips were becoming so frequent that newly promoted Private First Class B. was sent to the hospital. A thorough examination on the medical service revealed no organic cause and he was returned to duty. Five days later, he was back in the hospital, again for a long stay. Further study including psychiatric examinations resulted in a diagnosis of psychoneurosis, but the soldier did not seem incapacitated and was again sent back to work. This time he remained out of the hospital for just three days.

By this time his headaches were almost continuous and he was very upset because he was unable to gain any relief. At Christmas he went home on furlough, but an attempt to return to duty failed. He became weak and nauseated as soon as he started to work and the pain in his head was excruciating. During his fourth and final hospitalization, G.B.B. was very nervous and depressed. He frequently burst out crying in a manner reminiscent of his mother's behavior. He told the doctor: "I'm so disgusted, I don't know what to do with myself. I like to be like anyone else, and the first thing I know I am in the hospital." Starting to cry, he continued: "I would rather be cured than be discharged, but if I have to suffer, I would rather suffer at home. I am at the end of the rope. I can't stand it this way." Within a month he was discharged.

As a civilian, G.B.B. worked for about a year at his former job with the airplane manufacturing company. However, his difficulties continued and as the war came to an end, he decided to return to farming. Over the next ten years, he gradually built up his farm into a quite profitable enterprise. In 1950, he took some training in farm management with the Veterans Administration, but soon dropped out. Still, his farm continued to prosper and even more important his headaches became less frequent and less severe. His marriage has been quite happy and he now has two children. Apparently in recent years his health has much improved and he no longer suffers from crippling symptoms.

J.R.N. was the youngest of four children. His family lived in a large East Coast city and he was brought up as a member of the Jewish faith to which his family adhered. Although the father was a rather nervous and irritable man, he was away from home much of the time and seems to have had very little influence on his son's development. J.R.N.'s mother has always been the most important person in his life. From infancy she has pampered and spoiled him. She kept him at home with her throughout his early childhood and would not let him play with other children. As he grew older, she continued to dominate his life to the point where he was not allowed to think or act for himself unless the initiative came from her. Mrs. N. constantly complained about aches and pains, about the work she had to do, about the family income, and about other people. The household was constantly disorganized. Meals were rarely on time. Dishes sometimes stayed in the sink for days. Mrs. N. frequently got up late in the morning and did not bother to dress. She would scurry about the house in a rather excited state, talking to herself and scolding the children. J.R.N. spent much of his time from the age of three sitting at a large piano, picking out tunes under his mother's erratic but constant tutelage.

As he grew older, he began to have temper tantrums, headaches, and would vomit whenever he did not get his own way. At the same time, he was an intelligent child and got very good marks in school. His first year in high school he was on the honor roll and was elected president of his class. His mother was very happy. Then, as his schoolmates began to date girls, he started to withdraw completely from social activities. His interest in studies waned and he failed several subjects. He became very fearful and finally quit school because he could not concentrate or remember things. Often he would spend the whole day brooding at home. Gradually he began to think he heard voices which shouted at him and cursed him. He thought that people were always watching him, especially during meals, and when he walked on the street he would suddenly turn around to see if anyone was following him.

About this time, his older brother, who had always been nervous and who had stuttered all his life, broke down completely and was committed to a state hospital with a diagnosis of schizophrenia. J.R.N. made several attempts to work, first as a messenger boy, and later as a theater usher, but he would become confused and could not remember what he was supposed to do. Occasionally, he played the piano in a small restaurant. At the age of eighteen, on being called for induction into the Army, he became panicky and did not want to go. However, he was afraid to tell the doctors about his constant fears and the voices, and he was accepted for military service.

As a soldier, Private N. had many difficulties. He was frequently reprimanded and punished for his forgetfulness. He would become perplexed because he confused the voices that he thought he heard with the orders he was given. Once he almost got in serious trouble for cursing an officer, whom he thought was cursing him. Yet, he could not bring himself to tell anyone about his condition, not even his mother, who became quite worried about him after he had spent almost an entire furlough sitting at home with his eyes closed. In spite of these difficulties, Private N. completed basic training satisfactorily and started training with an infantry division for combat duty. His first summer was spent in very rugged training. The heat was almost unbearable. Then in the fall, the entire division was shipped north for specialized winter training. On these winter maneuvers, Private N. broke down completely. As his confusion mounted, he refused to bathe, and vomited after nearly every meal. The voices became more insistent, and one night on guard duty, he became lost, was completely unable to take care of himself, and almost froze to death.

When admitted to the hospital, his condition closely resembled that of his older brother. He evidenced a complete lack of interest in his surroundings. He spoke only when questioned and made statements such as: "I hear them. . . . They say, 'N., you are no good. You are a s.o.b.' The voice is inside my head or in back of my head. It comes back every once in a while. I feel that something is going to happen to me." He also had nightmares about people dying or about falling off a cliff which seemed at times so intense that they are probably better described as visual hallucinations.

When he was discharged to a V.A. hospital, there was little change in his condition. However, after two weeks he left the hospital against medical advice to return home. During the next few years, J.R.N. continued to spend most of his time with his

mother. The Veterans Administration tried to interest him in some
sort of training, but gave up after vocational testing revealed that
his emotional state precluded any further schooling. He did try
a few jobs, such as a mailman and pianist, but he always became
afraid and ill and he could not continue. Once he got a job as a
salesman in a department store, but was not able to bring himself
to report for work the first day. Finally, he gave up trying to work
and did nothing but give occasional piano lessons to young
children.

By 1950, the veteran's behavior had become quite bizarre. He
never left the house except at night and was quite hostile to his
parents. The Veterans Administration had to employ the unusual
procedure of having a psychiatric examination for pension purposes carried out in the home. He would not go out to a doctor's
office. When his parents die, an event which he constantly fears,
he will without doubt have to be sent to a mental hospital.

Little is known of W.G.'s early history other than the
fact that he was born and grew up in a large Midwestern city. He
went as far as the second year of college, married, and worked
for a number of years as an inspector for a candy company. In
1935 during his wife's pregnancy he became quite nervous, but
was able to continue with his work. Three years later, however,
at the age of twenty-four he began to drink rather heavily. As
the drinking continued he had periods of delirium when he
trembled all over and was very excited and anxious. Frequently
he started drinking in the morning to steady his nerves. He began
to stay away from home for periods of time on drinking bouts.
Finally, his wife divorced him for drunkenness and was given
custody of their child. At this time W.G. was employed as a
government clerk, a job which he lost shortly before induction because of his drinking.

Private G. took his basic training with the Signal Corps in late
1942 and early 1943. Military life, with its new demands and pressures, led the soldier to increased drinking. Toward the end of his

three-month training period, he went on his first drinking bout, which lasted four days. As a result, his final weeks at the Signal Corps Replacement Training Center were spent at hard manual labor. Nevertheless, because of his education and intelligence he was assigned to relatively responsible duties as a clerk in a signal supply organization. But the alcoholic pattern continued. In the next four months he was absent without leave twice and spent over a month in the stockade. His imprisonment would have been longer, but his outfit was alerted for overseas shipment and he went with them to the port of embarkation.

While waiting to embark, Private G.'s company went through the usual training exercises. During one of these—an obstacle course—the soldier jumped from a high platform and broke a bone in his foot. He was hospitalized and his company shipped out without him. This was the beginning of a period of almost a year during which he was shifted from one hospital to another. As his foot began to heal, Private G.'s anxiety increased and his need for liquor, which he could not obtain in the hospital, became almost unendurable. He started going AWOL to get a drink. One drink led to another and sometimes he was away from camp for as long as three weeks at a time. In seven months he was absent on five separate occasions for a total of fifty-four days.

Finally, after returning from his last bout in a delirious state he was transferred from the medical to the psychiatric ward where he was kept in confinement for the next several months. The restriction only increased his craving for liquor and on his release he got drunk again. Again he was admitted to the psychiatric section in an alcoholic delirium. At that time the doctor decided that since Private G. had real capabilities and since he wanted to return to duty, he should be given one last chance. Although the soldier signed a pledge to abstain from all liquor, within two weeks he was back on the psychiatric ward in an intoxicated state. At that point the Army decided that nothing further could be done to help the soldier and he was discharged "without honor." At the board proceedings, the soldier said of himself: "I cannot seem to give the cause of the first drink. However, when I drink a little bit I cannot stop for several days. Then I will quit for a period of time, nothing at all, no alcohol. However, in the Army, with the seriousness which I think is due to the pressure of Army life which all of us in the service know is prevalent, it is worse."

On returning home, W.G. continued to drink heavily. Nine months after his discharge he was admitted to the V.A. hospital for alcoholism with acute complications. Within twenty-four hours he died of heart disease. W.G. literally drank himself to death within six years. When his widow applied for a pension on behalf of his child, it was denied on the ground that the character of his discharge barred payment of death compensation or pension benefits.

There is a clear connection between the severe emotional illness of these three soldiers and their ineffective performance in the Army. In each instance their illness was sufficiently serious to have interfered with their civilian work and adjustment. Had any of these men called the examining physician's attention to their difficulties at induction, they might have been rejected. There is no doubt that J.R.N. would have been. Once a man was in uniform the Army had to exercise reasonable caution before it could release him. It had to be sure that G.B.B.'s headaches were truly disabling, and that W.G.'s alcoholism had reached a stage where it could no longer be arrested. The fact that both men were above average intelligence made the Army more interested in seeking to retain them.

MOTIVATION

Our democratic society is so structured that all adult males are under an obligation to put forth the effort required to support themselves and, if they have a family, their wives and children. The war confronted all males in the draft-eligible ages with still another demand—namely, that they risk their life for their country.

Most young men were able to rise to the occasion, but a small minority sought to avoid military service entirely or, more frequently, refused to make much of an effort once they had been inducted. Only a narrow line separates the emotionally disabled from the inadequately motivated, but the following cases suggest that there appear to be at least three different types of men characterized by low motivation. There is the psychopath who will do what he wants, not what he is told or directed to do. If the orders which he receives suit him, he will carry them out; if not, he will disregard them. Then there is the malingerer who deliberately refuses to meet the demands made upon him because he calculates that he will be better off if he is discharged from military service, or at least if he can escape from being assigned to combat. Finally, there is the disorganized and lazy man who appears to be unable to put forth any sustained effort required to perform effectively as a soldier.

C.L.A., a Negro, had spent most of his life working as a longshoreman in a Southern port. He never went to school. In his early twenties, he was married for a short time, but divorced his wife for infidelity. In the course of his years on the waterfront, he suffered a number of injuries; perhaps the most serious was when he was thirty when he fell 25 feet into the hold of a ship. His left foot was broken, and he lost consciousness. Although not hospitalized at that time, he was, several months later, when an abscess developed at the site of the fracture. On another occasion he incurred a cut tendon in the left wrist, and just prior to induction into the Army he was struck on the head while at work and knocked unconscious. For a number of years he had suffered from "spells" during which he became weak and perspired profusely. None of these conditions, however, had ever made it impossible for him to continue working.

Induction into the Army at the age of thirty-six was something that Private A. would have preferred to avoid. He had a steady job, was supporting a teen-age child, and had a girl friend whom he hoped to marry. Suddenly, he had to break completely with this life, and although assigned after induction to familiar work as a longshoreman in a port battalion, he had to adapt to an unfamiliar social and physical environment.

Although his work was satisfactory, he soon began to report for sick call with a variety of complaints: his old foot and wrist injuries bothered him; he had colds, and then there were the "spells." While the doctor did not feel that any of these conditions were incapacitating, Private A. became so insistent in his claims that he could not work that he was first assigned to light duty, and later, after four months of service, he was admitted to the hospital for further observation.

Orthopedic tests were made of the foot and wrist. The examination proved difficult because of the patient's resistance and marked anxiety. However, the final conclusion was that full, painless, and free motion was present and that the patient's limp seemed to be somewhat exaggerated considering the full motion and power of the various leg muscles. Further observation on the ward indicated that Private A. had no difficulty at all in walking as long as he did not know he was being watched. It was clear that he was deliberately acting on those occasions when he limped into the doctor's office.

On the other hand, there was no doubt that he did have anxiety attacks, or "spells" as he called them, when he would perspire all over, his heart would beat very fast, and he would feel weak and afraid. These, however, occurred at most twice a week and lasted for only about fifteen minutes. Further, they were no more frequent since induction than they had been in civilian life. While hospitalized, these periods of anxiety were noted only when his foot was being examined.

The final conclusion of the doctor was that Private A. was engaging in a great deal of conscious malingering. Although tense and anxious, the source of these difficulties appeared to be the soldier's fear that he was not sufficiently incapacitated to be discharged. Nevertheless, since it was practically impossible to obtain any real duty from him, and since he did have a psychiatric condition in addition to very poor motivation, he was discharged with a diagnosis of psychoneurosis, anxiety state, in April 1943.

After leaving the Army, he drew unemployment compensation for a number of months under the V.A. plan of fifty-two weeks of $20 allowance per week (52–20) and then returned to his old job as a longshoreman. In 1954, he was earning as much as he received before the war, and had purchased a home with the assistance of the Veterans Administration. He had married and was supporting five children.

Until the age of thirteen, when he completed grade school in a Southern city, A.J.S. had lead a rather uneventful, if not always happy, life. For the next six years, however, he was almost constantly in trouble. He served several sentences in reform schools, left home because of conflict with his parents, and traveled all over the United States, hitchhiking and riding freight trains. He worked occasionally as a painter, or carpenter, and once for eight months as a truck driver. He could never keep a job very long. At one time he joined the Civilian Conservation Corps, but did not like the restrictions on his freedom. Before long he found a way to get himself discharged.

On being drafted, Private S.'s initial reaction to Army discipline and restrictions was similar to his reaction to the CCC. He stayed at the reception center for one unhappy week and then, thoroughly disliking what he had seen, returned to his home, where he stayed for a month. During this time he got married. On returning to camp he was court-martialed and sentenced to the guardhouse, but actually spent most of his confinement in the hospital with a foot infection. Four days after his release he went AWOL again, and this time contracted syphilis which he transmitted to his wife. Again he was court-martialed, sent to the guardhouse, and spent most of his time in the hospital, this time being treated for syphilis. After having spent four months at the reception center, he was shipped out to his first assignment directly from the hospital.

During his next two months, which were devoted to Field Artillery basic training, Private S. worked as a member of an ammunition platoon. He was hospitalized for one brief period. Otherwise, he performed regular duty. However, he was unreliable and seemed to resent every order. The other soldiers did not like him, and he did not like them. Soon, he began to talk about getting out of the Army, saying that he had gotten a discharge from the CCC and that he had tried it here, but it had not worked as yet. This seemed to be his favorite topic of conversation, and he was apparently willing to accept even a dishonorable discharge.

In early April, Private S. again absented himself from military control and as a result spent a month and a half in the stockade. Yet, within two weeks of his release he went AWOL again. It was at this point, after the fourth period of absence from duty, that Private S.'s plans to obtain a discharge began to materialize. He was referred for psychiatric examination and presented a long list of complaints to the psychiatrist: heart trouble, nervousness, headaches, syphilis, fainting spells, among others. None of these appeared to be truly incapacitating since the soldier had never done anything about them. Nevertheless, the psychiatrist felt that he was dealing with a psychopath whose prospects of rehabilitation were hopeless and who would continue to perform poorly. There seemed to be no way to keep him from going AWOL except continuous imprisonment. Private S.'s total service of slightly less than a year was terminated by a discharge "without honor" for "traits of character which render his retention in service undesirable."

Although his objective had been achieved, the eventual cost was greater than he had anticipated. Civilian life brought the responsibilities of supporting a wife and, in time, three children. The nature of A.J.S.'s discharge made it difficult for him to get a good job. He could not get support from the Veterans Administration for his plans to further his education. He held some jobs as a cook, truck driver, painter, and laborer, but they did not last. Finally came divorce and unemployment. A.J.S. would have liked to reenlist in the Army, but he had closed that door himself. At the time of his remarriage in 1954, he was having an extremely difficult time maintaining himself.

R.V.A. was the youngest child born into a farm family in the deep South. He was the baby and was treated as such, especially by his mother and oldest sister. Much younger than his brother and sisters, he almost always got his own way. Until he entered the Army he never spent a night away from home unless he was with another member of his family. Under these circumstances R.V.A. never learned to accept responsibility. He expected other members of the family to take care of him, remind him of things that he had to do, and help him whenever he got into difficulty.

In school he did relatively well until the seventh grade. Then he began to complain that the work was hard, and he lost interest completely. As a result he failed several grades and finally left at the age of seventeen having completed one year of high school. Taking a job in a cotton mill he again found the work too hard and quit after two years. Until he was inducted into the Army at the age of twenty, he worked periodically at helping his father on a small farm. He never worried about supporting himself; he felt that others should take care of him. Once he bought an automobile on the installment plan, but could not meet the payments even though he was working at the time. His brothers and sisters paid them for him.

Initially R.V.A. was assigned to the Chemical Warfare Service. After basic training he was sent to a testing area in the desert where he performed a variety of duties. Much of his work, however, centered around the testing of various gases and methods of protection against gas. This he detested thoroughly. Frequently he did not appear for duty and had to be called from the barracks. Of the seven months Private A. was in the desert he spent over two in the hospital with hay fever and sinus trouble. On one occasion he overstayed a furlough for five days and was court-martialed.

Finally he was transferred to a medical detachment on the West Coast in the hope that he would make a better adjustment. His irresponsibility continued, however. He never had his uniform cleaned; he always looked dirty. His bunk area was untidy and often smelled of rotten food. Frequently he slept all night in his clothes. He didn't seem to care how he looked. It was almost impossible to get him to clean up or perform duty. As one of his NCOs put it: "About the only way you can make this boy do any duty and perform it right is to give him a specific detail to do, and, if he does not do it by a certain time, not give him anything to eat until he does it."

Assigned to work as a hospital orderly, he was expected to assume a considerable responsibility for patients, especially at night when it was not always possible to have a nurse for every ward. Private A., however, spent most of his off-duty hours in town sometimes working at odd jobs, sometimes in a penny arcade where a friend worked. The result was that he did much of his sleeping while on ward duty. Often he was found stretched out in a chair in the waiting room with his shoes untied, face unshaven, and hair uncombed when he should have been attending to patients. On one such occasion he was awakened by a nurse, who demanded in no uncertain terms that he tidy himself up and get to work. He responded by threatening to kill her if she reported him. The next day his commanding officer talked to him and then sent him to the hospital where he was placed on a psychiatric ward.

During a stay of more than a month, the doctors found the patient to be totally irresponsible, but they did not consider him to be suffering from a mental disorder. As one psychiatrist described him: "He would rarely, if ever, do anything spontaneously and had to be reminded to bathe and comb his hair. He was taken off KP because he had to be told to do everything. He is not a typical psychoneurotic, but it seems he is unable or incapable of adjusting himself to the Army, and I feel that, on the basis of his impulsive behavior, his disinterested attitude, and his unkempt habits, it would be best to discharge him." After almost twenty months of active duty he was brought before a board of officers and found inadaptable to military service. He appeared for the hearing in the wrong uniform, had his sleeves rolled up, had not brushed his shoes and was wearing a shirt which had not been cleaned for a year. However, he considered his grooming acceptable.

Almost immediately after leaving the Army the veteran married and about a year later a child was born. However, he did little to support his family and his wife eventually left him. His work history during the postwar years has been poor although he has spent a sizable amount of time taking courses under the G.I. Bill. First he entered vocational training in the field of refrigeration. This lasted only briefly and he shifted to a music school. Next came a six-month course in a beauty college, followed by another course in the same field. This too was never completed. In 1951 he did, however, take and complete a six-month course in barbering.

These three men have only one thing in common: the Army was unable to get them to put out the requisite effort to become effective soldiers. By his pre- and post-military experience, C.L.A. clearly demonstrated his ability to accept responsibility not only for himself but for those dependent upon him. A.J.S. had a long history of nonconforming behavior, devoting most of his energies to fighting authority. R.V.A.'s behavior is so aberrant as to suggest that he might be schizophrenic. The Army might have been able to whip some recalcitrants into line had it wanted, or been permitted, to employ harsh punishments. But the line between malingering and illness is very narrow and as the Patton incident so clearly demonstrated, the American public had no intention of tolerating any abuse of the sick, even the emotionally sick. Hence the Army was under pressure to discharge the poorly motivated. Only one man was executed because he steadfastly refused to fight.

Chapter Three: THE SOLDIER
AND HIS FAMILY

THE DEVELOPMENT of industrial capitalism has led to an increasingly sharp differentiation between a man's activities at home and at work. Yet, what transpires within his family frequently exercises a significant influence on how a man performs on the job. Home and work remain closely associated in farming which continued to be the principal occupation of a large segment of the population prior to World War II.

It was very difficult for a physician at an induction station to evaluate a young man of eighteen or nineteen who had never spent a single night away from home and whose work consisted of helping his father run the family farm. In the absence of specific information which would have alerted him, the examining physician had to proceed on the assumption that the young man would be able to stand on his own feet and make an adequate adjustment to the Army. We have previously presented cases of men whose dependency on their family was excessive, witness T.W.P., who turned all of his earnings over to his mother, or R.V.A., whose parents and siblings had always taken care of him.

Some men had so little intelligence that they had to be told when to take a bath and when to go to town to have their hair cut. It was not easy for the Army to spot these potential ineffectives, although caution was indicated in evaluating older selectees who continued to live at home long after their siblings had married and established themselves as heads of families.

It was not only the poorly educated who became disturbed on being separated from their loved ones. A considerable number of men of average or even superior education who were tied very closely to their mothers or wives became disturbed and unable to perform effectively when forcibly separated from home. These men had developed a tenuous equilibrium for themselves through their dependency. As long as they had special support, they could cope successfully with the strains and stresses of the outside world.

Army service upset this equilibrium. Sometimes a wife was able to accompany her husband while he was transferred from one camp to another during training. But when his unit was alerted for overseas shipment this makeshift arrangement had to come to an end. The tremendous importance that most soldiers placed on mail was proof that homesickness was widespread, almost universal. Fortunately most men were able to endure it, as long as they received reassuring letters from their loved ones.

This helps to explain why many soldiers with good performance records collapsed when they learned of threatened or actual trouble in their family. In answering the call of his country a man did not free himself of his feeling of responsibility for his wife and his attachment to his children. Hence when a soldier learned that one of his immediate family was seriously ill, he felt trapped because he was so far away from home and unable to lend assistance when it was most needed. It was also very upsetting to receive a letter from one's wife or fiancée that she had decided to dissolve her ties and break the relationship. Many a soldier broke under the double blow of losing a loved one and not being able to fight to keep her—because he was thousands of miles from home. Some commanders feared the mail from home almost as much as the enemy's bullets because of the havoc that it raised with their men.

SEPARATION

Homesickness has always been a challenge to the military. It has been claimed that almost 10 percent of the men discharged from the Northern Army during the Civil War were released for this cause. During World War II the Chinese Nationalists had to fly recruits to points a thousand or more miles from their homes in order to hold down the desertion rate.

Separation from one's family involves not only the loss of direct personal relations with loved ones, but also the transfer from an environment that one knows intimately to one that is more or less completely alien. At home one knows what others like and dislike, how one can gain their support, and what will make them angry. The Army is a new and strange world, and it takes considerable time and effort for a man to get used to his new surroundings and to feel at ease with others who only yesterday were total strangers.

For schematic purposes one can distinguish the following stages in a soldier's separation from his family: induction which takes place near home; shipment to a training center which may still be located near home; transfer for unit and divisional training usually far from home; maneuvers or special field training often in isolated areas; embarkation for overseas; overseas service. Some men became anxious about military service even before they were inducted and many more developed varying degrees of anxiety as their unit was alerted for overseas shipment. In almost every instance the soldier's anxiety was heightened by his approaching separation from his loved ones.

A.F.M. was the oldest of six children born to rather poor parents. He was nervous and easily fatigued as a child; he wet his bed until he was thirteen. The family lived in a small Midwestern community and were always quite close. A.F.M. first left home at the age of nineteen to attend the State Teachers College. After one year, he suddenly decided to discontinue his education to marry a home-town girl whom he had known for many years. However, the death of his mother who had been ill for some time coinciding with a rather severe emotional disturbance at about the same time delayed the marriage for a number of months. His fiancée spent many hours at this time helping him overcome his feelings of depression. After their marriage, his wife continued to work at her former job while A.F.M. held a series of jobs as a service station operator, sporting-goods store manager, and bus driver. He also took part actively in church work and was a Boy Scout leader.

Although by 1942 there were two children, Mrs. M. continued to work. Husband and wife were very close and lived in a comfortable home of their own. The only difficulty in an otherwise happy life was the fact that at times A.F.M. experienced rather severe depressions. Combined with these depressions were headaches which seemed to occur whenever he was under emotional strain. However, with his wife's help he usually was able to work out of his difficulties quite rapidly. In fact, Mrs. M., a rather independent and confident person, was always the one who made decisions and took responsibility when difficulties arose, and her husband was too upset to take charge. Actually, it was his suggestion that since the family was not dependent on his income, he should enlist for military service even though he had been deferred. His wife, although with some misgivings about how he would adjust without her, supported his decision and in late 1942 he was inducted.

Assigned to a Quartermaster Company for training, Private M. showed promise of developing into a very good soldier. He was efficient, worked hard, and seemed to have a strong wish to serve his country. However, he found it hard to do things that he knew he should do. He thought frequently of home, of the children, and most often of his wife. He became a little bitter when he thought of how much he had given up in comparison with other soldiers. Sometimes he was afraid. His headaches kept recurring and there was no one to comfort and encourage him. The headaches were increasing in intensity. One day after he had been in camp for about a week, a headache developed which did not stop as usual. It lasted through the night and the next day and the next night. Then, as he got up after having hardly closed his eyes, the pain started to subside. In its place came a clicking sound. Private M. collapsed on the floor of his barracks.

He awoke in the station hospital. He could not speak and his whole left side was paralyzed. His speech soon returned, but the paralysis lasted for several days. At first, the doctors thought that he was suffering from a brain tumor, but neurological examinations were negative. When the psychiatrist talked to him he was convinced that Private M. had had a hysterical attack. His listlessness and apparent indifference about his symptoms were typical of that type of neurosis. As A.F.M.'s dependency on his wife was revealed, the psychiatrist became convinced that no permanent cure could be achieved unless the patient was discharged and returned to his wife, who had been instrumental in helping him out of prior emotional difficulties.

At home A.F.M. recovered rapidly. With his wife, he could regain a feeling of composure, a conviction that everything would be all right. Eventually he took an administrative job with the Village Department of Public Works which he has held for over ten years. There are four children in the family. To the veteran his brief Army career seems very dim and distant.

Born and raised in a small city in the South, D.F. was never away from home for more than a day until his induction into the Army. His father was a cripple suffering from palsy, who was able to eke out a bare living for his family working as a night watchman. The mother was a nervous, high-strung, anxious woman, extremely solicitous of the welfare of her two sons. D.F. himself was quite nervous as a child and was especially afraid of his teachers in school. Nevertheless, he graduated from high school, although not until the age of twenty-four. Later, he worked at a variety of jobs around his home town: as a laborer in a lumber mill, a waiter in a cafe, a W.P.A. laborer, a farm laborer, and a carpenter's helper. Since he had no wish to leave his home, his employment was restricted to the very limited opportunities available in his particular area.

At the age of thirty-eight D.F. had never really thought seriously of marriage. He describes himself as a "home boy" who has a very strong attachment to his mother. His interests were restricted to those which could be satisfied locally; roller skating, attending movies, watching baseball games. In his religious life he was extremely devout and read the Bible without fail every morning and night. When his father died in the late 1930s, he was rather emotionally upset. However this event seems to have only brought him closer to his mother.

D.F.'s Army career was very brief. Inducted in late 1942, he was in the hospital after less than two weeks. After two days of drill, he had felt unable to continue and went on sick call. When seen by the doctor, he was suffering an acute anxiety episode with widely dilated pupils, rapid breathing, and "bizarre tremors" of both hands. He seemed to feel he might have palsy like his father and said: "My nerves are all unstrung, I get nervous thinking about home. It shot me all to pieces. I've never been away from home. Getting up here has tore my nerves all apart." He went on to talk at some length about his mother; he said that she was in poor health, had had her teeth pulled, and had a bad stomach condition. He was afraid she might die and begged to be transferred to an air field near his home so that she could visit him. With considerable anxiety, he stated emphatically that he could not be away from his mother because "I love her so." The psychiatrist felt that the patient's attachment to his mother was so pathological that the only possible solution was to return him home. Although during his hospitalization the tremor had disappeared and a reduction in anxiety occurred, the doctors had little doubt that a return to duty would only result in continued and more severe anxiety attacks.

After less than two months away from home, D.F. returned to his mother. Although he has continued to be nervous at times, he has in general adjusted very well. Living in his home town amid familiar surroundings, the harrowing emotional episodes of his Army life have gradually been forgotten and lost their force. His occupational pattern has remained much the same: three years at one laboring job, four years at another, and so on. At the age of forty-five D.F. married, but otherwise his life is little different from what it was before he was inducted.

Both of these men were able to get along in civilian life because of the support which they received from members of their family, A.F.M. from his wife, D.F. from his mother. Both collapsed almost immediately following their separation from their loved ones. Their dependency was so great that the Army doctors realized that they could never make a successful adjustment away from home, no matter how much they tried.

BREAKUP

During the war most men were able to keep going under very adverse conditions because they were sustained by a hope of the future when the war would end and they could return to their loved ones. Their family was their anchorage, their tie to the past and to the future which made it possible for them to endure the almost intolerable conditions of the present.

If a man was considerably older than the average soldier, or if he had a special skill which he knew had gained deferment for others, he might resent being in the Army far away from his family, while others remained at home in comfort and security. Frequently he had these feelings even if he acknowledged that the draft had operated fairly in his case. Usually such resentful attitudes were transitory. They assumed significance only if the soldier was victimized by developments at home as was so clearly the case with H.H.V. below.

Many soldiers were upset by gossip reported in letters from home. Some mail was deliberately malicious, but for the most part it reflected thoughtlessness. A soldier who received several letters written within a fortnight from friends who reported on the enjoyable evening which they had spent with his wife could become very restive about what was happening at home. His restiveness might be increased if he was feeling guilty about his own behavior.

H.H.V. spent his childhood on a Midwestern farm. Although prone to occasional temper tantrums, he was in general a happy child who enjoyed the pampering and indulgence of his parents. In school he did fairly well and was promoted regularly. He was interested in sports and social activities. Most of his spare time, however, had to be spent at home working with his father. When he was seventeen, his father became ill, and he left school and took over the management of the farm. The next year, after his father died, an older brother returned from the West and assumed responsibility for the family. A quarrel ensued and H.H.V. decided to leave home despite his rather close attachment to his mother.

With some friends he purchased a car and followed the harvest for several months. Finally they settled in a manufacturing town where he took a job in industry. Soon he became homesick and was able to prevail upon his mother and sister to join him. His sister introduced him to a girl, and after several months of friendship they became engaged; and five months prior to his induction into military service they were married. His wife was his first love and he was very closely attached to her. She loved him just as deeply and was very jealous when he paid the slightest attention to another girl.

When H.H.V. left for the Army reception center, his wife became almost hysterical. However, she followed her husband immediately and remained close to him at the various camps where he was stationed prior to departure for overseas duty. Originally assigned to limited service because of a hearing difficulty, he was given brief basic training and then assigned to a trucking unit. This organization, however, was soon alerted for overseas shipment and Private V. was told that he would be discharged because of his hearing disability. Instead, he was transferred to a replacement detachment where he remained for a month. During this period he became quite nervous and reported to the dispensary several times. After assignment to a medical unit, however, his condition improved and his work was excellent. Throughout this first year of his military service, his wife followed him from one station to another and, without doubt, her presence was instrumental in easing his adjustment to Army life. When the day of his departure for overseas arrived, his wife again became hysterical and had to be carried forcibly off the train.

The soldier spent the next eighteen months as a medical technician and ward attendant in Hawaii. Although nervous at times, he enjoyed his work and was promoted. He spent his evenings quietly and avoided going out on pass for fear he would have to go out with girls that the other men would pick up. He was never unfaithful to his wife; he rarely spoke to other women. Much of his free time was spent in writing letters to his wife and nearly every day the mail brought a letter from her.

Suddenly the letters ceased. For almost three months he heard nothing from her in spite of repeated and increasingly frantic inquiries on his part. As time went on, H.H.V. became anxious and depressed. Several times he spoke with the hospital psychiatrist. Finally a letter arrived; Mrs. V. had been going out with other men and enjoying herself; she felt that they should get a divorce. Within a few hours the soldier was a patient on the psychiatric ward of the hospital. He was tense, unable to sleep; he did not seem to care if he lived or died. Yet he seemed to feel that if he could get home things could be straightened out.

Accordingly, an emergency furlough was arranged. At home he found that his wife, who had previously been living with her mother, had taken an apartment with a girl friend. She had been unfaithful to him, had spent all their savings, and had even sold most of their household effects and furnishings. When he arrived at her apartment, she was not there although he had notified her of his coming. Much later that night she arrived home from a date with another man. H.H.V. went back to camp in far worse condition than he had been before his furlough.

Since the doctors felt that further hospitalization would only increase his anxiety, a discharge was arranged. The ensuing period of obtaining a divorce was very difficult for H.H.V. However, within a year he married again and about a year later his first child was born. This marriage lasted about three years. The second wife, like the first, was unstable; she could not take care of the baby and shortly she left home. Throughout the postwar period, H.H.V. has suffered from almost constant tenseness and anxiety. He has had a number of jobs but has lost one or two days from work a week because of his emotional condition. At present, he is employed as a press operator, lives in an apartment, and pays a household helper to take care of his child while he is at work.

The most important influence in D.D.W.'s early life was his alcoholic father. When drunk, he would frequently terrorize the household, assaulting anyone who happened to be in his way; at other times he would become depressed and threaten suicide. He was always extremely strict with the children. By contrast, the mother was sickly and a constant worrier. D.D.W. himself was prone to temper tantrums and suffered from frequent nightmares from which he would awake in a state of terror. Nevertheless, he adjusted fairly well at school, although he left at the age of fourteen, primarily because of a lack of interest. During the next seven years, he worked on the family farm, keeping a constant eye on his father, whose outbreaks of violence and occasional attempts at suicide were a continuous problem to D.D.W. and his brothers.

On being drafted, Private W. was assigned to a newly formed infantry division. The next eighteen months were spent in intensive training which terminated with full-scale maneuvers. He was constantly worried about conditions at home, but since he was stationed at a Southern camp not far from his home town and had frequent furloughs and passes, he was able to keep in touch with his family. His performance of duty was excellent and before leaving for overseas service, he was made a squad leader with the rank of sergeant.

The division was assigned to duty in Hawaii. Although there was intensive training and Sergeant W. was in charge of guarding a radar station, he had a good deal of leisure time to spend on amusements or "just to think." His mother wrote frequently and her letters were filled with reports of the father's drinking. D.D.W.'s fears that his father would either kill his mother in a drunken rage or commit suicide were intensified by his being many thousands of miles from his family. Soon he began to have rather intense stomach pains which, although not incapacitating, were most disturbing. Later, a rash broke out on his face for which he was hospitalized over a month. As the letters from his mother became more frantic, the stomach pains became more intense; he began to vomit frequently after meals. Obsessed with fears that his father would either commit murder or suicide, he became morose and depressed. Since there was a possibility that Sergeant W. might have an ulcer, he was examined extensively in the hospital, but nothing was found.

Returning to the States after fifteen months of overseas service, the sergeant was immediately sent home on furlough. It was a hectic time. During the month he was with his family the father was drunk many times. Once he stabbed an older son with a knife and on another occasion was found just as he was attempting to hang himself. He bitterly berated his sons for leaving him alone in his old age when he most needed their help. On returning to the hospital, Sergeant W. spent many hours in psychotherapy, physical rehabilitation work, and occupational therapy. However, he remained preoccupied with his problems. He was frequently nauseated, suffered from pains in his chest and from alternating constipation and diarrhea. The only hope for his recovery seemed to be a return to his home, where he would be in a position to do something about the ever-threatening breakup of his family.

After discharge D.D.W. worked intermittently at carpentry. Within a year he was married. During 1947, he tried farming on his own, but did poorly. He still suffered from nausea and stomach pains. Later he entered on-the-job training as an automobile mechanic under the G.I. Bill, and in 1952, having completed the course, was employed as a solderer. During that same year, he spent nine days in a V.A. hospital for his stomach condition. Apparently, the return to his home environment has kept his psychoneurosis from getting worse, but he still suffers from occasional severe attacks when under emotional strain.

Both of these soldiers were performing effectively until they were overwhelmed with bad news from home. Although the Army gave H.H.V. an emergency furlough, his marriage was already so near dissolution that he could no longer save it. Whether it would have held together in the absence of war is hard to know. Likewise, there was little that the Army could do to quiet D.D.W.'s fears of a catastrophe at home other than to follow the humane approach of separating him prematurely so that he could return home and help to prevent it. While "separation" triggered D.D.W.'s difficulties, they were clearly more pervasive as indicated by the fact that he did not become completely well after his return home.

Chapter Four: THE IMMEDIATE GROUP

AS SOON AS the child goes to school his dependency on his family begins to lessen and as he grows older other institutions assume added importance in his life. By the time he is an adult the adjustment is likely to be significantly determined not only by his basic relations to his parents but also by the extent to which he has been successful in developing effective relations with his classmates, social acquaintances, and fellow workers. Many men derive major satisfactions from their participation in various organizations—business, church, political, social.

Among the disruptive effects of war is the severing—or suspending—of all these ties, with the result that men enter the Army deprived of the support of their immediate family and these additional community ties. This means that their adjustment to the Army will depend in considerable measure on how quickly they can develop new relationships to replace, or at least to substitute for, those they had known in civilian life.

Assigned by the Army to a specific unit, they are not able to choose their companions, but must do their best to establish themselves as members of whatever group they are in. All too often the Army assignment system put a stray Southerner into an otherwise exclusively northern group, or vice-versa, with the result that he was likely to find himself an outsider. Unless he was accepted, he might well be miserable, for a man had to depend on his immediate group for support: barracks mates ate together, trained together, played together, worshiped together, slept together.

But even if a man had the good luck to be assigned to a group to which he could make an easy adjustment, difficulties often arose. Men were constantly pulled out of one unit and assigned to another. This was particularly true of Air Forces training where men were assigned as individuals until late in their training cycle. It was better in the Ground Forces, especially for soldiers assigned to a division. The worst problems were encountered by soldiers trained as individual loss replacements, who were sent overseas as casuals and who were distributed to understrength units. Such men entered combat in a strange unit. To make matters worse, the members of the unit to which the replacement was sent often adopted a withholding attitude towards the newcomer who, not being battlewise, might act in a way which would jeopardize not only his own life, but theirs. Although the Army became aware of the special emotional stress to which the individual replacement was exposed, it never fully solved the problem of training, transporting, and assigning them in groups.

Many men were able to perform effectively because of their identification with their immediate group, and some groups became so closely knit that they carried ineffective members for a long time. This type of behavior is also characteristic of certain work groups in civilian life where fellow employees frequently cover up for the lack of skill, alcoholism, or other defect of a fellow worker. However, combat took a heavy toll of these well-integrated groups, which frequently fell apart after key members were wounded or killed.

The British have long employed a regimental system of call-up in order to gain the specific advantages of group identification. This policy has much in its favor but is not free of drawbacks. For when men from the same area participate in a battle where the casualty rate is high, the impact on their communities can be devastating.

The extent to which soldiers received support from their immediate group was much influenced by the quality of leadership of the noncommissioned and junior officers. During training, a soldier was constantly in contact with his noncommissioned officers. His lieutenant and captain were rather distant figures. In combat, this was different. Here the officer was in constant and direct contact with his men and to the extent that he was competent and courageous he was able to support them; and to the extent that he was incompetent or cowardly he added greatly to their insecurities and anxieties. The fact that soldiers could not complain about their leaders when they found them wanting, nor find another assignment with more congenial leadership, was a serious burden. They were forced to make the best of what was frequently a very bad situation. A soldier knew that he might lose his life unnecessarily because of the lack of skill or judgment of his superior and there was little, if anything, that he could do to prevent it. There was much talk about men who had shot or planned to shoot their officers—an indication of the tension that prevailed.

But there was not much security, especially in combat, even for the soldier who was fortunate enough to have good leadership. The losses among sergeants and lieutenants ran very high and many a soldier who kept going for a long time finally broke down when the leader who had long supported him was injured or killed.

COHESION

A soldier did not have to be well liked by all of his thirty-nine barracks mates to receive the support that comes from close ties with others. Often all that he really needed was one buddy. But some men, because of age, personality traits, or other reasons, were ostracized by the entire group. As long as they were not singled out and made the butt of the group's aggression and hostility, they might still survive by developing a relationship with soldiers from other companies. But that was not easy to accomplish at home and next to impossible overseas.

However, when a soldier such as J.U.S. was singled out as a target by the entire group, there was little likelihood that he could long stand the pressure. The various ways in which group cohesion can influence a man's performance are suggested by the following cases.

L.S. is a Negro, born and raised in the South. He went to school until he was fifteen, completing one year of high school. For the next ten years he drifted from one job to another, all in the same large city where he had lived as a child. He worked as a laborer on construction jobs, in a lumber yard, and for one period of eighteen months on W.P.A. His health was always good and he had many friends, both male and female.

In late 1942 he was inducted and took basic training in the Quartermaster Corps near his home. Later his outfit was moved to the West Coast where he worked as a bugler and messenger. A year after induction he was promoted to private first class. His next assignment was as a laborer at a West Coast port of embarkation. Shortly after being transferred L.S. began to have occasional headaches which gradually became more frequent and severe. However, he was with a group of soldiers who were very good friends. They worked, went to the PX to drink beer, went on pass to the nearby city—always together. He felt very much a part of this group, and, as he said; "They would build up my morale and the headaches didn't worry me." As time went on they met girls in town and frequently went on dates together. Some of the girls became in many ways a part of the group and in mid-1944 Private S. married a girl whom he had been dating for several months. From then on he lived off the post, but continued the close association with his buddies. His work was excellent and, with congenial friends always around, he enjoyed life. Whenever his headaches began to bother him, the presence of his friends and their good-natured banter cheered him up.

Then, rather suddenly, he was sent for further training to a remote camp in the Rocky Mountain area. Far from his wife and friends he felt alone and lost. The headaches, which before had been almost forgotten amid the friendship and support, became continuous and much more severe. He spent a large part of his time thinking about his wife and buddies back on the West Coast and worrying about his condition. Because he was shifted frequently from one training unit to another he didn't seem to be able to make new friends. He became anxious, hated each new camp, and wanted only to get away. He felt that if a discharge would free him from the detested place and return him to people he knew and liked, that he would take it. His work became quite poor and much of the time he felt unable to do any duty at all. After two months his commanding officer sent him to a psychiatrist. A complete physical examination revealed no organic basis for the headaches. The doctor felt that the headaches were not a sufficient basis to warrant a diagnosis of psychoneurosis. He recommended a discharge for inaptness and lack of adaptability for military service; the discharge board concurred.

L.S. returned to the West Coast and a month later his wife gave birth to a child. He worked for several months in a shipyard and later as a porter. During this time he continued his education under the G.I. Bill. Back with friends again, his headaches became much less frequent. In 1947 he started working for the City Park Commission, a job which he still holds. He has completed high school and one year of junior college.

A.W.G.'s father died when he was very young and he, along with his six brothers and sisters, was brought up by his mother. As soon as the children were old enough they went to work to supplement the mother's meager earnings. A.W.G. never attended school. He suffered from many fears as a child and had frequent nightmares. At twelve he left home to earn his own living. As he put it: "My mother was always looking for a new man and we didn't like the new man." Until this time the children had always been very close and, since the mother was away from home all day working, they relied on each other for many of the things that in a more normal family situation would have been supplied by parents. For the next twelve years he worked at a variety of odd jobs, mostly as a laborer on construction projects. He married at the age of twenty-two.

As an infantry rifleman, Private G. received extensive training over a period of eight months. He joined a division immediately after induction as one of a number of replacements. Although he had some difficulty because of his illiteracy, his buddies helped him whenever he had to read or write. Largely because of this need for assistance in any situation calling for literacy, the soldier developed a strong feeling of closeness and loyalty to his immediate group. They helped him and he in turn would do anything he could for his friends. It almost seemed like being back with his brothers and sisters again. Under these circumstances he performed very well and was promoted to corporal shortly after his outfit returned from maneuvers and before they went overseas.

Specialized training in jungle warfare and invasion tactics continued for over a year while the division was in Hawaii and later in New Guinea. It was on the latter island that Corporal G. saw his first combat action—some sporadic fighting while on patrol. In early 1945, however, the division participated in much heavier fighting while engaged in capturing an island which was soon to serve as a stepping-stone for the invasion of the Philippines. Corporal G.'s company was involved in one of the initial assaults against the Japanese positions and came under heavy fire from snipers in the trees. As they advanced they had their first experience with short-fused demolition charges hurled at them from above. Finally they reached the Japanese position and fierce bayonet fighting ensued. Although the attack was successful, casualties were heavy and Corporal G. realized for the first time that as the fighting continued the group of friends with whom he had lived and worked for the past two years would not remain intact. Already it had started to dwindle.

A month later they were fighting in the Philippines, first in patrol actions aimed at eliminating pockets of Japanese resistance and then in a desperate effort to hold the line against enemy counter-attacks. Shortly after the initial landing the soldier was promoted to sergeant. Casualties among the noncommissioned officers had been heavy. As the fighting continued, Sergeant G. saw his group of buddies still further reduced; one was killed by a sniper, another was sent to the rear on a stretcher. He began to feel very much alone. Then in early April came a drive to relieve another company which had been surrounded by the enemy. In the thick of the attack he saw first one and then another of his friends killed. Sergeant G. was practically the only member of the group left. Suddenly he was overwhelmed with an intense feeling of helpless loneliness. There didn't seem to be any reason to continue living. The attack failed, but the soldier didn't find that out until much later. He had lost control of himself completely and tried to end his life.

Three days later he woke up in the hospital. He was severely depressed; he spoke only of the buddies he had lost and of his guilt at not being able to carry on in combat. His hands and sometimes his whole body trembled; his sleep was constantly interrupted by vivid dreams of battle. When he found himself with a group of people, he became panicky and wanted to run away. With the gradual disintegration of his group of friends, the stresses of combat had increasingly taken their toll. When the last two were killed, it had seemed as if there was no longer anyone who could help him. He was left powerless and feared that the enemy would now certainly torture and kill him. Although the patient's condition improved somewhat during his subsequent five months of hospitalization, he continued to experience marked anxiety. In addition there were occasional bouts of malaria.

After discharge A.W.G. remained anxious and depressed for some time. His malaria bothered him and there were times when his dead buddies seemed to talk to him. He talked to them, too. However, with time his condition improved. He went to work first as a construction laborer and more recently as a carpenter's helper for a railroad. For about six months he went to school, and he learned to read and write. There are now five children in the family. The veteran is to all intents and purposes an average citizen with a steady job and a happy family life. Of his Army experiences he says: "Well, I think sometimes it was just like a dream, and that it was a miracle that I am still here."

J.U.S. was born on his parent's farm in the Midwest. From an early age his life was devoted almost entirely to planting crops, caring for animals, and helping to harvest. He started school at nine and attended irregularly until the age of sixteen. The farm work, however, always took precedence and lessons were difficult and uninteresting for him. He completed only the third grade. For almost thirty years thereafter J.U.S. worked on the family farm first with his father and then, when his father died, with his brother-in-law. He enjoyed the work, wanted nothing more from life than an opportunity to stay on the farm. There he belonged, he was healthy, and he could care for the animals that he loved.

The war, however, upset all this. Although initially considered too old, he was accepted for military service in late 1942 at the age of forty-five. Sent to a Field Artillery training center on the West Coast, he felt completely out of place. The people were different. They did not know or care about crops and horses, and he did not know about anything else. Used to a group of people who loved and talked about the same things he did, he found the chatter of his barracks mates, many less than half his age, almost incomprehensible. All they talked about were girls and military subjects. He felt too old and set in his ways to get very interested in either. Furthermore, because he did not understand these people, he began to fear them. He did not have any way of knowing what they would do next. They always seemed to do the unexpected. He tried avoiding them to protect himself. But the difficulty did not stop with Private S.'s isolation from the group. The group began to notice that he was different, that he did not know the things they knew, that he cared little for what was important to them. Soon he became the butt of jokes and teasing. An outcast, he was fair game for anyone. Private S. responded at first by playing the fool. He was annoyed and upset at the way they treated him, but on the other hand he did want to be part of the group, to be accepted. He felt that if he put on a show for them, that would make them laugh. Even being laughed at was better than being completely alone. And so he tried to hold back his anger and contempt for these stupid children, and act the role of a silly, overaged yokel. But soon he was not acting any more. He had completely retreated within himself.

When first admitted to the station hospital, the patient was quiet; he would not even answer questions. Frequently he burst out crying. He had auditory and visual hallucinations. When he did speak, his words were confused and indicative of extreme fear, such as; "I took a spear from a German because I wanted it. I didn't lock my suitcase. I wore this spear on my necktie to tell them secretly. Now I think they will court-martial me. They will kill me some way." Later, as he began to improve, he said: "Since coming here I have been thinking that I had been tricked into enlisting or maybe I was drafted. The way people act they are going to get ahold of me and kill me. If they put me on the farm I could work, I could." When asked why he would not talk, he said: "I told a Baptist preacher I wouldn't talk." Still later, "I want to be with the horses. I have worked on a farm all my life and I miss the horses. I could always get along with them."

Discharged and transferred to a state mental hospital near his home he had an opportunity to do farm work and associate with his own kind of people. In eight months he had improved considerably and was sent to the V.A. hospital. By that time, however, his psychosis had completely disappeared and a month later he returned home. Back among people whom he understood and whose behavior seemed predictable, J.U.S. has never had a recurrence of his emotional disorder. He has worked at a number of jobs: farm labor, bridge construction work, carpentry. More recently, nearing sixty, he has had difficulty finding employment, but he has always been able to make enough to support himself.

G.B.G. was the youngest of six children born to a middle-class Negro family in a small Southern city. As a boy he was somewhat effeminate and preferred playing with dolls to participating in more strenuous activity with the other boys. He finished grammar school and later held several jobs, as a tobacco

factory worker, and as a janitor. However, from the age of fourteen until the time he entered the Army at twenty, he was frequently financially supported by other men in a homosexual relationship.

During this period his main desire was to have some man take
care of him; he wanted to be a woman. His affairs usually lasted
for long periods. He preferred to wear women's clothes and frequently went out in the evening or attended a dance wearing a
dress. He used lipstick, nail polish, and other types of make-up as
well as perfume. In spite of the fact that he lived with and was supported by another man for over 18 months prior to Army induction, he was able to keep the nature of his activities from his family
and other members of the community. He lived and associated
primarily with homosexuals like himself among whom he considered himself, and was considered, a woman.

Private G.'s Army experience was in many respects quite unusual, even for a homosexual. He was stationed in the United States
for approximately eighteen months. During this time he was able to
maintain his homosexual activities without difficulty. His first assignment was a ward boy in a hospital where he avoided watching
surgical operations because they made him sick. Later he was transferred to an Engineer organization as an assistant clerk. In late 1943
he joined a Quartermaster battalion where he worked periodically
as a supply clerk. He was hospitalized on a variety of occasions
most frequently for syphilis and related conditions, but also for
a recurrent stomach disorder. Since his duty was always of a special medical and clerical nature, he was able to obtain frequent
passes during which he could satisfy his needs for homosexual activity. But even with his effeminate manner, marcelled hair, and
cosmetics he was not picked up by the military authorities.

On arriving in England, however, the situation changed. Passes
were infrequent. He was assigned to duty in the kitchen where
his effeminate ways immediately attracted the attention of other
men. Used to considering himself a woman and acting as such, he
found the demands for masculine behavior distasteful and disturb-

ing. For the first time since the age of fourteen he not only was unable to participate in sexual acts with other men but was forced to remain a member of a group that was not willing to accept his feminine patterns of behavior. The other men considered him a man and expected him to behave as such. He was teased unmercifully and sometimes quite maliciously. Faced with this conflict between the way of life he had adopted and the expectations of a social group from which he could not escape, Private G. became quite upset. He had headaches and pains in his abdomen. The latter always seemed to occur when his homosexual desires were aroused but not satisfied. Then, too, he had developed a rather painful eye condition probably as a result of syphilis. Finally he went to his commanding officer and told him: "I won't do this work. I'm not a man, anyhow. I don't like men's work. I can't do what men do." Even then his C.O. did not seem to understand, but further explanation eventually convinced him that Private G. was a homosexual and should be sent to the hospital.

There, the patient became quite articulate as regards his homosexual activity and his need to escape from a group of people who expected him to be a man. Leaning over the psychiatrist's desk he said, "Before I went overseas I was going with a boy of twenty-three. I loved the ground he walked on. It tears me apart to be away from him. I dream about him and in my dreams I hold him in my arms, and when I wake up and he isn't there I get sick." Asked what he would do if given the opportunity to do what he liked, he replied: "I'd marry me a good-looking man and settle down." During the interview the patient requested that every effort be made to get him out of the barracks because he was suffering greatly especially from the teasing of the other men.

Private G. spent exactly two months in Europe, most of that in the hospital, and was returned to the States. A board of officers decided that he should be returned to civilian life with a discharge of "other than honorable" because of "lack of adaptability for military service and traits of character which render his retention in the service undesirable."

Back in his home town, the veteran found it very difficult to adjust. Before, he had always accepted himself as a woman and among his homosexual friends had been accepted as such. Now, having been exposed to a social group that had actively condemned this way of life, he did not know what he was. For the first time he wondered whether he should support himself rather than be supported by other men; whether he should learn a trade and act like a man, although he did not have any particular skill and was not eligible for veterans' benefits. Presently he had what he, in his own words described as a "nervous breakdown," from which he has only recently begun to recover. As of 1954, however, he was working full time as a hospital orderly.

These cases provide concrete evidence that "no man can be an island unto himself." The need of individuals to be accepted by the group is illustrated by the efforts that J.U.S. made—he was willing to act completely out of character in order to gain acceptance. The cases further illustrate the importance of group support in enabling men to perform effectively. L.S. broke down following his isolation from his friends; A.W.G., after his buddies had been injured or killed; J.U.S., after he was rejected by the group; and G.B.G. after the group refused to accept him on his own terms.

Among the important contrasts between military and civilian life is the much greater need of the soldier to be accepted by his immediate group, for all alternatives are closed to him. G.B.G.'s pre-induction history shows how much latitude frequently exists for civilians even with major behavioral deviations to find congenial associates from whom they can receive the emotional support which will enable them to adjust, even to perform effectively.

LEADERSHIP

As we explain in our companion volume, *The Lost Divisions*, the Army, because of its rapid expansion, was not always able to select the ablest men for leadership positions. Some who became officers were immature and insensitive and were unable to cope effectively with their responsibilities. Many soldiers were victimized by poor leadership.

One of the difficult tasks that the Army faces is to help civilians make the transition to military life. When the Army is under the pressure of time, it is likely that many recruits will be poorly handled; this was clearly the case with W.L., reported below.

Another major challenge to Army leadership occurs in combat. Here the men are quickly separated from the boys. If the noncommissioned and junior officers do not provide effective leadership, soldiers are forced to look to one of their own for direction. Such "informal leadership," well known in civilian life, played a significant part in the Army. This is illustrated by the case of P.W.K., which follows that of W.L.

Because his parents died when he was four, W.L. was brought up by relatives and friends in a Southern farming community. The town was isolated and very poor. Until he was ten he lived with a sister and her husband. When they moved away, he stayed on with the new residents of the farm helping them work the fields. Several attempts were made to send him to school but he refused to stay because the other children made fun of him because he had no parents. And so he never learned to read or write. Outside of two periods of enlistment in the Civilian Conservation Corps the second of which ended when he deserted to return home, he spent his whole life prior to military service working on a farm. Although of low intelligence he was a good steady worker and always managed to support himself. With the exception of one occasion when he got angry and beat up a neighborhood bully who had been teasing him, he never had any trouble with the law. At the age of twenty he married a local girl and they had one child.

Inducted into the Army at twenty-two, Private L. was assigned for training in the Armored Infantry. His troubles started immediately. He had been able to do farm work because he had had many years in which to learn. Now he was expected to become a soldier almost, as it seemed, overnight. His mind could not work that fast. He did not understand the words the officers used during lectures and even when he did understand he could not translate what was said into action. On the drill field he was completely confused. Further, because of his inability to read he never knew when his name was posted on the bulletin board for a work detail. Learning his general orders was impossible. He had flat feet and on hikes would develop large protuberances which were very painful. Frequently his feet hurt so much that he had to rest.

The officers, both commissioned and noncommissioned, completely failed to realize that they were dealing with a man of very low intelligence who had, in addition, a very painful foot condition. To them Private L. was just one more green recruit who did not want to become a soldier. They felt that all he needed was to be toughened up and taught discipline.

Consequently he was subjected to constant criticism whenever he made a mistake. He became the butt of many jokes. The other soldiers, taking their cue from the noncommissioned officers, teased him unmercifully. He was assigned extra work as punishment for his failures. On hikes when he quit because of his feet, the NCO's dragged him along behind the marching column.

Always sensitive to teasing and criticism, Private L. reacted with anger to this treatment. But he could not fight his officers as he had the neighborhood bully at home. As time went on he began to be increasingly depressed. Caught between his own physical and mental incapacity and the constant demands of his superiors, he did not know what to do. Finally, he mentioned to a barracks mate that he intended to hang himself. To him it seemed the only solution. When word of this got to his platoon sergeant, he was taken to the hospital.

The patient remained hospitalized for almost four months. Intelligence tests indicated that he had the mental ability of a five-and-a-half-year-old child. Although severely depressed on admission, he improved rapidly as he came to realize that in the hospital the officers did not tease him and try to force him to do things he did not understand. Nevertheless, he continued to think that if he were returned to his company he would kill himself. When asked why he did not run away instead of thinking of suicide, he said, "That would be wrong." It was obvious to the doctors that the failure of his superiors to recognize his very marked mental deficiency had contributed to the patient's emotional state.

After discharge W.L. went to work as a laborer in a factory near his home. His income was very low and he and his family lived in two small rooms partitioned off from a grist mill. Because the Veterans Administration was in doubt as to whether he was suffering from a true mental disorder, he was hospitalized for observation several months after discharge. The tests at that time revealed severe mental deficiency but no psychiatric condition. His flat feet and a curvature of the spine were also noted. Since his release from the hospital, W.L. has farmed on a share-cropping basis. Although, because of his intelligence, he is restricted to a marginal level, he has been able to support his family which now includes three children. Working at a job which he has had many years to learn, he has made a passable adjustment.

P.W.K. was raised by very strict parents. He did not become fully toilet trained until the age of six and his mother frequently whipped him when he wet the bed at night. As a child he suffered from intense fears, especially when he was left alone in a dark room. His friends were all boys; he rarely went on dates and never learned to dance. Although his basic education ended with graduation from grammar school, he attended a business school for eighteen months. With this background he obtained a job as an office clerk in a brewery which he held for thirteen years until inducted into service. During these years he began to have sharp stomach pains and a sensation of burning which occurred whenever he ate fried or greasy food. He was able to continue working, however, and in fact was a very satisfactory employee, perhaps because his job required little initiative or responsibility.

Shortly after induction into the Army at the age of thirty-two,

Private K. married. His wife was a rather independent woman who had been used to supporting herself. As time went on she came to make an increasing number of decisions for her husband. However, at the time of their marriage most of the soldier's decisions were being made by his military superiors. He was assigned to an armored division where he stayed throughout most of his military career first as a supply clerk and later as a jeep driver. After almost two years of training, the division was sent to Europe in late 1944. Just prior to overseas shipment Private K. had increasing difficulty with his stomach. However, he was not hospitalized and was able to enter combat with his outfit.

The soldier kept going for just one month after his company made its first contact with the enemy. Although exposed to heavy shelling at times and although he sustained a minor flesh wound in the thigh, Private K. experienced his major difficulties not directly as a result of enemy action, but because of conditions within his outfit. Accustomed all his life to having decisions made for him, first by his mother and later by his civilian supervisors, military commanders, and wife, the soldier found himself for the first time forced to act on his own initiative in combat and even to lead others.

Most of his fellow-soldiers and even noncommissioned officers were far younger than he. Many looked to him for help and direction because he was older. Further, because the primary mission of his group was reconnaissance, he frequently worked with a small group under a single officer. However this officer, a lieutenant, was a poor leader. In fact in many situations he was not a leader at all, and the responsibility fell on Private K. as the oldest man. The lieutenant was quite young and apparently incapable of inspiring any confidence in his men.

The company commander, although older, came from the deep South and was in charge of an outfit comprised almost entirely of Northerners like P.W.K. His frequent derogatory references to Negroes as well as his strict discipline only aroused resentment among his troops. Morale was extremely low and Private K., as he was again and again denied the kind of firm but friendly leadership that he needed, became surly and was almost on the verge of insubordination. Although he had several opportunities to kill enemy soldiers, he never did. He always made it a point to miss them.

As his resentment toward his officers for failing him increased and he was forced to take more unwanted responsiblity, his stomach condition became much worse; he had extremely painful cramps and began to vomit. At times he would shake all over and suffer from chills. When his division was placed in reserve for a few days, he went on sick call and was hospitalized for a suspected stomach ulcer. Extensive tests by the medical service over a period of many months eliminated the possibility of an ulcer, but the patient came to revel in the constant medical examinations. To be given the attention that he now received, after the complete lack of attention he had experienced in combat, was extremely satisfying to him. By the time he reached the psychiatrist it was obvious that, although his stomach condition resulted from intense emotional reactions, it was so entrenched as to make his return to duty highly improbable.

After his discharge P.W.K. returned to his former work at the brewery. However, his stomach complaints, nervousness, and irritability continued. He left his job and for two years took courses in commercial art and photography. Since 1950 he has worked for his wife who along with an older man operates a business making and selling small ornamental objects. He helps cast the figures while his wife and her partner handle the selling. The veteran is fairly satisfied with his work, although when his wife is away from home collecting orders and he is left alone to cope with the problems of filling requisitions his anxiety and stomach pains return. He and his wife still have no children. Although P.W.K. continues to maintain himself adequately, it is apparent that this is accomplished only with the support and guidance of his wife.

Poor leadership results in poor performance in a great variety of ways. The fact that W.L.'s unsuitability for military service was not noted until he threatened to hang himself points to the incompetence of his superiors. They tried to turn him into an effective soldier when they should have proceeded to discharge him expeditiously.

P.W.K.'s eventual collapse was dictated by his inability to assume the leadership which was thrust on him because the duly designated leader was incompetent and his fellow soldiers had to turn to someone. It is impossible to calculate the number of men who became ineffective because of poor leadership but it was undoubtedly substantial.

Chapter Five: THE MILITARY ORGANIZATION

THE ARMY dominated the life of everybody in uniform. No man, day or night, weekday or weekend, could get free of it. The aim of this chapter is to illustrate how various organizational policies and procedures affected the performance of the individual soldier. No attention will be paid to the unique problems that soldiers faced as a result of the stress of combat. Such situational factors will be dealt with in Chapter Seven.

No organization can benefit from the advantages of specialization without strict adherence to established principles and procedures. The larger the organization, the greater is the need for basic policies to guide those in subordinate positions. It has been said that the great virtue of this approach for the Army is that it enables a sergeant to carry on even if all of his officers become casualties.

The fact that the Army expanded more than thirtyfold in less than four years precipitated problems for which satisfactory answers could not always be readily found. This chapter will call attention to some of the policies that had an adverse effect on the performance of particular groups of soldiers. We are not seeking to reach a judgment about these policies and procedures. The Army and the other armed services did succeed in defeating the Germans and the Japanese. Our sole interest is to illustrate how organizational factors can have an adverse effect on the performance of particular individuals.

Four facets of military organization—investment, planning, discipline, and assignment—have been singled out for specific consideration. The Army could never have expanded so rapidly had it not devoted major resources to the task of converting civilians into soldiers. In addition to investing in their training the Army had to devote considerable resources to supportive activities. For instance, all Americans insisted that the Army supply excellent medical service for the soldiers who became ill or injured. The investments that the Army made in its men had a considerable influence on their effectiveness as soldiers. Pressed for time, it was not possible for the Army to make an optimal investment in each man to bring him to his highest level of performance. It had to be satisfied with making a reasonable investment.

The Army's lack of experience in screening and training very large numbers obscured some of the steps that it might have taken to reduce unnecessary losses. The Army's only direct experience with large-scale mobilization was in World War I. Time dimmed some of these lessons while changes in resources and requirements made others obsolescent. Planning lagged behind these changes. It was not until the third and fourth year of mobilization that the Army developed mental hygiene clinics and special training units to help handicapped soldiers. Entering the conflict with incomplete and inadequate plans the Army had to fight and learn at the same time. Inevitably it paid a price for improvisation.

No organization, large or small, can exist without basic discipline: the members must have a clear understanding of what is required of them and realize that failure will lead to punishment. The Army had an elaborate system of discipline. But no system is better than the men who operate it. The Army had to rely primarily on recently commissioned officers who had no experience with its traditions, who knew little about the men for whom they were responsible, and who frequently had never before held a leadership position. As a result gross inequities often developed in the administration of military justice. Soldiers guilty of the identical offense might initially receive sentences varying from three to thirty years in prison.

But not all the difficulties, or even most of them, arose because of excessive severity. Often it was failure to enforce discipline that led to the ineffective performance of many soldiers. Officers found it easier to get rid of a troublemaker by reassigning or discharging him than to prepare formal charges and hold him for trial by court-martial.

The Army's disciplinary problems were compounded by the fact that the American public insisted and the Army agreed that a soldier whose ineffectiveness grew out of emotional illness should not be disciplined. Since the sick were entitled to the best medical attention, everything possible was done to restore a soldier to health. And it was not until late in the war that the Army came to recognize that the discrepancy between conditions in combat—where injury or death might come at any moment—and those prevailing in rear hospitals was so great that many soldiers sought to escape from the front lines by becoming or remaining invalided. Most of them were not malingerers; they were more the victims of their own unconscious fears and anxieties. The war was over before the Army was able to resolve the dilemma between its desires to provide the best hospital treatment for those in need of it and to prevent soldiers who feared to return to duty from holding on to or exaggerating their symptoms.

Among the most important personnel decisions that the Army made was the duty to which it assigned a soldier. If a man was assigned to work beyond his capacities—either physical, intellectual, or emotional—it was only a matter of time before the strain made it impossible for him to serve effectively.

It was often just as difficult for men who were given work far below their capacity. Although most soldiers could accept such assignments, a minority could not tolerate work that made a mockery of their capacity, training, and aspirations. Among the many who were underassigned some developed such deep frustrations that they broke down.

INVESTMENT

We have noted earlier that no man could become a soldier unless the Army made an investment in converting and training him; and that in the midst of a major war the Army was under great pressure to invest only in those who were most likely to prove effective. It could not afford to devote too much time or too many resources to conversion and training, but neither could it afford to skimp for in that case large numbers would be inadequately prepared to perform effectively.

Optimal investment for the Army was a function of four variables: the size and quality of the nation's manpower resources; the time schedule that the enemy was forcing on the Army to get trained divisions into the field; the risk that the Army was willing to assume with respect to men who might fail if they were forced through an accelerated program; and finally the number of trained instructors that the Army could allocate to the training task. The following cases indicate some of the consequences for the performance of individual soldiers which resulted from the Army's attempts to balance these complex variables.

Little is known of C.B.E.'s early life, other than the fact that he was born in a rural area of the South and was brought up on a farm. He did complete three years of schooling. Later he worked as a farm laborer until drafted for military service at the age of thirty-three.

After leaving the reception center he was shipped across the country to the West Coast and joined a newly formed infantry division. His group arrived shortly after basic training had started and, because of further delays in processing, they missed over a week of the thirteen week training period. Private E. found the work very difficult from the beginning. Because of his limited intelligence, he could not absorb new material as rapidly as many other soldiers. Military drill was particularly difficult. Nevertheless, he was healthy and in good physical condition from his work on the farm. He had no difficulty keeping up with the others on hikes in spite of the fact that he was somewhat older. Furthermore, he liked the Army and felt strongly that it was his duty to serve. He was generally well-liked and was considered a man who tried hard to be a good soldier.

Ten weeks of training, however proved rather conclusively that Private E. would not make the grade without some special instruction and assistance. He had learned some things, but was still far behind the majority of his group. Accordingly, he and five other soldiers were removed from regular training for special classes, in accordance with a recent directive from division headquarters. Over a two-week period they received twenty-eight hours of instruction in basic military subjects from one of the company officers. The rest of their duty hours were spent in performing various work details around the company area. On the latter Private E.'s performance was quite satisfactory as long as he was told exactly what to do and was guided until he understood clearly what the work entailed. It took a long time to instruct him, but once he had learned what was expected, he worked hard. In the special classes, however, it was a different story. Twenty-eight hours were quite insufficient and he failed a test given at the end of the two-week period. Possibly with the twelve to sixteen weeks of special training that the Army later introduced for such individuals, he could have become a soldier, but two weeks were certainly not enough.

At this time in early 1943, it was official Army policy to discharge any soldier who, after a reasonable trial at duty, was considered so lacking in the necessary intelligence that, even with intensive training, he might not be able to meet minimum requirements. In other words the Army, already faced with a tremendous training burden, did not want to increase this burden by investing in intensive instruction of soldiers who might have to be separated from the service anyway. In the division of which Private E. was a member this policy was interpreted to mean that any soldier who could not satisfactorily complete the special two-week course, should be evaluated with a view to discharge. A board of officers was established for this purpose.

After failing the test of basic military subject matter, Private E. was immediately sent for psychological testing. He was found to have the intelligence of a child of eight-and-one-half years old. His I.Q. of 60 was sufficiently low to bring into question the advisability of further military training. It was possible that he might eventually be able to learn the necessary material, but how long that would take remained in doubt. There was no certainty that he could ever absorb enough to be a competent soldier. The board of officers felt that the Army should not make the investment in further training and accordingly he was discharged with just over four months of service.

As a civilian C.B.E. has made a quite satisfactory adjustment at a level consistent with his limited intellectual capabilities. He has been employed primarily as a farm laborer, but he has done some highway construction work. In 1950 he married a woman who had recently been widowed and shortly thereafter started farm management training under the Veterans Administration. He continued for sixteen months performing quite satisfactorily. At present he is share-cropping his own farm.

As a child, V.T.F. was always very much attached to his mother, who had become an invalid when he was thirteen. This close relationship continued for many years. In school he did very well. He graduated from a Midwestern state university at twenty-one, having majored in pharmacy, and was married the next year. He became a registered pharmacist and took a job in his father's drugstore which he held for three years. However, he began to have difficulty with his wife as well as his father, and his drinking, which from the age of sixteen had been quite heavy, increased.

Over the next eleven years V.T.F.'s life followed the course of a chronic alcoholic. He drifted from one job to another as a pharmacist, musician, and a piano tuner. On four different occasions he was fired for drinking. After his mother died he reacted by becoming intoxicated even more frequently. His wife divorced him the next year. Three years later they remarried because of their three children, but that lasted only six months. A third marriage, this time to a different woman, was always on the verge of break-up. V.T.F. usually drank about a quart of liquor a day when on a bout, but when his money ran out he resorted to hair tonic and shaving lotion. He was arrested on twelve occasions for intoxication and twice was sent to the penitentiary for passing bad checks in order to buy liquor—once for six months and once for a year. He was hospitalized seven different times for psychiatric treatment.

In spite of this history he was accepted for military service in late 1942 at the age of thirty-five. His basic training, which he underwent as a member of a medical battalion in a West Coast camp, was continually interrupted. Although officially with his unit for four months he spent two months in the hospital with a hernia and another two weeks on furlough. Private F. was then assigned to the camp medical detachment as a pharmacist. He had very favorable recommendations from his previous commanding officer. At first his work in the pharmacy was good; he was intelligent and knew his job well. Then he began to drink again. Once he was absent without leave for three days after a three-day pass. At other times he reported in for duty intoxicated. After one month he had to be transferred; even though he was a good pharmacist when sober, the risk that he might make a mistake was too great. The officer in charge and other supervisory personnel were far too busy to spend their time watching Private F. to see that he did not drink or at least to make certain that he never worked while under the influence of alcohol.

Assigned next to the medical laboratory, he almost immediately went AWOL and was picked up, drunk, by the military police. While in the hospital recuperating, a psychiatrist talked with him. At that time a discharge for alcoholism was considered, but the doctor felt that since he was a highly skilled worker of well-above-average intelligence every effort should be made to retain him. There was also some hope that he could be rehabilitated, since he had vowed to stop drinking. The feeling at that time was that although it might be necessary to make a considerable investment in rather close supervision, this investment should be made in view of the nature of the patient's prior training. After release from the hospital he received his first court-martial and was sentenced to the post stockade where he stayed for about a week. Over the next five months the soldier worked hard and well; he stayed sober. Then he began drinking again and was assigned to the kitchen because it was thought that there he could be supervised more closely than was possible in the laboratory or on the wards.

During a month he did not report for work three times and was found on every occasoin in his quarters thoroughly intoxicated. Each time he had to spend several days in the hospital and was then court-martialed. After the third episode he was sent to the stockade for two months. Back with his outfit the same thing happened again. Then he was AWOL for a day. In describing his own experiences during this period the Mess Sergeant said: "Private F.'s work under my supervision was fine except every once in a while he would go off and get out of control. I was told to keep in touch with him, but just couldn't. He was on the run all the time. You would try to keep him in the Mess Hall, and you would have to have a man at the front and back door as he was always wanting to get out. He would be there an hour and take off an hour. While he was sober, his work was satisfactory."

The final decision to release the soldier from the Army came after he failed to return from a furlough to his home. Although he claimed, when picked up by the military police, that he had been drugged and all his belongings stolen, it was quite obvious that he had been drinking heavily. At first another court-martial was considered, but in view of the constant repetition of this same pattern, it was felt that further punishment would do little good. The probability of successful psychiatric treatment in such a case of confirmed alcoholism was recognized to be rather low. Further, the Army at that time, mid-1944, did not feel that it should invest in long-term treatment of alcoholics because of shortages in hospital space and, more crucial, in trained psychiatrists and psychologists. The only alternative was to supervise the prisoner's activity so closely that he could not get drunk. That, however, had been tried in the pharmacy, in the laboratory, and in the kitchen. In every case it had failed. The final decision of the discharge board was that time spent in further attempts at supervision would probably be futile unless he could be watched constantly by a noncommissioned officer who had practically no other duties. In spite of Private F.'s qualifications as a pharmacist, this was felt to be too much of an investment for the Army to make. Furthermore, even this degree of supervision might well not succeed. Accordingly, a discharge "without honor" was decided upon.

Returning home, the veteran worked with his father again until the latter died in 1945. Since then he has held numerous positions as a pharmacist and professional musician. His drinking continued after his discharge, but stopped almost completely when he joined Alcoholics Anonymous. For five years he appeared to be cured. Difficulties with his wife became more pronounced, however, in 1950 and he started drinking from one to one-and-a-half quarts daily. Four months of this resulted in a separation from his wife and brought about his admission to the V.A. hospital for acute alcoholism. Later he was divorced from his wife. At the present time he is remarried again and is operating his own business.

M.E.O. completed the eighth grade in school at the age of seventeen, having failed several grades because of irregular attendance. For the next three years he worked in a sawmill. After that, he drifted from one job to another working usually as a welder or mechanic. Although he traveled a good deal, he always remained in the deep South. Except for one hospitalization during which he was treated for syphilis his health was good. In 1941 he married and a child was born shortly. He and his wife lived near an Army base where he worked.

In the summer of 1942 he began to feel weak and began to think that he was rotting away. His family physician referred him to a mental hospital where he was found to be suffering from an acute psychosis. He remained in the hospital for two weeks during which time he was given electric shock therapy. Although considerably improved, he did not get a job after returning home and this combined with many family problems led to frequent fights with his wife. Finally, they separated. Shortly afterwards, an induction order arrived and M.E.O. entered the Army. At that time his mental condition appeared to be quite normal and he did not inform anyone that he had been discharged from the hospital only four months previously.

Although his performance in basic training was satisfactory, Private O. reported on sick call several times during the first month complaining of what appeared to be mild convulsions. The doctor at the dispensary, suspecting epilepsy, sent him to the hospital for a more complete study. There, he appeared cheerful, mixed well with the other patients, and did not exhibit any signs of epilepsy or other illness. He seemed quite normal. For the first time, however, he discussed his prior hospitalization for psychosis.

Army policy at that time barred the induction of all individuals who were known to have been hospitalized for a psychotic condition. This policy had been adopted because such men tended to become psychotic again, thus frequently making any training investment valueless; moreover, once these men broke down again, an extensive investment in treatment was required to rehabilitate them, an investment which in many cases did not yield satisfactory results. The Army's objectives were military, not medical, and it was policy to avoid extensive medical treatment of soldiers who probably could not be returned to full duty.

Accordingly, Private O. was given a medical discharge, even though he was not psychotic at the time, because the Army did not want to take the risk of investing in training a man likely to break down in the future. He was, in fact, returned to duty, although not to training status, and served for over a month while awaiting his release. At no time did he exhibit any psychotic symptoms.

In civilian life M.E.O. maintained a relatively good adjustment, although he did not go back to live with his wife and they later were divorced. His work pattern was similar to that of his pre-Army period, although possibly more irregular. He held jobs in many different parts of the country. Employment was easy to obtain and having worked as a welder and mechanic, he was paid well even though he rarely stayed on a job for more than three months. He was killed in 1946 as a result of an accident which occurred while he was repairing some farm machinery.

These three cases illustrate some of the difficult problems that the Army had to resolve in determining whether to train a man and how much of an investment to make in him in the hope of securing an effective soldier. In the case of C.B.E. it was willing only to give him two weeks of remedial instruction. Later in the war, when manpower became tighter, the Army was willing to make a much greater effort to bring the uneducated up to minimum standards.

An alcoholic such as V.T.F. who has scarce skills always presented a tantalizing problem because the Army hoped that if given another chance, he might become an effective soldier. The fact that at one point he was able to remain sober for five months added to the uncertainty about what policy to pursue with respect to him. The Army was clearly willing to make reasonable investments as long as it believed it could receive reasonable returns.

Only in the case of M.E.O. was the cause clear of doubt. The Army had a firm policy that men who had suffered from a psychosis would not be accepted for military service and if they slipped through the screening, they would upon identification be discharged. The likelihood of their future ineffectiveness was too high to justify holding them or investing in their training.

PLANNING AND IMPROVISATION

In establishing standards of performance the Army was hampered by the absence of reliable experience data which would have enabled it to judge the advantages and limitations of various criteria. The prewar Army had operated on such a small scale with such different personnel that its experience could not be safely used as a guide for wartime decisions.

Moreover, during the early years of the war there was relatively little understanding of, or sympathy for, operational or any other type of research that might have provided a more solid foundation for the decisions of the General Staff. Most senior officers believed that they had accumulated sufficient knowledge over their years of service to reach sound judgments about manpower policy. Therefore, instead of being based on careful planning, manpower policy in World War II was largely one long effort at improvisation. How lack of planning could adversely affect the performance of individual soldiers can be seen in the following cases.

J.A.H. was born and raised in a small town in the Middle Atlantic area. Although he completed the eighth grade at the age of fifteen, he had a great deal of difficulty in school and never learned to read or write anything but the simplest material. Newspapers and magazines were incomprehensible to him and sometimes he made a mistake in spelling his own name. Actually, he had been promoted from grade to grade without having mastered the material. Since he did not learn to read in the earlier grades, the subject matter to which he was exposed later was largely meaningless.

Duller than many of his classmates, he needed more time to learn, but instead of getting more time, he was rushed through school at a rate which left him bewildered. At an early age he developed a tendency to react with tenseness and fear whenever he did not know the answer to a question. The prospect of being asked to recite in class was a continuous nightmare. He expected to be criticized when he failed and he often was. As a result of his limited intelligence and fear of failure he learned practically nothing during his last five years of school. Nevertheless, after he had left school he was able to obtain a job as a presser in a dry cleaning establishment where he remained for four years. His income of $25 a week was sufficient for his needs and, free of the pressure to learn things faster than was possible for him, he was happy.

Inducted into military service in the final months of 1942, Private H. found himself in a situation which reminded him in many ways of his earlier school experiences. Again he had difficulty in learning and as he was rushed from one thing to the next, he began again to fear that he would do or say the wrong thing. Then, after only a week of training he came down with the grippe and had to spend three weeks in the hospital. He never did catch up with his group. For a man of J.A.H.'s limited intelligence, to take a thirteen-weeks' course in only ten was quite out of the question, especially since he had missed much of the earlier, fundamental subject matter. He was constantly preoccupied with problems of close-order drill and rifle care which the others had learned while he was in the hospital. As a result he had no time to absorb the more advanced training. Frequently the officers took him aside for individual instruction, but at these times he felt so self-conscious at being singled out for special attention that he only became more confused. The instructors, in turn, became impatient and considered him much more stupid than he really was.

Although he tried hard Private H. had not learned enough at the end of the thirteen-week period to qualify him for more advanced training with his company. Consequently psychological testing was requested to determine if he should be discharged. To the surprise of his officers, he was found to have the mental age of an eleven-year-old. His I.Q. of 80 was above that of many other soldiers who had performed quite satisfactorily. But he needed some type of special training which would include reading and writing as well as a longer period of instruction on military subjects.

Private H. was not in that group of soldiers who have been termed screening errors because the examination at induction failed to reveal characteristics which if known would have resulted in their rejection. In every sense—physical, intellectual, and emotional—he met the current requirements for military service. There was every reason to believe that with appropriate training he would become a satisfactory soldier. The Army had deliberately accepted large numbers of men with intelligence as low as Private H.'s and even some with lower I.Q.'s, realizing that special training might be required for them.

Although adequate special training units did exist on some posts in early 1943, Private H. happened to be at a camp where facilities appropriate to his needs had not been provided. He was discharged as inapt, not because he lacked the ability to serve, but because the Army had not provided the type of specialized instruction required to convert him into an effective soldier. In fact he had not even had a full period of training and no procedure then existed that would compensate for the period of enforced hospitalization. Later, he would have been assigned to a new outfit and started his training again on leaving the hospital, but at that time such action was seldom taken.

As a civilian, J.A.H. returned to his former job as a presser. About a year after his discharge he married and he now has two children. Although he has never continued his education and is still practically illiterate, he is a good worker and supports his family adequately.

G.G.T. had been a rather timid child who tended to avoid other people. At the age of nine he was in bed for a year with tuberculosis, but he recovered and has since been in good physical health. As he grew up he concentrated on his school work and did not participate in athletics or social events. He entered a Southern state university which was located near his home and did quite well his first year. As a sophomore, however, he lost interest in his studies and became quite disturbed over the thought that he was a homosexual, in spite of the fact that his homosexual activity had been confined to several minor episodes many years before. He was able partially to overcome these disturbing thoughts and continue his education, majoring in mathematics.

At the time of his induction into the Army in the middle of his senior year in college, G.G.T. was a rather emotionally unstable individual. Nevertheless, he scored very high on the intelligence test and with his background in mathematics, seemed to be a person that the Army could well use. Certainly his emotional problems were not of sufficient magnitude to justify his rejection.

He was immediately sent to the West Coast for training in the use of anti-aircraft weapons. The physical work was extremely difficult for him. He had always withdrawn from physical activity and people to his school books and now that this was impossible he began to experience shortness of breath, a rapid pounding of his heart, and high blood pressure. With the other soldiers talking about girls all the time, he became extremely conscious of his own lack of interest in the opposite sex and his former fears of homosexuality were revived. After about ten days his company commander noticed the difficulty he was having with drill and marching as well as his tendency to withdraw from the other soldiers. He was sent to the Neuropsychiatric Clinic where an extensive examination was carried out. The conclusions of the psychiatrist were as follows:

Were it not for the fact that this man's civilian training, namely, mathematics, might be utilized in our school, I would recommend that he immediately be given a C.D.D. However, the soldier himself states that he would like very much to remain in the Army in order to be "able to do something." I do not believe that his latent homosexuality will in itself be a problem with this boy. For the present, therefore, I would recommend that he be reclassified Limited Service on the assumption that he can be assigned to the school for teaching mathematics. If this recommendation is accepted I will want to see this man in the Neuropsychiatric Clinic approximately once a week for follow-up interviews.

In spite of this recommendation and the very real need for men with his training, Private T. was discharged approximately one month later. The examining psychiatrist was overruled by higher authorities who were unwilling to make available the type of assignment and the outpatient treatment that were necessary. Although later, outpatient facilities became a regular part of the Army medical establishment, there was no regular provision for them in early 1943. Thus a soldier who, although suffering from a neurosis, could have been maintained on duty in a critical specialty was discharged because of a lack of appropriate procedures for his retention.

In civilian life G.G.T. has become a teacher of mathematics. After three years of graduate study he worked for two years in a research institute and for the last five years has been employed as a university teacher, first as an instructor and later with the rank of assistant professor. His mental health seemingly remained good, and he received no psychiatric treatment until 1953. At that time he became quite disturbed and spent six months in a state mental hospital. His recovery has apparently been quite satisfactory. He is still unmarried.

The Army's neglect of manpower planning and its costs in the loss of manpower are illustrated by these two cases. So many illiterates like J.A.H. were lost to the Army because they were not given simple additional training that the Army eventually acted to remedy the situation by establishing formal Special Training Units at reception centers in June 1943.

Likewise, many competent men such as G.G.T. could have been salvaged had they been able to receive some psychiatric support to ease them over the rough spots. Here, too, the Army eventually acted but not before many had been discharged. Industry has learned this lesson and has come increasingly to recognize the importance of easing the adjustment of new workers.

DISCIPLINE AND OVERPERMISSIVENESS

As we noted, the Army was not an excessively disciplined organization. This can be primarily explained by the moderating influence of civilian attitudes and values which made themselves felt through

Congress, the press, the senior officials of the War and Navy Departments, and above all by the prior conditioning of the officer personnel, the vast majority of whom were civilians in uniform.

It is a well-known fact that during the war Negro soldiers were not generally held to the same strict account as were white troops, which helps to explain at least in part the extreme case of J.Y. below. Moreover, as has also been pointed out earlier, soldiers who were hospitalized were granted many special privileges. But the greatest privilege for the patient was his relative safety. It was not until the latter part of the war that the Army took steps to insure that in its efforts to provide good medical care it did not undermine the fighting morale of the troops by offering them a respectable escape route.

Psychiatrists, especially those serving with combat units, came to recognize that they had to temper their humanitarian approach to the individual patient with a concern for the impact of their professional decisions on the morale and efficiency of the group. Frequently they kept men in the line whom they would have preferred to send to a rear hospital because they did not want to encourage other soldiers to seek relief in the same manner.

Although J.Y. attended Negro schools in a small Southern city for four years, he has been illiterate all his life. He worked in various jobs as a truck driver and laborer. A big man, he was a good worker, but was at times prone to outbursts of rage. However, when made to understand that these would not be tolerated, he caused little trouble. At home however he was able to dominate his family by threats of violence and on several occasions, after his marriage in 1939, ran his wife out of the house. These rages were most likely to occur when he had been drinking, although J.Y. was by no means an alcoholic.

On entering the Army in late 1942 he was first assigned to an Infantry division and later to two different Quartermaster battalions, all at a Southwestern post. His total period of service was approximately four months. Throughout this time he was in almost continuous trouble because of his fighting and insubordination. Yet he never was court-martialed nor did he spend any time in the stockade. His punishment consisted of a transfer to another outfit, or, on one occasion, a week at hard labor. At no time was he made to feel that he had to behave as a soldier.

His actions were in many ways quite unusual. He initiated several fights in his barracks, sometimes when he came in drunk, but at other times when he was quite sober. Once, in a rage, he took the top off a commode and threw it on the floor. When several other soldiers tried to stop him he threatened to kill them and was successful in terrorizing the whole barracks.

He also precipitated difficulties in the mess hall. When he did not like the food, he demanded an order of bacon and eggs and a bottle of milk. When they did not appear, he threw his food on the floor and stalked out. He once asked for a second glass of milk before the other men had been served. Told that he could not have another cup until the rest had had a first, he deliberately upset the milk container which had ten gallons of milk in it. On the one occasion when he was disciplined, he had been in bed and refused to obey an order to get up and take his bedding out for airing. The noncommissioned officers were unable to do anything with him. He considered drill a big joke. Many times the NCOs went to the company commander because they were afraid of him. Yet the CO did little. As a result morale in the whole company was poor. Private Y. felt that he could do practically anything he pleased.

Several times the company commander sent him to the dispensary because he thought the soldier might be mentally ill or might have very low intelligence. Although the medical officer did not agree with either of these opinions he finally sent Private Y. to the hospital for further study. The psychiatrist there felt that he was not suffering from any mental disorder and that, although he was somewhat mentally retarded, there was no real mental deficiency. The soldier was returned to his company with a recommendation that his conduct be corrected by disciplinary means; his problem was not of a medical nature. A month later Private Y. was discharged under "other than honorable" conditions, still believing that in military service he could act just as he had at home. Certainly his officers had never given him reason to believe that he would have to conform to military discipline.

Shortly after J.Y.'s separation from the service his wife died. There were no children. Later he returned to work as a manual laborer handling machinery and scrap iron for his former employer. After about three months he began to be absent from work frequently and was fired. During the next five years he worked on several different construction jobs, always as a laborer. No information is available on J.Y.'s history since late 1948. However, until that time he had adjusted to civilian life on a level commensurate with his education and prior work experience. He had not remarried.

T.J.M. was born in a large Midwestern city of immigrant parents. His childhood was a happy one and his family was quite close. At the age of sixteen, after two years in a trade school where he studied a variety of subjects including machineshop, typing, and baking, he went to work as a truck driver. A good worker, he enjoyed his job and spent the ensuing twelve years at it. Then he was drafted. T.J.M., although quite willing to serve his country, was loath to leave what had been a very pleasant life. He knew that he would miss not only his parents, his fiancée, and his job, but also the participation in athletics—boating, horseback riding, baseball—that he enjoyed so much.

Nevertheless, he was a good soldier. Although the training was especially difficult because of an extremely severe winter, he rapidly developed into a very competent infantryman and was assigned to duty as a jeep driver in a heavy weapons company. Except for a month when he was hospitalized for a tumor operation, he was in good health. After almost two years of training, his division was sent to England and shortly thereafter to France. In early September 1944, T.J.M. entered combat. However, it was not until the first of the year that he was exposed to very heavy fighting. During January and February his division participated in some of the heaviest fighting in Europe as they approached the Siegfried Line.

In late February, while attacking across a river, Private M.'s outfit was reduced from a strength of eighty men to nine. As he was pulling up the bank on the far side two shells landed very close to him and while in the act of jumping out of his jeep, he was hit by a third. He lost consciousness and awoke in the basement of a house with the medics attending him. Within seven hours he was on the operating table. His body had been badly cut by shell fragments; he suffered a large wound on his hip, another on his ankle, and a broken finger on his left hand. None proved to be serious. In two days he had been transferred through Paris to a hospital in England. Suddenly the front seemed much closer to England than he had ever realized. Two and a half months later he was flown to Scotland and from there to the United States. He still had the feeling that it was only a matter of a day's trip back into the terror of combat. Perhaps this feeling was reinforced by the realization that his wounds had healed completely and that he might be sent back into combat again.

Quite suddenly he developed a nervous tremor and rather severe back pains. It was almost as if he had decided he wanted to stay in the hospital longer rather than return to duty. And yet his symptoms were completely real. Subsequent experience with patients of this type has led the military to adopt a policy of returning those who have recovered from wounds to duty as quickly as possible. In T.J.M.'s case, however, the long period of hospitalization had already contributed to the development of psychological symptoms. His life in the hospital as contrasted with combat was pleasant; he was taken care of and, most important, as long as he stayed there, he would not have to fight again. It was not that he did not want to return to combat; he just felt that he was sick and could not return.

The medical authorities, rather than assuring T.J.M. that he had no physical disorder and returning him to duty in the hope that his symptoms would disappear, further reinforced his conviction that he had received a back injury when wounded which had only later manifested itself. He was fitted with a brace and then transferred to another hospital without appropriate neurological studies.

Finally, after two months in the States he was referred to a psychiatrist because there seemed to be no physical basis for his backaches and tremor. By that time, after almost five months in various hospitals, after being returned to this country because of his wounds, and after wearing a brace for a month, it was impossible to convince him that he was not suffering from a serious injury. T.J.M. was discharged for psychoneurosis.

Within a month the veteran was back at his old job as a truck driver. For a while his back pains continued. He lost about a day a week from work and once in a while he went to see a doctor. His conviction of the physical nature of his complaints was once again reinforced when he received a pension from the Veterans Administration for anxiety neurosis and spinal sprain. His pension was eliminated, however, at a later date after an extensive physical examination. By late 1948 T.J.M. was no longer losing any time from work. Although he still suffered occasionally from pains in his back, his condition was greatly improved.

Frequently men perform effectively, especially in difficult situations, only if they clearly perceive the consequences that will follow upon malperformance. No doubt J.Y. had an ugly temper, but he was able to restrain it sufficiently in civilian life to hold down a job. He could probably have been made into an effective soldier had his officers held him to account.

In T.J.M.'s case the hospital environment was so pleasant in contrast to the dangers of combat, that it sapped his will to continue to perform effectively as a soldier. The military has special need to avoid such situations, for unlike civilian life, where a man wants a job and tries to hold on to one when he gets it, there are obvious gains for a soldier when he is judged to be medically unable to perform his work effectively.

ASSIGNMENT

It was inevitable that in classifying and assigning millions of men the Army under great pressure would make many serious errors. Sometimes it was able to catch and correct these errors but often soldiers who were overassigned or underassigned came to the attention of the authorities only after they broke down.

The most serious cases were the overassigned. Since a higher assignment gave a soldier more rank, money, and privileges, it was likely that he would struggle to perform adequately and many undoubtedly outdid themselves. But strong motivation is not enough. No matter how hard a man tries, lack of skill or intelligence can lead to failure. Among the underassigned who broke were some who, disturbed on other counts, found an excuse in the way in which the Army treated them to justify their failure. They could not tolerate frustration and took the view that since the Army had broken faith with them, they were under no obligation to do their best for the Army.

P.W.A. was a member of a socially prominent family residing in an Eastern city. His father was a successful lawyer and both sons studied for the bar. P.W.A. attended local schools and graduated from a college near his home. Although not an outstanding student he did well and was active in social affairs; he was a member of the golf team as well as a frequent speaker at student gatherings. After completing college in 1942 he entered law school while working part-time in his father's office. During this period, as before, he was frequently in conflict with his father. The latter was prone to occasional alcoholic bouts and on several occasions the son had to go out and "round up" his father. Other than this, the family life seems to have been normal and P.W.A. gave no evidence of emotional disturbance.

In the summer of 1942, however, he had a disturbing experience in connection with some Civil Aeronautics Authority pilot training. Prior to graduation from college he became interested in flying and attempted to enlist in the Naval Air Corps. Rejected for physical defects, he was later accepted as a member of the Army Air Corps Reserve with the provision that he would be called to active duty for pilot training as soon as needed. Wishing to get some prior experience, he entered the Civilian Aeronautics Authority Training Program during the summer. From the beginning of the course he was a complete failure as an aviator; he lacked coordination but this was attributed to the fact that he was frightened all the time he was in the air. After about eighteen hours of flying it was quite apparent that he would "wash out." Before this happened, however, he himself decided he would never make a flyer and resigned from the program. At this time he was emotionally disturbed, realizing he was terribly afraid of flying, but at the same time not wishing to admit his failure.

Several months later he became an Air Cadet. Wishing to try once more to overcome his fear and thus convince himself and others that he was not a "sissy," he did not mention his prior failure. Air Corps selection procedures at that time did not include techniques that would reveal a fear of flying. He found even the initial instruction difficult and was rather relieved when after three weeks he entered the hospital with pneumonia. During the next two weeks he improved rapidly and was apparently emotionally normal, although he talked almost incessantly about an affair with a girl at home. A convalescent furlough followed during which he became increasingly nervous. His parents were especially concerned because his apathy and listlessness were in marked contrast to his earlier ways. As the time for his return to flight training approached, he worried almost continually. Driving back to camp with his parents, he became upset every time he heard a plane fly overhead. His behavior in the squadron orderly room when he checked in was so peculiar that he was sent back to the hospital.

For the next five months P.W.A. remained in the hospital suffering from an acute psychosis. He talked to himself, wandered about aimlessly, smiled inappropriately and was careless about his appearance. He also wrote on the walls. At times he rolled his eyes up in his head and leaned back against the wall while staring at the ceiling. Later he explained that he had been listening to voices. At other times he would sit quietly and write the names of the states over and over again. His speech was disorganized. "Well, I think President Roosevelt was about right. I suppose you might say I was yellow. I can't figure just how I landed here. There are better men than I dying around here now." Again, for no apparent reason at all, "I would not want to disturb an old barracks roommate of mine on his career in aviation." The feeling of antagonism toward his father was especially evident in his discussions of "homopatricide." Once he seemed to think he had killed his father, but later denied it. When brought before a medical board for discharge, he was obviously psychotic and a transfer to a civilian mental hospital was recommended. However, his parents finally obtained permission to take him home.

For a little over a year he remained at home doing very little. Gradually his thoughts of flying and glory and crashes and death began to recede. My mid-1944 the world of aviation had become a thing of the distant past and he was able to take up his career again. Entering law school he worked hard and within two years had passed the bar examinations. Later he worked as a law clerk and by 1954 was an assistant district attorney of his county. He married in 1949, but to date he has had no children. He is now doing very well and has an income exceeding $10,000 a year.

D.B.D. was born on a farm in the deep South of Negro parents. His school attendance was sporadic and at the age of twelve after completing only four grades he left. His ensuing occupational experience was quite varied, but in every case he was employed at a relatively low-level job consistent with his limited education and intelligence. He worked as a waiter in restaurants, a laundry helper, a factory laborer, a highway laborer, a janitor at a university, and finally for over three years as an able seaman in the Merchant Marine. Sometimes he was laid off because of insufficient work, sometimes he left because he did not like the job; rarely was he fired. At the age of eighteen D.B.D. married a girl who claimed she was going to have his child. However, the child died shortly after birth and D.B.D. left his wife. Although neither husband nor wife made any effort to obtain a divorce for many years, she started living with another man. D.B.D. was inducted into the Army shortly before his twenty-ninth birthday a healthy man, physically and emotionally.

Although he received a very low score on the intelligence test at induction, the soldier did very well in basic training. Along with many other low-intelligence inductees he was assigned to a Negro guard battalion at an air base. Selected for further training at a cooks and bakers school, he found the work difficult and was just barely able to pass the course. Nevertheless, after he returned to his company he was again considered an excellent soldier and was rapidly promoted to staff sergeant and placed in charge of the company mess hall. His company commander was especially impressed by the soldier's conscientiousness and his rather domineering attitude which seemed to suggest leadership ability.

Shortly after his promotion the guard battalion was disbanded and he was sent to an Engineer company. Here he continued as mess sergeant, but he found the job very difficult. With his very limited ability to read and write he had trouble making out menus. Then, too, frequently soldiers tried to get extra food from the kitchen and on many occasions they outwitted him. He began to get very irritable and as a result was unable to gain the respect of his subordinates. He knew that they considered him stupid. Frequently, he became enraged over minor incidents which as often as not resulted from his own lack of comprehension.

This situation lasted for a year during which the unit went overseas, first to England and later to France. The morale of the kitchen force became steadily worse. Things came to a head when a sergeant, who had often been in conflict with him and who had, on occasion, bullied him quite unmercifully, demanded a can of water from those Sergeant D. was filling. When Sergeant D. refused to give him one, he became abusive and a scuffle began.

Sergeant D., conscious of the fact that he should be able to demand obedience from his opponent but unable to cope with the situation, became enraged and in desperation picked up a rifle, shooting his tormentor in the leg.

Yelling wildly he was taken to the stockade by other soldiers. There he was seen by several medical corpsmen who had him transferred to the hospital because they were convinced he was insane. He remembered nothing about the incident. For five months he remained in the hospital in England while he received insulin shock treatment because the doctors had diagnosed him as psychotic. Returned to the States and given a furlough, he improved rapidly although he remained irritable and extremely sensitive to noise. He was quite vehement in stating that he did not want to be a mess sergeant. The responsibility and intellectual demands of the job were more than he would be willing to assume again. The doctors, however, felt that his emotional condition, although improved, was still severe enough to warrant discharge. Even after another four and a half months hospitalization in this country he remained impulsive, tense, and restless.

Just prior to his discharge the soldier obtained a divorce from his wife of fourteen years and within a month married another woman. On returning home in June 1945, he took a part-time job as a cook's helper in a hotel. However, he was quite disturbed, and when seen by the V.A. staff five months later seemed so confused that he was sent to the hospital. There he improved and soon returned to his home. His tenseness and irritability continued, however, and he was unable to hold a job for long.

His second wife divorced him in 1949 and two months later he married for a third time. Throughout this period the veteran received periodic outpatient treatment for his mental disorder. He also obtained training through the Veterans Administration as a cook and as a shoe repairer, although he never worked at either occupation. Throughout the period from 1945 to 1951 D.B.D.'s marital life, his occupational history and his schooling were extremely unstable. He was not able to recover from his experience in military service and he was not able to adjust as well as he had prior to induction.

Until entering military service at the age of twenty, A.S.V. spent most of his early life on a farm in the deep South. The family was large, the land poor, and both parents in bad health; often there was barely enough to eat. A.S.V. lived a long way from school and attended only when the weather was good and the farm work completed. His parents did not care whether he went or not. At thirteen after finishing four grades he stopped going at all. He worked on the farm and later, for a year and a half, with the Civilian Conservation Corps.

Always shy, he preferred hunting and fishing by himself to social activities. He even kept away from his brothers and sisters. Many times he experienced fear—when in his bed at night, when fixing the barn roof, or when asked to go swimming. He did not know why, but these and other situations disturbed him intensely. A.S.V. had his first date at the age of nineteen. One year later he married the same girl. She was then fourteen. About the same time he was in an automobile accident and suffered rather severe cuts and bruises on his face and head. Shortly after his recovery, draft papers arrived and, in spite of the fact that he was afraid of the future and wanted above all else to remain at home, he was forced to enter the Army.

As an infantry private he was sent to a camp in the far North for training in winter warfare. His division was selected as one of the first to test new equipment designed for use under conditions of extreme cold. He hated the Army that had taken him from his home and placed him in this land of snow. He was afraid, and he had frequent fainting spells. After two months he began to go AWOL for short periods of time. He was sent to the stockade. His brother died and while home for his funeral, Private V. decided he would not return to duty. For twelve months in late 1943 and early 1944 he stayed at home, worked the farm, and dreaded the possibility of being returned to military life. When the military police finally arrived, he was taken to another camp in the North and court-martialed. His former outfit had already gone overseas, and was making final preparations for the invasion of France as Private V. came to trial. Sentenced to six months in the stockade he served less than a month before he was placed on board ship. After two days at sea he was released from confinement. To the Army the soldier was a shirker who had deserted his outfit in order to avoid fighting. Now he would be forced to fight.

Two weeks after landing he was assigned to an Infantry division in reserve. Seven weeks later his outfit was thrown into some of the bitterest fighting in the Italian campaign. For eight days Private V. lived in a constant state of panic. He could not control himself and was more of a liability than an asset to his unit. Just before he broke down completely he received a slight shrapnel wound on the hand and was evacuated to the hospital.

A week later he was sent back to duty, but had to be returned to the hospital the same day because he was shaking all over and could not even pick up a rifle. This time, after another two weeks of medical care, he was temporarily assigned to the division's military police. The doctors were now convinced that he could not stand combat. But by then even a job directly behind the lines was too much for him and within ten days he had to be hospitalized again. From then until July 1945, when he returned to the States, he was assigned to jobs far behind the lines—in replacement depots and air bases. Even there his performance was of dubious value. He began to drink heavily and was court-martialed on one occasion for being drunk in public.

Following a month's furlough at home the soldier continued to work at an air base. Never really well, he now became more and more confused and deluded. He thought he was going to be shot and that people were trying to terrify him. He felt that German spies, or maybe the F.B.I., were after him and wanted to grind him up for sausage. He kept hearing voices. When admitted to the hospital he was drooling and muttering incomprehensibly. Started on insulin shock therapy he improved sufficiently to be returned home by late 1945.

A.S.V. was in a V.A. hospital in late 1946 because of heavy drinking, which always followed attacks of shakiness, vomiting, and fear. On one occasion he bit his tongue. A year later he was back again. Again in the fall of 1948 he was hospitalized; this time he was jerking all over, drunk, and talking gibberish. Tests showed that he was suffering from epilepsy and it was the opinion of the doctors that the fainting spells, trembling, attacks of confusion, and panic during his Army career were all probably closely related to an epileptic condition. Twice in 1949 he had to be hospitalized after drinking bouts during which he had epileptic seizures and was completely out of his mind. In December of that year his wife divorced him.

Within a year he had remarried and since then has not required further hospitalization. However, he is still emotionally disturbed and ekes out a bare living with the help of his pension on a farm which is so poor that the Veterans Administration will not authorize its use for farm training. They feel that the land is not worth planting and that they can never help A.S.V. to improve his farming methods there. He and his wife and child live in a two-room shack and pay $54 a year rent for 52 acres, of which only 14 can be tilled.

The early life of W.S.N. was one of almost constant turmoil. His father, an alcoholic, was frequently away from home on drinking bouts and his return always brought on periods of quarreling between the parents. A brother was seriously injured in an automobile accident and has since been mentally deficient. W.S.N. was often beaten by his father. As he grew up he was forbidden to go out with girls and most of his social life had to be hidden from his family. In spite of being forced to live in this far from healthy environment, he never suffered any severe emotional upsets although he was prone to occasional temper tantrums and headaches. In school he did very well and on graduating from high school would have liked to go to college. However, because of his father's irresponsibility and intermittent employment, he had to give up his dream of further education. For a year he worked in several low-paying jobs as a laborer and mail clerk. Then, he obtained a good position as a clerk with an automobile manufacturing company. One year later he was drafted.

After four weeks of basic training in a Field Artillery battalion, Private N. was shifted to a position as battery clerk because of difficulty with his feet which made field duty impractical. Soon he was promoted to technician fifth grade. In the spring of 1943 he learned of the Army Specialized Training Program under which soldiers were sent for college courses at various universities. His application was accepted, but with the proviso that he would have to accept a reduction in grade to private. This was the stipulation for all ASTP graduates. It was expected that they would be made either commissioned or noncommissioned officers on completion of their course. W.S.N. was happy to give up his rank in order to obtain college training and he was soon engrossed in studying engineering.

By early 1944, with the increasing need for ground troops, especially infantrymen, produced by the build-up for the invasion of Europe, it became apparent that the ASTP program would have to be abandoned. There was a sizable shortage of manpower, especially at the higher intelligence levels, and the ASTP students were the best source immediately available. Private N. was bitter, not only because he had been led to believe he would get at least two years of college, but because he had expected either a commission or high enlisted rank. Nevertheless, the Army needed these men badly, and prior commitments had to be revoked because the war situation itself had changed. Combat losses had been higher than estimated and the invasion date had been advanced. Moreover, most units had filled all their noncommissioned officer positions. Thus, there was no alternative, but to return many ASTP trainees to regular duty in ranks below those they previously held.

Private N. disappointed at having to leave college after only ten months, applied for air cadet training in the hope of still obtaining a commission. Although he was accepted, the training facilities were full at that time, and he was sent to an infantry division in training to await call. Several weeks later pilot training was all but eliminated for the same reasons as those which closed down the ASTP program and many cadets were shipped to the Infantry. Deprived of his rating, a good job, a college education, and a commission by events he did not entirely understand Private N. was angry and frustrated. Moreover, all he had to look forward to now was infantry training, pain from his feet, combat, and maybe death.

After less than three months of infantry training, the division was put to work packing equipment for movement overseas. By October 1944 they were in combat. Already bitter and upset by what he considered completely unjustifiable treatment at the hands of the Army, Private N. began to have severe headaches. Sometimes, he became nauseated and vomited when emotionally upset.

As his division entered more severe fighting in early 1945 he had periods when he sobbed uncontrollably and became quite confused. He was angry at the Army for exposing him to physical hardships, suffering, and death when it had promised him so much. He felt cheated and yet he was ashamed of himself. The other men kept going, they did not sulk and cry. He had to fight with himself to live up to their expectations of him. But always when the fighting was severe he would think again that he should not be suffering so, that it was not fair, and that he would be justified in quitting. Once when ordered to crawl back from an advanced position, he was so confused that he stood up straight and ran back a hundred yards through machine gun fire. It was a miracle he was not hit. Finally, after four months of fighting and while his company was off the line for a short rest, the soldier gave up and begged to be sent to the hospital. There, he was very depressed, stuttered when he talked, and suffered from vivid dreams of battle which would awaken him out of a sound sleep, sweating profusely. He was returned to the States and discharged.

As a civilian, W.S.N. has gradually improved. He returned to his old job at the automobile company and stayed for almost two years. He left to look for a job in Florida, but later returned to his home in the Midwest. He has since worked steadily, first as a cemetery salesman and more recently as an automobile salesman, a job which he enjoys very much. In 1951 he was "going steady" with a girl, but did not feel financially able to get married although he was making $4,000 a year. He still suffered from occasional headaches and nightmares and still stuttered a little.

Each of these soldiers were given assignments which added greatly to their difficulties in performing effectively. However, there was not much that the Army could have done to save P.W.A. from himself. There are always some people whose emotional problems lead them to pursue educational or occupational objectives that insure their failing. D.B.D. was a clear case of overassignment; the Army had mistaken a domineering approach for leadership and had then neglected to note his lack of capacity to cope effectively with his assignment.

A.S.V. represents a more difficult case to evaluate because Army policy was to pursue deserters and force them to fight in order not to open the doors to many others who wanted to escape combat. The fact that A.S.V. broke down almost immediately upon entering combat must not be considered apart from the larger purposes of this policy.

Most men were able to tolerate the Army's breaking its promise once or twice but W.S.N. was the unfortunate soldier with whom the Army broke faith repeatedly. That he was able to perform effectively for a considerable time before he broke down reflects the effort that he made to swallow his disappointments and keep going. Only when the full impact of his bad luck became clear to him in combat did he finally collapse.

Chapter Six: CONFLICT OF
CULTURAL VALUES

WE HAVE referred to the Army's task of converting millions of civilians into effective soldiers when the war was already under way and when strategic considerations required that trained men be placed in the field in the shortest possible time. Considering the changes required, it is remarkable how thorough a job of conversion was done within such a relatively short period of time. Men with soft muscles whose daytime concern in civilian life had been with earning a living and whose nights were spent with their families were transformed into hardened soldiers who could march twenty or thirty miles with full pack, and who could, when necessary, sleep in mud, live off short rations, and fight to kill the enemy.

We know that while millions were able to make the transition, many failed in the effort. One of the causes of their failure was an inability to put aside the values by which they had always lived. The most serious conflict that many experienced was between their strong civilian indoctrination against killing, and the Army's training them to destroy the enemy. Postwar studies revealed that many soldiers in the front lines had not fired their weapons. While an immobilizing fear probably inhibited many, others failed to fire because they could not bring themselves to take human life even in war. They understood, on an intellectual level, the need of their country to fight—which is why they did not seek classification as conscientious objectors—but they were unable in combat to pull the trigger because they were so strongly emotionally conditioned against taking human life.

Indoctrination about the sin of killing takes place within the home as well as within the church and community; the full weight of authority establishes these values for the individual. And once firmly established, they are not easily changed. Forcing a man who had been brought up to abhor killing to participate in bayonet drill and later in hand to hand combat with the enemy was certain to lead to serious conflict for him if he could not readjust his value structure in light of the exigencies of war.

Since men found service, particularly combat service, very onerous, many sought to escape, especially if they could do so without branding themselves or being branded by others as cowards. To say that one was frightened and could not go on was thought to be cowardice, but to state that the war violated one's deepest convictions had an aura of respectability.

If the Army could be made to appear remiss, the individual was in a better position to justify, at least to himself, his unwillingness to make the effort and sacrifices required to serve effectively. There is no doubt that many Negroes born and educated in the North were very resentful when they were assigned for training in the deep South where segregation was most intense. As was pointed out in *The Negro Potential*, General Marshall at war's end held that the Army had been in error not to train Negroes in the North. It was not easy for the Negro to do his best for the Army when he had repeated evidence that Army policy was insensitive to, and tended to violate, his basic rights as a citizen.

The Army did, of course, recognize certain conflicts of values and tried to avoid them. For a long time its selection policies were structured to prevent the induction or enlistment of men with prison records, and it refused throughout the war to accept known homosexuals. Army policy was thus made so that young men from good homes should not be forced into close association with those who had broken the law once and who might break it again. It was only after the manpower pool started to diminish rapidly that the Army decided to give the delinquent or minor offender a chance to serve. But believing it was unwise for inductees to come in close contact with homosexuals, the Army pursued from beginning to end a strict policy toward these deviants, discharging those who had slipped by the screen as soon as they were identified —irrespective of whether their military performance was good or bad.

The most significant aspect of Army policy which took account of cultural values were the regulations affecting rotation and demobilization. In recognition of the American commitment to the doctrine of equity and fair play, the Army early established objective criteria for the relief of troops from combat or other overseas duty. If some men were favored over others, rotation could result in a decline rather than an increase in effective performance. Except for the Air Force, however, rotation never affected large numbers. But demobilization affected everybody. And the Army determined the preference of the troops themselves as to who was to be let out first before establishing its point system for demobilization.

Another area where conflicts of values arose related to sexual behavior. Although war represented a great deprivation sexually for most soldiers, some who had grown up in a strictly controlled environment suddenly found themselves in a group which was much more casual about sexual morals. Those who considered sex outside of marriage a sin were sometimes seriously disturbed by the promiscuity that they frequently saw in others.

The impact of cultural values on effective performance can be summarized in these terms. Some men failed to perform effectively because they did not have a sense of personal responsibility or a feeling of patriotism. Lacking one or both, they had little incentive to endure the difficulties and dangers of military service, particularly combat. Others became ineffective because of a conflict between the basic values which had guided their lives prior to induction and the conditions of Army life in which they found themselves. They could not change the Army or the demands which the new environment made on them; but neither could they free themselves from a commitment to ingrained values.

EQUITY

The extent to which the concept of equity permeates American life can be illustrated by the efforts that employers make to establish rules and regulations that by their intrinsic fairness gain the support and respect of their work force. A European visitor to the United States was startled to find pickets carrying posters saying that the employer was "unfair." In Europe it is taken for granted that an employer is unfair; this happens in an environment in which even those who are not Communists believe that there is a basic conflict between the wealthy and the poor. While the Germans have a word for just and unjust, they do not have a word for "fair" —they use the English term!

The Army was faced with a dilemma during World War II in reconciling equity with efficiency. Its major mission was to win the war as quickly as possible with the least loss of life. But so deeply ingrained was the concept of equity among all Americans that time and again the Army had to shape its policies to take this value into consideration.

Most men realized that it would be impossible for the Army to carry on the war effectively if it had to weigh every move to be sure that it was fair to all. However, if a small group was required for patrol, most men preferred that they be given a chance to volunteer—or to draw lots—rather than to be arbitrarily assigned. If it was inevitable that some be injured and others killed, luck, not authority, should be the arbiter.

J.G.S. was born and raised in a small Northeastern town. A member of one of the few Negro families in that area, he experienced little discrimination and was generally accepted as an equal by his schoolmates. He completed junior college at the age of twenty with a very good scholastic record and thereafter held jobs as a public stenographer and chief clerk with the draft board. Just before his twenty-second birthday, he enlisted in the Army. Until then he had had only very limited contact with the manifestations of prejudice against his race. He had deliberately sought out an environment in which he could expect to find people, both Negro and white, who would not feel that he should act differently just because he was a member of a minority group. In this way, he was able largely to avoid discrimination and developed cultural values much closer to those of the white middle class than to those of his fellow Negroes in the South.

In the Army, however, J.G.S. found himself treated differently from other soldiers because he was a Negro. He had no choice as to where or with whom he worked. He was constantly and directly exposed to a set of values which differed radically from his own and to the manifestation of these values in discrimination, segregation, and rigidly prescribed patterns of behavior. He received his basic training in the South; later he was sent to clerical school and then assigned as a clerk, specializing in courts-martial, to an anti-air-craft artillery group.

Intelligent and relatively well educated, he was promoted rapidly and became a technician fourth grade in less than a year. Nevertheless, he was in constant conflict with many of his officers, especially those from the South. He resented any system which assigned Negroes to segregated units and on many occasions found himself in serious disagreement with his fellow Negro officers and enlisted men who accepted a second-class status. As a court stenographer he saw or heard about many instances of discrimination, which affected him in a very personal manner. Furthermore, as an educated Northern Negro he was considered by many of his white officers as a troublemaker. Several times he was threatened with court-martial for treason. He was forbidden to give books to other soldiers and just before going overseas his commander denied him a pass to go to his home which was nearby; instead he received a two-hour lecture designed to make him give up his "liberal" values and accept his status as a Negro.

Early in his Army career the soldier began to develop psychiatric symptoms. During basic training he went on sick call several times with nausea, headaches, tenseness, and stuttering. While in clerical school he consulted a psychiatrist, but was not hospitalized. The symptoms continued after he joined the anti-aircraft group and became quite severe after his outfit left its former location in the Deep South and went overseas to North Africa. At times his stuttering was so incapacitating that he was unable to speak at all.

The morale of the outfit was poor primarily because of the discord between the white officers and Negro enlisted men. In May 1944, however, after about a year of overseas duty, the organization was disbanded because of reduced need for anti-aircraft protection, and J.G.S. was placed in charge of a quartermaster laundry receiving office. For two months until the replacement depot closed he supervised both white and Negro enlisted men. There was no difficulty and his headaches, nausea, and stuttering improved considerably. He was next sent to Italy and spent another two months working on courts-martial before being assigned to clerical duty with an Infantry division. Although he saw only intermittent combat, his symptoms now became quite severe. Again he was involved in a good deal of strife with white officers. Morale among the Negro troops was low and many resented being led by officers who seemed to hate them as much as the enemy. In addition there was frequent strife between Negro and white soldiers in rear areas. All this had a marked effect on J.G.S. and he spent almost a month at one time in the hospital because of his stuttering. Nevertheless, he was able to return to duty and served until returned to the States in the spring of 1945 after more than two years overseas.

Back in this country and on furlough, he became extremely disturbed over any evidence of discrimination, especially against Negro soldiers, who he felt deserved better. At that time he decided that he would never marry because he did not want a child of his exposed to the discrimination that he had experienced. On returning to camp he was hospitalized with a severe speech impediment and constant headaches. Several months later he was discharged.

Shortly after leaving service the veteran began receiving treatment for his speech disorder through the Veterans Administration while working as a government clerk in the Northeast. Free once again to avoid people who might be prejudiced against him because of his race, he gradually improved. By late 1947 when the treatment was terminated, he was making a good adjustment. He had married and had one child; he was happy in his home life. He had started taking courses with a view to obtaining a degree in business administration. By 1950 he was well on the way to accomplishing his educational objectives, although the necessity of holding a full-time job to support his family left him little time for studies.

B.C.R. grew up in the Midwest where he attended school until the age of eighteen. He completed the last two years of high school at night while working as a salesman during the day. Brought up in a strongly religious environment, he developed very rigid concepts of right and wrong which he applied to others as well as himself. His parents, particularly his mother, were quick to punish him for any sign of dishonesty, lack of fairness, or deviation from the precepts of the Church. Lying was particularly condemned. As a result he came to demand very high ethical standards not only of himself, but of his associates. In actual fact most of his friends held values very similar to his own. Whenever they deviated, he quickly dropped them. His friends were largely women.

B.C.R. worked for about ten years as a men's clothing salesman in his home town. Then he went to Florida and held a variety of jobs as a salesman, automobile mechanic's helper, and in an advertising office. In late 1942 he received his draft notice and entered the Army. He was then thirty-one years old and unmarried.

After infantry basic training Private R. was assigned first to a division that was being used to supply replacements and later to a replacement pool. By the spring of 1943 he was on his way overseas. Two months after joining his new division he participated in the assault on Sicily. A series of short but extremely fierce engagements ensued. The terrain was very rocky and mountainous. When the campaign, which lasted a total of thirty-nine days, ended Private R. was a seasoned infantryman. Sailing from Sicily to the

British Isles the division spent almost ten months in training for the invasion of France.

On D-Day the soldier landed with the first wave of troops. After two weeks of heavy fighting during which he was decorated for bravery, the lines stabilized. A little later he spent several days in the hospital with a pulmonary condition, but was back with his outfit to participate in the breakthrough out of the beachhead and the race across France. By October they had entered Germany and were engaged in intensive, close combat with bayonets and hand grenades as the enemy was pushed back inch by inch. Private R. was again hospitalized for a few days with pains in his chest which apparently resulted from exposure but again he returned to duty.

In December he was on the line when the German counterattacks came. As the fighting continued it began to snow. Drifts of four and five feet piled up. Exposed to the elements for days at a time with no opportunity to dry out and get warm, the soldier began to suffer once again from severe chest pains. By early January he had to be hospitalized and was returned to England. It was late March before he was released and assigned to an Air Force unit. The doctors felt that he should not be returned to combat. He, himself, felt that he should either be sent back to his unit or home to the States. He knew nothing about the Air Corps, had no special skill that could be utilized, and actually had very little to do most of the time. As an infantryman he felt he deserved something better than this rather pointless duty.

When the war ended in Europe his hopes of going home were revived. For a while he was quite cheerful. With over two years overseas, a decoration for valor, and credit for participating in five separate campaigns he had enough points under the system of demobilization to be returned to the States. But nothing happened. The war in the Pacific ended and he still had not received his orders. Most of the men in his old division were already home. Checking into the situation he learned that his records had been lost in combat.

His story of the fighting in Sicily, France, Belgium, and Germany fell on deaf ears. No officer would take the responsibility of writing orders for him without adequate records and the records could not be found. The officers were following directions: only men with a specified number of points could be sent home. To send a man home without specific knowledge of the soldier's military record would be impossible. Private R. on the other hand knew that he was eligible for discharge. He felt that either the officers were calling him a liar, which he never had been, or the promises embodied in the point system were being deliberately broken. He felt that either they were accusing him of dishonesty or they were cheating him. He believed that in either case, he was being unjustifiably persecuted by the Army. Out to get what he felt was his due he succeeded in creating a good deal of trouble. But still nothing happened. By mid-September he was thoroughly convinced that he was being deliberately discriminated against. He was irritable and apathetic in turn. He became fearful of everything about him and he refused to associate with other men. Finally his commanding officer sent him to the hospital.

By mid-October he was back in the States—but as a hospital patient suffering from a severe paranoid disorder, not a soldier returned for discharge. He was, however, released from the service toward the end of 1945, although still quite fearful and harboring a variety of complaints against the Army. By this time his ideas of persecution had become so expanded that his whole Army career represented to him a series of attempts by the military to cheat him, humiliate him, and deprive him of his just due.

At home with his parents he rapidly expanded his delusional system to include the Veterans Administration and his mother. Often he was quite belligerent toward those he thought were taking advantage of him. For almost three years he moved from one place to another always trying to escape people whom he was convinced were trying to persecute him. Occasionally he held a job for a brief period and intermittently attended a training course under the G.I. Bill. He wrote many threatening letters to the

Veterans Administration; he refused to take physical examinations. In late 1948 his sister prevailed upon him to go to the Veterans Administration and find out why they were mistreating him. He was so obviously disturbed on arrival that he was hospitalized.

During the following ten months he received extensive treatment and spent most of his time writing threatening letters to the President and various high Army officers describing his mistreatment prior to discharge and since. However, the veteran did improve and by mid-1950 was working part time as a salesman and taking a course in dental technology. Although he has since discontinued his training and still writes occasional hostile letters to congressmen and the Veterans Administration, he is able to hold a full-time job as a salesman of women's shoes. The doctors feel he is not psychotic at the present time, but may well become sick again if any major change occurs in his very circumscribed and withdrawn pattern of life.

These two cases call attention to the effect on performance of a serious value conflict. This can drain the energy of a man so that he is unable to direct his efforts towards the accomplishment of a specific goal. From many points of view it is remarkable that J.G.S. was able to keep going for as long as he did, as the conflict within him reached such a pitch that he lost his power of speech. B.C.R.'s case reminds one of the classic picture of the individual's helplessness in confronting a bureaucracy. Although we could never be certain that B.C.R. might not have broken down for other reasons, his record leaves no doubt that his acute psychosis was precipitated by his unfortunate experiences in the Army.

RELIGIOUS AND MORAL VALUES

The average child is willing to accept what his parents tell him is right and wrong. When parental indoctrination is reinforced by church and community influences, the values which a child acquires are likely to become very deeply rooted. If in adulthood an individual is forced, or desires, to break free of these commitments, he is likely to develop confusion and guilt because of the conflict between the old and the new values.

While deviant sexual behavior, more particularly homosexuality, is not, strictly speaking, a religious or moral value problem, such behavior is dealt with in our society largely in moral terms. Moreover, it is a problem that has long been of serious concern to the military and one to which they have tended to respond in terms of principle. Hence several cases involving homosexuality are included in this section.

Most laymen find it difficult to understand how it happens that some young people grow up feeling attracted only to members of their own sex, and as adults adjust their entire life in terms of their deviation. Since many homosexuals are intellectually well-endowed, they are able to do well in high school and college and at work and frequently they succeed in avoiding being conspicuous in civilian life.

Many homosexuals undoubtedly served with distinction during World War II and their deviant sexual proclivities never came to the attention of the authorities. It was Army policy, however, that if a man admitted that he was or could be proved to be a homosexual, he must be discharged "without honor." The Army would not expose normal men to possible seduction by homosexuals, especially since the latter might be in a position to take advantage of rank. The Army's severe attitude reflected not only its desire to avoid organizational difficulties but a sensitivity to the public's lack of tolerance for this type of sexual deviation.

A truly religious man is one who not only accepts certain beliefs but regulates his life accordingly. It is easier, however, to conform to a particular set of beliefs in a community where others do likewise and where social forces help to reinforce the individual's own commitments. Among the soldiers who encountered serious problems in this area were some who had been brought up in a strict religious community and who, until their induction, had lived according to their beliefs. Army life presented them with temptations from which they had been guarded at home. Moreover, most of their fellow soldiers did not share their values and frequently mocked them. Many of these religious persons experienced emotional conflicts in the Army which finally prevented them from performing effectively.

Born to a very religious Midwestern family, P.P.T. started attending church at an early age. As well as being the religious center of his community, the church was also a major factor in much of its social life. As he grew up, graduating from high school and taking his first job, he came to accept the religious precepts as basic to his way of life. He attended services twice a week and participated actively in church affairs. Religion was his guide as well as his solace. To flout its doctrines was to flout not only his God and his family, but the whole community of which he was a part. After leaving school P.P.T. worked for four years as a truck driver and construction laborer before entering the Army at the age of twenty-two.

During the first nine months of his service career he was shifted rapidly from one air field to another—Florida, Utah, Colorado, Washington, Oregon, Nebraska. By the time this training was completed he was qualified to work as a gunner on the large bombers and had attained the rank of sergeant. Although this was not the type of duty he would have chosen he accepted it. Next he was sent to England and joined a bomber squadron that had already amassed an impressive record in raids over France and Germany. His first mission was an easy one, but after that it was very difficult. The flak was almost always heavy and enemy fighters were everywhere. His pilot was killed on one raid, his bombardier on another. Once they just barely made it back to England after losing three engines and putting out a fire in the cockpit.

P.P.T. was frightened, but even more, he felt terribly guilty. Every time his plane went up its only purpose was to drop bombs on defenseless people. His job as a gunner was to kill enemy fliers and he did his job. But it seemed all wrong to him. This was contrary to his religion and everything that he had learned prior to entering the Army. He felt that he was guilty of participating in a never ending series of heinous crimes for which his family, his community, and his God must always condemn him. He became jittery, could not sleep, and vomited frequently. Yet he kept going and completed his twenty-five missions in a commendable manner. Seven months after leaving the United States he was on his way home again.

After a furlough, he returned to duty still completely obsessed with guilt. If anything, his state was worse than when he had been in combat. He didn't want to do anything, could not eat or sleep and had the sensation that ants were crawling all over his body. Hospitalized, he poured forth his preoccupations to the doctor: "There was the raid the day before Christmas. We had to go. I didn't want to kill those poor people. . . . I shot down a man, a German. I feel guilty about it. We shouldn't kill people. Here they hang people for that. . . . I guess that is what bothers me most. I killed somebody. . . . I think about that German I shot down. I know it was him or me, but I just can't forget that I saw him blow up. Up to then it was just an airplane. Then I realized that there was a man in the plane. . . . I keep trying to think that it is all behind me, but I can't. I just think about it and get upset. I can't read or go to classes without thinking about it. You have fighters coming at you in bed and you can't do anything about it. I keep dreaming about it. I just can't help it." The doctor tried to convince him that he had only been doing his duty, but to no avail, and he was finally discharged virtually unimproved by his hospital stay.

Within two months of leaving the Army P.P.T. started work in a steel plant. At first he found it difficult to work; he was plagued with frequent thoughts and dreams of combat. He did not go to church or associate with his old friends. Gradually, however, he began to participate in community activities and finally started going to church again. By 1948, although still rather restless and suffering from insomnia, he had almost fitted himself back into his old pattern of life. He enjoyed his job, went hunting and fishing for recreation, and was thinking of getting married. He felt far less guilty than he had when he returned from Europe. Later he married and had two children. He feels very much a part of his community again and has, as he sees it, returned to a religious way of life.

D.L.M. spent his early life in a small Midwestern town. His father was a farmer with a comfortable income. When D.L.M. was thirteen, however, his father died and shortly thereafter the family lost its savings because the local bank failed. Although he wanted to continue in high school D.L.M. had to devote all his time to working the farm. For the next eighteen years he lived at home with his mother, who became quite nervous after her husband's death. At the age of twenty-eight he gave up farming and took a job as a sheet-metal worker in a factory. Three years later, and several months before he was drafted, he married a local school teacher. They continued to live with his mother on the farm.

After he was drafted, D.L.M. was assigned to a newly activated infantry division which had just started training on the West Coast. For six months he went through intensive training including desert maneuvers. Then the division went to Hawaii where he spent another ten months in training and guard duty. During this time he had two operations for a chronic eye disorder, but otherwise he was in good health. He went with his outfit to New Guinea where, as a newly promoted private first class, he first saw combat in the summer of 1944. The fighting, mostly patrol action against isolated Japanese units, lasted until early 1945, when the entire division was sent to the Philippines. Relieving one of the invasion units, D.L.M.'s regiment was immediately thrown into heavy fighting. The advance was slow both because of the mountainous terrain and the stubborn Japanese resistance. In thirty days they had advanced only 13 miles. Casualties were heavy.

On one occasion D.L.M.'s battalion was instructed to take a small mountain that had been the site of fanatical enemy resistance for several days. One attack failed and a second advance was ordered under the cover of darkness. As a member of a squad which had been reduced to seven men, D.L.M. advanced through the underbrush and emerged close to the Japanese lines just as the sun was rising. The fighting was continuous and fierce for two days. Enemy mortar fire was heavy and accurate. By the end of the first day D.L.M. and a buddy were the only ones in his squad still alive. Pinned down in a dugout, he did not notice when this buddy crawled off to the side in an attempt to circle around and advance a few yards closer to the enemy position. Then he suddenly saw a figure stooped over and running directly at him. Automatically he opened fire and with some satisfaction saw the figure crumple. Only when the figure began to shout at him in English did he realize that he had wounded his own buddy. Completely shattered by this experience, D.L.M. broke down completely. Although the mountain was soon captured, he felt no sense of elation. His thoughts centered constantly on what he felt was his unforgivable sin. Depressed and afraid, he was evacuated to the hospital.

There he was constantly upset; he jumped at the slightest noise and swore that he would never pick up a rifle again. Although the doctor tried to convince him that he had done the right thing and that if the oncoming figure had been Japanese he would have been killed, he refused to believe him. Again and again he mulled over the events of that day and always came to the conclusion that he was guilty of a terrible crime. To shoot an enemy was bad enough, but necessary. To shoot a friend was not only bad, it was unforgivable. He trembled all over when he thought of it, and there was a constant ache in his back. By the time he reached the States he was suffering from malaria as well and had lost 20 pounds, because he often refused to eat. Discharged in the fall of 1945, he was somewhat less anxious, but far from recovered.

Nevertheless, on returning home, he refused psychiatric treatment from the Veterans Administration because he was afraid that his friends and neighbors would condemn him for and laugh at his weakness. During the first year after his discharge, D.L.M.

was unable to work at all. His back hurt; he was nervous and depressed. Then he took a part-time job with a roofing company. His income was small, largely because he found it very difficult to do much work. His family were supported by his pension and his wife's teaching. However, by 1951 he was working steadily for the roofing company and had been put in charge of several branch offices. The prospect of his actually supporting his family proved stimulating. Then the company went out of business and about the same time his wife became pregnant and had to stop work. D.L.M. started his own roofing business, but to date he has been able to realize only a very small profit. He spends much of his time moping around the house and still is preoccupied with what he considers to be his guilt. The events of that day in April 1945 are etched on his mind in bold-face type. Not a day goes by but what he thinks of them and shudders imperceptibly.

A.L.A. was adopted as an infant by a relatively well-to-do Midwestern couple who reared him as their only child. He preferred to play with girls and did the things little girls do: he played with dolls, cut out paper dolls, collected pictures of movie stars. Other boys laughed at him and called him a "sissy," but he did not seem to mind. At the age of eight or nine he began to think of himself as a girl and shortly thereafter he began to participate actively in homosexual activities. In junior high school he had a crush on another boy and the two had frequent homosexual relations until they entered the Army. A good student, he had done outstanding work in school and had just started his senior year in a college near his home when he was called for active military service in the spring of 1943. He had joined the Enlisted Reserve Corps the preceding fall.

Immediately after induction Private A. was put to work as an Air Corps personnel clerk at a field located near his home. He remained in this position throughout his thirteen months of military service except for two periods of a month each of special schooling. His work was always excellent and he was promoted to corporal after being in the Army for only five months. Soon after entering service the soldier began to meet other homosexuals through his friend of junior high school days. However, he never had any sexual relations with the enlisted men whom he met in this manner. In fact he had no sexual relations at all with service personnel during the five months following induction. Then one Saturday night while sitting in a bar in town he started to talk to a young lieutenant. After the bar closed they stayed together and eventually headed for an isolated spot in the country where they had homosexual relations.

Shortly after that, while on detached service in an Eastern city A.L.A. met an ensign in a night club which he knew to be a homosexual meeting place. After several drinks they went to the officer's hotel room. On another occasion he met an Army lieutenant through his friends at the post cafeteria. Later he got word through the same friends that the lieutenant was interested in him. As a result of a telephone call Corporal A. was invited to have dinner with the officer and to meet him in his room. They had homosexual relations and later went out to dinner together. Several days later while sitting smoking in the men's room of a movie theater the corporal began to talk to an Air Force lieutenant. The same pattern was repeated.

Shortly thereafter one of the soldier's enlisted friends, who had been particularly unhappy in the Army, went to the medical officer in the hope of obtaining a discharge for homosexuality. As he talked about his own activities he began to mention other names. Soon the Inspector General's Office was called in and a full-fledged investigation of homosexual activities at the field was initiated. Corporal A. was summoned, sent to the hospital for several days, and then placed before a board of officers. There he told his full story, adding: "I have, since the first hint to myself that I have had homosexual inclinations, accepted it. It is just as normal for me to want to have and to have homosexual relations as it is for someone else to have normal relations with the opposite sex. I am aware that I am not like other people in that women hold no sexual pleasure for me.

I enjoy the company of women and can go 'Oh' and 'Ah' over the picture of a beautiful woman, not because it arouses sexual desire in me, but because I think I can appreciate things that are beautiful." A month after the board met he received a discharge under "other than honorable" conditions for "habits and traits of character rendering retention in the service undesirable."

After leaving the Army A.L.A. immediately returned to college. After he finished his undergraduate work he entered graduate school and received a master's degree in English and journalism in 1947. His grades were all high, most of them A's. Since then he has worked toward a Ph.D. degree and taught English as an instructor at a large Midwestern university.

As a child W.S.U. was insecure; he was afraid of the dark and had frequent temper tantrums. Sometimes he stuttered when he talked and there was a marked nervous twitch about his eyes. His parents were very strict people, strongly religious. The father was in poor health and the mother rather nervous. The family—W.S.U. his two brothers, and his parents—were a very close group and kept somewhat to themselves. W.S.U., the youngest, was particularly close to his mother. Even when he was young she read to him from the Bible and emphasized that those who did not live by its precepts were bad.

As he grew older he associated only with those whom his family considered "good" people. In high school his friends were limited to a small circle who shared his interests and ideals. He did not go to dances or mix with the general run of students because he felt that most of them had no morals or high values. At the age of eighteen he left high school after three years and took a job as a machine operator in the large Midwestern city where he lived. Four months later he enlisted in the Army. He expected to be drafted soon and hoped that by enlisting he would get a good assignment.

After basic training in the Air Corps he was sent to armament school and then worked for several months as an instructor at the school. During this time he was promoted to corporal. He was transferred to another field where he worked briefly as an armorer. However, he soon began to go on sick call frequently and after a thorough examination was reclassified because of flat feet. For the next nineteen months he worked at a switchboard. A good worker, he was promoted to sergeant after ten months. Nevertheless, he continued to go on sick call with a variety of complaints.

Gradually he became more and more nervous and had increasing difficulty sleeping. He was irritable while working and refused to associate with his barracks mates and co-workers. He complained that his back began to ache. Several times he went out and got drunk with his fellow soldiers and once was punished by his commanding officer for being drunk. After these bouts he would not talk to the others for several days. Twice he had intercourse with a woman he described as an "old bag." This upset him terribly. For days he was irritable and withdrawn. He could not get along with the WAC switchboard operators at all and finally asked to be transferred to a night shift in order not to have to work with them.

His commanding officer sent him to see a personnel consultant about the possibility of being reassigned. There he poured out his complaints: he could not stand the work he was doing; he was sure he would have a nervous breakdown if he continued at it. He detested the Army. He said that the men he lived with were degenerate; their filthy talk and low ideals had so degraded him that it would require a year after he was "free" before he could rid himself of their stigma. He blamed them for his drinking and sexual promiscuity. He said that he had never been like this before he entered the Army. The WAC telephone operators he described as "lousy and crummy" women whose only interest was to get a man. "All I can think of is getting away from these degenerates—these crude, rowdy, and stupid people." Sitting on the edge of his chair, his eyes twitching, he condemned the whole Army and especially the people around him, who had degraded him and forced him to be "bad." Shortly afterwards he was transferred to another outfit as a duty sergeant.

Although Sergeant U. liked his new job he continued to be nervous and irritable. He could hardly sleep and his back ached constantly. After two months he was sent to the hospital. There he repeated his condemnation of the Army and its degenerate soldiers. He said that being forced to associate with such people was more than he could stand. He resented the officers and the system which so controlled him that he had to remain in close contact with people who did not know or care about religion, morality, or high ideals. The doctors were unsuccessful in their attempts to treat him and in the fall of 1945, the soldier was discharged as suffering from a severe psychoneurosis.

Several months after becoming a civilian once again W.S.U. started a three-year course in dental technology. At that time he was seriously thinking of getting married. However, after a year of training he left the school even though he had been doing very good work. He was still nervous and irritable, still had difficulty sleeping and suffered from occasional terrifying nightmares. Next he worked for almost a year delivering furniture. Quitting, he drifted from one job to another: salesman, bottling company employee, machine operator in a lightning rod company, stock clerk in an automobile company, gas station attendant. In May 1949 he had just taken a position as a bartender. Each job seemed to make him more nervous than the last. He lived at home with his parents and, although constantly planning to get married, never seemed able to bring himself to set a date.

R.B.V. was an only child. His parents and his grandparents were divorced. Without the guidance of a closely knit family, he developed his own philosophy of life at an early age. While still in his teens he decided that killing in any form was wrong and that one's actions should reflect this belief. As he later stated, "The fundamental law of civilization is to 'do unto others as you would have done unto yourself.' Since your own survival instinct causes you to seek protection from those creatures and forces which do not or cannot understand or respect your right to life, and to expect consideration of this right on the part of those creatures capable of reason, you must be willing to grant this same consideration to all sensate beings. In other words, realizing that all animals 'human' or otherwise feel the same desire to live as you yourself must feel, you have under no circumstances the right to extinguish or cause to be extinguished, their lives." It was the adoption of this philosophy, which he felt to be as strong as a religion, that led him to become a strict vegetarian at the age of sixteen.

While still in high school in the Far West, R.B.V. met a girl who was also a vegetarian. He described her as "understanding and sympathetic of his philosophies and willing to face the rocky life that their pursuit against the obstacle of an unsympathetic world must bring." The two youngsters, firmly believing in their philosophy, became engaged. R.B.V. grew restless under the restraints of the school program, even though he was an avid student of politics, economics, and philosophy. Leaving school upon completion of his junior year, he started work as a sheet metal worker. When he had saved a little money, he married. He was only nineteen. Shortly after changing to a better paying job a year later, he was called up for induction into the Army.

This was a severe blow to him, but he resigned himself "to subservience under threat of man's punishment by law, on condition that he be forced to serve only in a non-combatant status." Conscientious objection to war, if based on intellectual rather than on religious training and belief was not, under the law, grounds for placing a man in a work camp or assigning him to non-combatant duty in the military service. Although R.B.V. did not belong to any religious sect, his local board gave him the benefit of doubt by ascribing his conscientious objection to religious beliefs but refused to send him to a C.O. camp since he was employed in defense work which they felt to be incompatible with his claim of being opposed to war in any form. He was drafted as a conscientious objector and designated for non-combatant military service.

Initially assigned to a rifle company of an infantry regiment at a West Coast Army camp, Private V. went through normal basic training with the exception of rifle drill and marksmanship training. Then he was assigned to work in the medical detachment of the regiment. At first he was very interested in the humanitarian aspects of his medical work. He did his job well and was soon promoted to private first class and shortly thereafter received the rating of technician fourth grade. But as the days and weeks passed in the atmosphere of an infantry regiment training for war he came to feel that even his medical work was contributing directly to what he termed "legal murder on an infamously grand scale." This belief was reinforced by a tragic episode; he was on duty at the autopsy of one of his close friends who died in camp. He felt the autopsy was roughly done and he worried about it for a long time. Death became very real; his job palled. The principal function of a medical unit in the Army now appeared to be "to maintain its killing strength, or to be sort of a repair base for men who have become killing automatons." His letters became moody.

Obsessed with these ideas, R.B.V. became deeply depressed. He suffered from severe headaches and frequent attacks of dizziness. As time went on, his condition grew worse and he thought of suicide. He was unable to reconcile his belief that killing was wrong with his service in that type of Army unit most directly concerned with killing—an infantry division. Even his humanitarian medical work now seemed to contribute to the very end he opposed. Hospitalized for a month and returned to duty after his symptoms had subsided, he continued to be disturbed by the apparent conflict between his beliefs and his work. After a suicide attempt while very depressed, he was again hospitalized. After this hospitalization, fourteen months after he had been inducted, he was discharged from the Army.

So great was his distaste for the military and wanting no reward for his participation in the Army, R.B.V. refused to apply for any disability compensation. Nor has he ever availed himself of any of of the other veterans benefits due him. The first few years after returning to civilian life were difficult ones. But he finally settled down in a job far removed from war and war work. Older now and in an adult world, his childhood philosophy no longer directly dictated all his actions. Although still opposed to war, his extreme ideas underwent a subtle change as he matured. He cut the final thread with his old life when he divorced his wife who had shared his earlier beliefs. During the past eight years he has worked steadily with one construction company, earning good wages. He has since remarried and has one child. Looking back on his days in the Army, he commented in our questionnaire to him, "I was immature and maladjusted."

It is worth noting that each of these five soldiers was able to perform effectively for a considerable period of time until a conflict between their values and their Army life developed and made it impossible for them to continue on active duty. P.P.T. believed it was wrong for any human being to take the life of another, and eventually broke down under the emotional strain of having to kill, even though he had completed his missions and left combat. D.D.M. felt not only that it was wrong to kill but that it was an unforgivable sin to kill one's friend. He collapsed only after he had accidentally shot his buddy. A.L.A. was discharged under the general rule that, once identified, a homosexual could not be retained on active duty. His performance up to that point had been excellent, but his behavior conflicted with the Army's value system. W.S.U., who initially had been a good soldier, finally became ineffective because he could not tolerate the values and behavior he attributed to his barracks mates. R.B.V. was so deeply committed to the belief that killing was wrong that he became a vegetarian early in life. When he was directly confronted with death the anomaly of being a soldier depressed him to the point of ineffectiveness.

The good performance records of these men prior to breakdown suggests that for a considerable time they were able to mobilize their resources so as to keep their value conflict from becoming incapacitating. But it was an uphill struggle and the longer they had to cope with the problem, the more likely that they would be overwhelmed by it and become ineffective.

Chapter Seven: SITUATIONAL STRESS

THE ENVIRONMENT in which men find themselves can make their adjustment easy or difficult but in every case it plays a major role in determining the level of their performance. No one works harder than the Chinese peasant, but with his land worn out from centuries of use and abuse, with little animal or other power to assist him, he has a constant and unremitting struggle with nature. In years when rain is insufficient, there is the risk of famine, and in other years when the rains are excessive he may be flooded. There is little that he can do to alter his fate. In contrast, the United States is peopled by men and women whose forebears settled here because of the promising environment, and in every generation large numbers of Americans move from one region to another to find better conditions.

War makes it impossible for the individual to select his environment. Moreover, war forces the individual who has been drafted to endure situations where he is exposed to serious danger which may result in his injury or death. And as long as he remains in uniform, he must face this risk.

In *Patterns of Performance* we deal at length with the impact of varying orders of situational stress on the level of soldiers' performance. Here we will restrict ourselves to two types of situational stress—those of location and combat—in order to illustrate the importance of the situational factor for performance.

The exigencies of war necessitated sending men to almost every part of the world, frequently to places where climate and living conditions were greatly at variance with what they had known at home. One major effort of the American forces was to open the supply route to Russia from Iran through the Persian Gulf where the temperature was excessively hot throughout most of the year.

Other soldiers were assigned to Alaska or to the barren islands off the coast. Iceland was an important base during most of the war. The North African campaign was fought in mountain terrain and in desert; and the advance of the Fifth Army through Italy was impeded almost as much by the elements as by the Germans.

The Pacific Theater was characterized by tropical heat and excessive rains. The Air Transport Command had to cope with extremely difficult flying conditions in moving supplies over the Hump into China. And the troops that fought the Germans across France encountered abominable weather just at the time of the German's last offensive in the winter of 1944–45.

There was more to location than climate. The presence of a native population, the distance from home, the quantity and quality of Army facilities—all these played a part in facilitating or impeding a soldier's adjustment. But it was war itself—combat, with its prospect of injury or death—that took the greatest emotional toll. The average person, even if he dislikes the heat or cold, will be able to endure them when his country faces a major emergency such as war. But combat, especially prolonged combat, is the worst conceivable environment.

It is normal for men to fear mutilation and death. Yet in the Army they had to muster sufficient self-control to participate repeatedly in actions where it was likely that they would either be injured or killed. Fortunately, most men were able to meet these demands and were able to fight not for one but many days without breaking under the strain. But no one should minimize the strain. Only fools enter battle unafraid. Yet despite their fear, most soldiers were able to keep going. Some, however, broke in anticipation of the ordeal; others, only after they were forced to confront it; still others, only if they were kept in line for an excessively long period without a chance for rest and rehabilitation, and a few broke only after they were out of danger.

LOCATION

People who live in apartment houses, work in skyscrapers, and find their recreation in movie houses seldom appreciate what the out-of-doors—the field, the mountains, the ocean—means to the country person. Most people who have had a reasonably happy childhood will take their surroundings for granted. If born in the South, they will find pleasure in the sun; if brought up in the northern climes they may feel exhilarated by the snow. If as adults they are forced to live in a radically different environment from that to which they had been accustomed, they may suddenly become aware of how much they value what they have left behind. In war, men are forced to separate themselves from all that is most dear to them.

Military service can prove to be a particularly severe burden for the soldier who is assigned to a locale that he despises—a rugged mountain area or the tropics. Or the tension may even be greater if a soldier, believing that dampness is injurious to his health, is assigned to a wet region and cannot succeed in getting relocated. If a civilian finds that he must cope with an unfavorable environment for a short period of time in connection with a business effort, it is likely that he can adjust to it and perform effectively. But the soldier assigned during a war to an unfavorable environment has little prospect of early relief. In such circumstances he is likely to have an exaggerated response to an unfavorable external environment.

Prior to entering the Army at the age of thirty-five G.S.W. had spent his whole life in the deep South. Because his father traveled a good deal his schooling was intermittent and he finally stopped at the age of eighteen when he completed the fourth grade. He was ashamed to go to school with children who were so much younger than he. The family was a large one, ten brothers and sisters in all, but four died before reaching two years of age. In general G.S.W. had a normal childhood although his father was strict and beat him him severely for wetting his bed at night up to the age of twelve.

After leaving school he began to drink quite heavily—mostly bootleg whiskey when he was out with the boys. While on one of these binges he was shot several times in the shoulder and abdomen. He awoke to find himself in the hospital but did not know the identity of his assailant. After that he cut down on his drinking and began to work steadily. He held a variety of positions—as a sawmill worker, a stump blaster, a farmer, a sheet-metal worker. All were in the South. He would not have thought of living anywhere else. The warm climate, the verdant countryside, the feeling of being in a place where he belonged—all this he loved.

At the age of twenty-eight he married a divorcee whose first husband had deserted her. At the same time they adopted two children, nieces of the wife, who would otherwise have been placed in an orphanage. G.S.W. described his wife as having many of the qualities of his mother who had died when he was twenty. The marriage was a happy one and when he entered the Army in late 1942, Mrs. W. was able to accompany him on his initial assignment.

Private W. served for over eight months as a member of an air base security battalion at a post in the South. He was a machine gunner. In mid-1943 he was sent North to await overseas shipment. While at the port of embarkation he became somewhat depressed and began to suffer from pains in his back and legs. His stomach was often upset and he reported on sick call for the first time since entering military service. During the long dreary trip across the ocean his stomach trouble continued and he went to see the doctor several times. Finally the unit arrived in Iceland and was assigned to duty guarding an air base.

The cold, wet climate and the bleak terrain disturbed him, but Private W. adjusted to his new surroundings rather well at first. Although his stomach trouble continued to bother him occasionally he did not feel it was necessary to see a doctor. He was, however, hospitalized for a few days about six months after arriving in Iceland when he slipped on the ice and fell, breaking his wrist. Shortly before this he had been assigned to work as an orderly, carrying messages for the officers, waiting on table at the officers' mess, and occasionally helping out in the kitchen. He enjoyed the company of the men and felt that the officers treated him fairly.

As the second winter approached, however, he became more and more depressed and upset. The contrast between this land of snow and ice and howling winds and freezing temperatures, and the warm beauty of his native South was often in his mind. He felt separated from everything he loved. He did not belong here, and yet it seemed as if he would never escape from this land of frozen dreariness. The monotony of the countryside and of his life was almost unbearable. His back began to ache constantly and his stomach upsets became more frequent. He began to have nightmares during which he would shout and scream. He dreamed of beasts and men attacking and overpowering him—they were trying to kill him. The men in the barracks would awaken him. He went to the hospital and stayed a month before returning to duty. His depression continued, however, and soon he began to tremble all over. His voice would shake when he talked. He spent hours sitting and bemoaning his lot at being exiled to this forsaken country. In April 1945 the soldier was again admitted to the hospital. His condition was diagnosed as arthritis, apparently aggravated by the damp, cold weather, and a severe state of depression, and he was returned to the States after serving almost twenty-one months in Iceland. Two months later he was discharged.

He did not, however, immediately recover from the effects of this long period of deprivation. His arthritis continued to bother him and his heretofore happy marriage became rather stormy. Finally, he forced the two adopted children out of the house and they went to live with other relatives. He also forced his wife out of the house for a while under threat of bodily harm, but she and G.S.W. were later reconciled. He worked a small farm and with the aid of training under the Veterans Administration was able to make an adequate living for a while. After assistance from the

Veterans Administration ceased, however, he worked the farm only intermittently. His wife supported them from her earnings in a nearby textile mill supplemented by the veteran's pension. Although G.S.W. continued to suffer from arthritis, the V.A. doctors felt that this condition was in no sense incapacitating and that his failure to support his wife and himself was largely attributable to a severe neurosis dating from the time of his service in Iceland.

O.P.T. was raised on a farm in the South and attended school in a small town near his home. As a child he was often unhappy and fearful. He awoke at night trembling all over. Sometimes he would find himself unaccountably in the hall outside his room. He developed intense fears of being left alone in the dark and would go to considerable lengths to avoid closed spaces. From an early age he was afraid of the water. Even the taunts of his schoolmates failed to make him go swimming with them.

During high school O.P.T.'s anxieties became so widespread and pronounced that he finally had to leave school. For a year he stayed at home. Then he started working with his brother repairing watches. Gradually his fears subsided and eventually he left home and went to work in a paper box factory in the North. By the time he enlisted in the Army at the age of twenty he had almost forgotten about the nightmares and sleepwalking and anxieties that had marked his childhood and early adolescence.

As a soldier O.P.T. performed well for over a year. He worked at a variety of Air Corps assignments in the Midwest, South, and finally on the West Coast. After nine months of service he was promoted to corporal. Just prior to going overseas in the fall of 1943 he became a cook in a fighter control squadron.

The trip across the Pacific was long and boring. However, after about two weeks, the tedium was suddenly interrupted by a torpedo from a Japanese submarine. As the troopship began to go down, the order to abandon ship was given, but Corporal T. was unable to move. All his childhood fears of the water came back to him and he felt very much as he had when his parents had tried to force him as a child to learn to swim. As more and more men jumped into the water and bobbed up again in their life jackets his panic increased. He stood at the rail powerless to jump in spite of the constant urgings of his buddy who promised to jump with him. In all probability he would have gone down with the ship if an officer, whose duty it was to check on compliance with the abandon ship order, had not come along. The officer, after arguing for several minutes, in exasperation drew his pistol and Corporal T. went into the water with a gun at his back.

The sea was rough, however, and the two were soon separated by the waves. Drifting alone in his life jacket, unable to swim and far from any land, the soldier was completely overcome with panic. In his confusion he thrashed about in the water instead of conserving his strength. Soon his eyes were filled with oil and salt water. Within a few hours he was exhausted and completely blind. Luckily he was spotted by a search plane and was picked up a day later and taken to safety.

For two months he remained in a hospital in the Southwest Pacific. Gradually the ulcers in his eyes cleared. But his mental state remained poor. He had a constant smile on his face. His speech was often confused and he would wander from one idea to another almost at random. For a long time he could remember nothing of his twenty-four hours in the water. On returning to this country he improved rapidly at first and was placed in an Air Corps Convalescent Center. However, his confusion and anxiety soon returned. Although his physical condition was by now quite good, he continued to suffer from a severe neurosis. In fact his condition was so poor that it was not considered safe for him to go home on furlough. In May 1944, he was discharged and sent to a V.A. hospital for further care.

In the hospital O.P.T. improved rapidly and within a month he was discharged as completely cured. Returning to the Midwest he again went to work in a paper-box factory. He continued at this work for seven years. However, his fears returned, and for a while he received psychotherapy through the Veterans Administration.

He took several summers off because he was too nervous to work and felt he needed a long vacation. He lived alone in a rooming house. In 1946 he started special on-the-job training under the Veterans Administration which would have led to a promotion but was unable to complete the course because of his constant anxiety. By 1951 he had become so disturbed that he had to leave his job. As of early 1952 he was living with his brother and again repairing watches.

A man's ability to perform depends on a wide range of factors including his response to the environment in which he finds himself. While most people have considerable latitude for adjusting to different environments, others do not. G.S.W. was able to cope with the cold and barrenness of Iceland for one winter, but not for two. O.P.T. had particularly bad luck in finding himself in a situation which triggered his deepest fears about the water. He was so thoroughly immobilized that only the threat of death by shooting enabled him to jump. The fact that there was nothing that they could do to escape from an unfavorable environment probably heightened the tension of these soldiers and helps to explain why they became ineffective.

COMBAT

Men differ in their anticipation of the future. Many live from day to day, worrying little about what will happen tomorrow. There are others who are constantly preoccupied with the future. Some men were fearful about what might happen to them in the Army even before they were inducted. At the opposite extreme, there were men who did not show any unusual response to battle until after they had completed their combat tour.

In general, the closer men came to the front the greater their fear, although many became upset only after their initial exposure to battle. But all soldiers knew that the odds against them increased the longer they were exposed to combat. There were few things as unsettling to a soldier as seeing his buddy hit. He felt that the next bullet would be marked for him. Yet most soldiers were able to keep going for a considerable period before their fears got the best of them. In the following cases, L.D.L. broke while fighting; G.G.M. and A.R.C. collapsed after they were out of danger.

G.G.M. had a happy and relatively uneventful life prior to his enlistment in the Army at the age of twenty. He attended schools in a large Eastern city until the age of eighteen when he graduated from high school. Before entering the service he worked at several different jobs, but spent the longest single period —over a year—as a machinist's helper in a shipyard. He lived at home and was his mother's favorite among four children.

After his induction G.G.M. worked as a clerk at an air base in Texas. However, in spite of the fact that he did not particularly desire flying duty he was soon sent to school as preparation for becoming a gunner on a bomber. Approximately six months after his induction he had completed his training and was promoted to sergeant. A number of brief assignments in the West and South followed and then in October 1943 Sergeant M. departed for England as a replacement gunner. He was married shortly before going overseas. Throughout his period of service in the United States he had felt it necessary to keep his mother from knowing of his flying status, and in actual fact she did not learn of it until notified sometime later that he was missing in action.

Soon after his arrival in England the soldier witnessed the death of eight of his own crew when their plane blew up during a take-off. They were on a weather mission to which Sergeant M. had not been assigned. Later with a new crew he completed three missions over Germany before disaster struck again. In early 1944 while on his fourth mission, the plane developed engine trouble over Holland and had to leave formation. Almost immediately they were attacked by enemy fighters. The tail gun was knocked out and one of the fighters was able to shoot at them from the rear without fear of having his fire returned. A case of ammunition ex-

ploded and the right wing caught on fire. In his gun turret the sergeant could see the fire coming from the Messerschmidt's guns. He
tried to swing his waist gun on it, but the fuselage was in the way.
Bullets crashed into the bomber in a continuous stream. The fire
spread. Somehow the whole crew was able to parachute to safety.

The next four months were an almost constant nightmare. The
group was picked up by the Dutch underground and gradually
worked its way across Belgium and France into Spain. Sergeant M.
was wounded in the left leg and treated by underground doctors.
They were frequently fired on by enemy patrols and the knowledge
of being hunted was ever present. They were always moving,
largely on foot through the snowcovered countryside. Food was
scarce and there was often fighting among the members of the
group for what there was. Finally, they reached the Pyrenees and
armed with guns provided by the underground started over the
mountains. This first attempt ended in failure. Seven of the group
were captured by the Germans, and Sergeant G.'s feet were severely
frostbitten. A second trip was more successful and after almost
three months in hostile territory he was interned in Spain. A month
later he returned to England.

The emotional strain of the months of hiding and deprivation
had had its effect. He suffered from terrifying nightmares of being
chased and shot at. A frequent theme was of his being fired on by
a screaming Messerschmidt that seemed to follow him everywhere.
Often he could not sleep. He became somewhat confused and
seemed to be in a daze. Things seemed out of focus and unreal. He
was irritable and restless. The return to England and to his outfit did not help. In spite of the fact that he was promoted to staff
sergeant and given ground duty repairing and servicing machine
guns on the airplanes, his anxiety continued. When the plane
engines started up, he became scared and wanted to run away.
These symptoms became even more pronounced when he learned
that his mother had died of a heart attack while he had been missing
in action.

In late May 1944 Sergeant M. was returned to the United States and went on furlough. In the week following his return to duty he was on sick call three times. Finally he was hospitalized with severe headaches and almost constant anxiety. Released from the hospital three and a half months later, he was assigned to clerical work at a base in the East. His wife lived nearby. His difficulties continued, however, and he reported frequently for medical treatment of a variety of disorders. He was often depressed and irritable. By June 1945 he was back in the hospital again, and a month later he was discharged.

Soon after returning to civilian life the veteran went to work as a foreman in a dress manufacturing plant. As of 1950 he was still employed at the same type of work. He and his wife had a five-year-old daughter who had been born at about the time he left the Army. Although he has been quite successful in supporting himself and his family, he has never recovered completely from the effects of his experiences during the long trek through Holland, Belgium, and France. He still suffers from severe headaches, is tense, irritable and impatient. In addition he frequently develops a skin rash which is described by his doctor as having an emotional basis. He loses several weeks a year from work because of these disorders.

A.R.C. was raised on a farm in the South. His family was very poor and since the father was often sick and unable to work there were times when there was hardly enough to eat. A.R.C. started school at the age of six, but even at that age he had to spend long hours helping around the farm. When he was ten his mother died. He continued in school for two more years, but there was so much work to be done at home that he finally stopped without completing the sixth grade. For the next seven years he worked steadily plowing the fields and planting crops. When the war came he took a job in a defense plant for a short time. In late 1942 he tried to enlist for military service but was drafted before the processing of his enlistment could be completed.

Private C. received his basic training with an armored division in the Midwest. Continuing with this organizaton he was trained

first as an ammunition handler and later as a crewman on a reconnaissance car. In late 1943 and early 1944 he spent a number of
months on maneuvers with his unit. Throughout this period he
worked hard and was considered a good soldier although too
limited mentally to qualify for promotion to a noncommissioned
rank. In August 1944 Private C. left for Europe as a member of
the same division. He was then assigned to the mechanized cavalry
reconnaissance squadron.

By late October the division had been assigned to patrol activity
along the Luxembourg border. However, contact with the enemy
was minimal and the soldier saw little real combat. Then, in mid-
December came the massive German counteroffensive. Private C.
was in the midst of heavy fighting for several days before he was
hit in the leg by shrapnel from an 88 mm. gun. At the time the
medical evacuation chain was badly disrupted by the enemy attack
and hospital treatment was impossible. The next day the position
was overrun completely and he was taken prisoner. Two weeks in
a German hospital followed.

For the next four months the soldier was shifted from one prisoner-of-war camp to another as the Allies advanced further and
further into Germany. In all he was in four different camps and
spent nearly as much time walking through the snow and ice as in
the enclosures. His wounded leg bothered him and his feet began
to swell and cramp during the long night marches. Food and drinking water were scarce and Private C. found it almost impossible to
eat the food he received. He had frequent stomach cramps and
vomited after eating. He lost a good deal of weight.

As time went on he became increasingly nervous, especially
during the long treks through the snow. He had heard stories of
prisoners being shot because they could not keep up on these forced
marches and lived in constant fear that he would become too sick
to continue. At the prisoner-of-war camps he was put to work in
machine and wood-working shops, but was too nervous and sick
to do much. Sometimes he would break out in a cold sweat and
tremble all over just thinking about what might happen to him.

Much of his time was spent in trying to get medical attention. Finally, in mid-April the Germans gave up the attempt to keep their prisoners and Private C. was released from his fourth and last camp deep in Germany by troops of his own division.

By the end of the month he was on his way back to the States for a two-month furlough. On returning to duty, however, he was still jittery and upset. Within a week he was hospitalized and although his condition improved it became increasingly clear that he would be of little future value to the service. In October 1945 he received a medical discharge for psychoneurosis.

Since the war A.R.C. has had difficulty maintaining steady employment and has never been as effective a worker as he was prior to his experience as a prisoner of war. He worked for a while around his father's farm but was unable to put in more than three or four hours a day. Next he started an on-the-job training course as a cabinet maker under the Veterans Administration, but quit after four months and went to work as a construction laborer. However, he was so jittery and suffered such frequent stomach upsets that he could not continue.

Finally, in late 1948 he started sharecropping a small 16-acre farm and enrolled in the V.A. on-the-farm training program. He has continued farming since then, but has to hire someone to do most of the work because of his own weakness and nervousness. Most of his time is spent in walking back and forth and sitting on the porch. Soon after discharge he married a young girl he had known for some time. This marriage lasted less than a year, but the veteran remarried within six months of his divorce. He and his second wife have two children. The family makes a bare living from the veteran's disability compensation and the farm.

The sixth of eight brothers and sisters, L.D.L. was raised in a small Midwestern town. He started school at the age of six and completed the sixth grade at the age of sixteen. School work was very difficult for him and after failing several grades he finally left to do carpentry work with his father. A long-smoldering conflict between the two soon broke into the open, however, and L.D.L. left home to work in a nearby city. Much of the difficulty stemmed from the fact that the father was a rather heavy drinker. A series of jobs as construction worker, truck driver, and factory laborer followed. In spite of the fact that L.D.L. shifted positions rather frequently, he was a good worker and was never fired. He enjoyed living away from home and was relieved to escape the almost constant bickering that had marked his life with his family.

Just before Christmas 1942 he entered the Army as a draftee and was sent to a camp in the West for infantry basic training. He found the work difficult and suffered from frequent pains in his back and feet. His major difficulty, however, was in learning subject matter in any way akin to that which he had in school. He had this difficulty in spite of the fact that he was not of particularly low intelligence. Nevertheless, he completed basic training successfully and went on to participate in field problems at the battalion, regiment, and finally division level.

In May word got around that the division would shortly be sent overseas for duty in the Pacific area. L.D.L. had not as yet had a furlough and felt that he deserved one. He left the camp and was absent without leave for almost five months before being returned to military control. Once he got away from the Army he could not bring himself to go back.

Following this episode the soldier was court-martialed and sentenced "to be confined at hard labor for six months and to forfeit $33 of his pay per month for six months." He was imprisoned for a while near his home and then sent to a post on the East Coast where prisoners were processed for overseas shipment. In January 1944 he left for England being released from confinement while at sea. Assigned to a division that was preparing for the invasion of the European mainland he spent over two months in steady training. However, when it developed that this division would not be employed in the initial invasion, but would be held in reserve for several months, Private L. along with many others was transferred to another, understrength division that had been alerted for early commitment. He was on board ship in the English Channel when the first troops landed in France and went ashore during the second day of fighting.

The ensuing action was among the most grueling of the war. The soldier was almost constantly under fire for ten days. Then there was a short break while forces were regrouped for the push across France. There were, however, frequent skirmishes with the enemy as a result of patrol action. In late July the attack was renewed. The initial advance was slow and for a week the fighting was intense. Toward the end of this period Private L. became extremely upset and frequently trembled all over. His condition became steadily worse over a two-week period after his buddy was killed by a rifle bullet while crouching in the same fox hole with him. Every time the company was under fire the soldier became convinced that he would be killed just as his buddy had been. With each man killed and each man evacuated he became surer and surer that he would be next. When a shell burst near him he would crouch in his foxhole or behind any cover he could find and cry quietly to himself. When it became apparent that he could no longer continue, he was sent back to the hospital for a rest.

After five days of hospitalization he was returned to duty but placed on detached service with a quartermaster battalion behind the lines until he was sufficiently recovered to enter combat again. Two months later he was placed on a truck and carried across France to rejoin his outfit which had taken up positions in Belgium. As the convoy neared the front it came under fire from a German artillery battery and Private L.'s truck was hit. Several men were killed and he was extremely lucky to escape uninjured. However, the feeling of approaching doom that had been steadily increasing ever since the trip started, now took complete possession of him. He became too depressed to speak and stood woodenly in one place until someone led him off. Later at the hospital he began to hear voices asking: "Where are you going?" and when he turned around there was no one there.

Evacuated to England he remained withdrawn, was suspicious of everyone, and continued to hear the voices. He was surer than ever that he was going to be killed. By January he was back in the United States where his condition improved somewhat. By May he was well enough to be discharged to the care of his family. He was, however, still considered psychotic at the time.

The veteran went to live with his brother-in-law after discharge and attempted to work. He tried various jobs of an unskilled nature, but always became irritable, said the bosses were imposing on him, and quit. Finally, he gave up all efforts to seek employment. He has since married and his wife cares for him completely. She takes him wherever he wants to go and handles most of his financial affairs. In late 1951 a child was born. The family lives alternately with Mrs. L.'s parents in the city and with L.D.L.'s parents in the small town where he was brought up. The veteran has not worked for a number of years and without the care of his wife would require hospitalization. Their primary income comes from his disability pension which amounts to about $200 a month.

Both G.G.M. and A.R.C. were exposed to major stress, yet they were able to keep going as long as they were in danger. Their collapse after their return to safety suggests that they had depleted their emotional reserves in the effort and as of the last date of record they had not yet made more than a partial recovery.

The case of L.D.L. illustrates the vicious circle that can be set up between exposure to danger and fears of future danger. L.D.L.'s fear reached a point where he had to be removed from combat because of a complete breakdown in his capacity to perform.

Chapter Eight: THE FRAMEWORK FOR THE STUDY OF EFFECTIVE PERFORMANCE

IN CONSIDERING the many factors that might have contributed to a soldier's breakdown, we reviewed to the extent that our materials permitted the level of his performance prior to induction as well as during the period of his active duty prior to his becoming ineffective. We went one step further. In order that the reader might better be able to evaluate the breakdown we summarized the soldier's postwar experience to indicate whether he had been able to reknit his life or not. But our cases were selected to illustrate strategic factors in breakdown, not to illustrate readjustment.

In this section we are changing our approach and will present cases specifically selected to illustrate the factors that appear to contribute to a man's rehabilitation. We will include a summary of the veteran's pre-military experience as well as the major incidents in his tour of active duty so that the reader will again have the benefit of a longer perspective.

Since our objective in presenting these case materials, both those dealing with breakdown and those concerned with recovery, is to add to our knowledge of the strategic factors involved in performance, we have not included case records of soldiers who after their discharge to civilian life failed to recover to the point of again being able to function effectively. A more systematic treatment of what happened to soldiers who broke down during their Army service is presented in *Patterns of Performance*. In that volume we include a consideration of men who did not recover as well as of those who, after their discharge became even more seriously ill.

Recovery, as we have seen, did not necessarily begin on the day a man was separated from the Army. Many veterans did poorly for months or even years after their return to civilian life. Some of these who were still in the process of recovering and had only recently started to perform effectively by the time we closed our follow-up in 1953 are included in the following selection.

We have, of course, no way of knowing whether a man who was performing effectively in 1950 or 1953 might break down at some later date. Only a prophet would venture such an opinion without knowledge of the situational stresses that might confront an individual and of the supports which would be available to him.

The following chapter heads indicate that we have made use of substantially the same framework for the study of effective performance as we employed in appraising ineffective performance. Yet certain modifications in the schema were necessary. The Army was not only the soldier's home but also his place of work. As we have pointed out earlier, a soldier was under surveillance twenty-four hours a day but in civilian life there is a much sharper break between a man's work and his hours off the job.

Millions of men have never introduced their wives to their employer and never invite their fellow workers to their homes—they keep the two worlds sharply separate. Many others find it necessary or desirable to mix their work with their personal life but the two are never as commingled as in the Army in time of war. We have therefore substituted for "The Immediate Group" and "The Military Organization" a major chapter on "The World of Work." Since we are interested in the strategic factors that contributed to restoring a man to effective functioning, we have added a chapter on rehabilitation factors in order to take account of the various ways in which the Veterans Administration and other organizations helped the veteran to find his place in the civilian community.

The contrast between the Army and civilian life is nowhere sharper than in the way in which the situational stresses of war contributed to a soldier's breakdown and the way in which a booming economy facilitated a veteran's readjustment by easing the problem of his getting and holding a job.

Another significant difference between the military and civilian environment is illustrated by the element of time. Once a man broke down in the Army and there was little likelihood that he could be returned to full duty within a reasonable period, he was on his way out—just as soon as he had received the benefits of medical treatment and the elaborate paper work required to discharge him had been completed. In civilian life a man did not have only one or two chances to make good; they were unlimited. He was able to make his climb back to effective performance over a period of time. While time militated against him in the Army, it operated in his favor in civilian life.

One further word in clarification of the term effective performance. Successful readjustment to civilian life implies a man's ability to meet minimum performance demands. This means that a man is able to hold a job and to earn enough to support himself. It means further that if he is married and has children he is able and willing to discharge his responsibilities to them. Finally, it means that a man abides by the laws of his community and stays out of conflict with the police and the courts. Thus effective performance means that a man takes care of himself and his dependents and that he does not become a charge on his family or the community.

This concept does not, however, tell us anything about the relationship between an individual's potentialities and his level of accomplishment. If a talented artist or engineer is an alcoholic and works only intermittently but earns enough to support himself, he meets this minimum criterion. If he is married and his wife remains with him even though she and the children suffer because of his alcoholism, he has met the second criterion—even though he is only formally discharging his family responsibilities. If he stays out of trouble with the police, he qualifies as a law-abiding citizen.

This concept of effective performance is predicated on minimum criteria of social adjustment, not on maximum criteria of emotional well-being. Many veterans whom we have selected as examples of effective performance continue to suffer from nervousness, sleeplessness, periodic depressions, or other manifestations of emotional illness. Many are quite miserable. From a clinical point of view many could not be considered cured or well. But from the viewpoint of the performance criteria that we have employed, they can be said to be effective. This parallels the approach which we followed in the analysis of soldiers who became ineffective while in the Army. There too we used the concept of the minimum to determine effective performance.

As our society increases its knowledge and understanding of the factors which contribute to or detract from individual well-being, the concept of effective performance tends to be broadened from the narrow criterion of minimum social performance to the broader criterion of basic emotional stability. While it is important to take note of these broadening horizons and to hope that our knowledge will rapidly increase, a restriction at this time of the concept of effective performance to minimum social criteria appears reasonable.

Chapter Nine: PERSONAL ASSETS

MAJOR ADVANCES in the understanding of human personality have been made because sick people have sought medical help. However, this means that we know more about pathology, about deficiencies that lead to malfunctioning, than about how an individual's specific strengths help him to achieve and maintain a level of effective performance. We know that many people become ineffective because their health is impaired. But little attention has been paid to the way in which a strong constitution can help a man to perform effectively.

The advantage of a superior physical endowment can be noted by considering some of the world's leaders. It is reported that Napoleon was able to get along with only a few hours' sleep. The campaign schedule of presidential candidates is enough to break all but the strongest. As we suggested some years ago in *The Labor Leader*, physical stamina is a prerequisite for many types of leadership.

The war exposed many men to special health hazards, including such debilitating diseases as malaria. However, many were able to make a quick recovery once they left the unhealthy area. Their physical recovery was the determining factor in enabling them to readjust successfully. Sometimes the situation was more complicated, such as when an initial physical breakdown had precipitated an emotional upset. In such cases physical recovery did not necessarily assure a return to health. This often depended on the man's emotional stability.

We have noted that a lack of intelligence was responsible for some soldiers' ineffective performance. As we shall see, the reverse was also true. Many men were greatly aided in their efforts to readjust to civilian life by their superior intelligence. Here was a strength on which they could build.

One of the important lessons of the war was that men with severe psychiatric symptoms could recover very quickly once they were removed from the environment in which they had broken down. Time and again, medical officers commented on how quickly patients who had been subject to outbursts of rage, destructiveness, incoherence could regain their composure. Many seriously disturbed soldiers were already substantially recovered at the time of their separation. And they therefore encountered little difficulty in readjusting to civilian life. A relatively strong psyche, evidenced by such a speedy recovery, was a major asset.

What a man makes of himself depends not only on his physical and emotional strengths, but on his motivation. Just as some men become ineffective in the Army because they were not motivated to do their best, others succeeded in civilian life, often in the face of major obstacles, because they put forth a very great and continuing effort to stand on their own feet. Although a man with exceptionally severe handicaps may not be able to succeed no matter how great his motivation, many who were marginal were able to tip the balance in their favor by their determination not to fail.

PHYSICAL ENDOWMENT

Contemporary society does not place a premium on physical strength and endurance such as was necessary on the frontier. But a man's physical condition still helps to determine the level of his performance. The strength of a man's constitution will largely determine whether he will eventually master or succumb to an enervating disease such as malaria, which kept J.J.M. from performing effectively for such a long period.

J.J.M. had a happy boyhood in a small Midwestern town where his father worked as a butcher. He attended the local schools and graduated from high school at the age of nineteen after repeating two grades. He played football and basketball and was generally well liked. While in high school he worked part-time in a restaurant. Later he held jobs as a shoe salesman and bartender. At the age of twenty-one he married a girl of fifteen. They had difficulty from the start and after two years and the birth of a daughter were divorced. J.J.M.'s former wife soon married his brother and he himself remarried several years later. This second marriage has been a happy one.

In late 1942 he entered the Army and after basic training with a Quartermaster unit in the South was assigned as a cook. After less than six months service he was promoted to technician fourth grade. In mid-1943 his unit was sent overseas and after an extremely long voyage landed in India. The soldier went through several air raids, but he did not see combat. Approximately two months after his arrival in India he developed malaria. He became very weak. At times he was overcome with dizziness and vomiting. He began to lose weight. He had frequent headaches, his joints ached, and he had a sharp pain in his chest. He spent four of the next six months in the hospital as he suffered one attack after another.

As the disease continued he reached a state of physical and mental disintegration which is usually found only among natives who have suffered repeated malarial infections over many years. In July 1944 he was flown to the States and soon recovered sufficiently to return to duty. Within the next year, however, he was hospitalized on eight different occasions, either for observation or treatment. In all he had fourteen different attacks in the 21-month period between the onset of the disease and his discharge from service. Complications involving the liver and spleen developed. At times he suffered a considerable amount of pain.

As the attacks continued the soldier became increasingly irritable and anxious. During his brief periods of good health he lived in constant fear that the infection would break out again. He began to have difficulty with his co-workers. There were arguments and finally, just after he had taken over as mess sergeant of his outfit, he broke camp restriction and went into town without a pass. He was picked up while drunk, court-martialed, and reduced to the rank of private. Private M. was finally separated for psychoneurosis, but there was a question as to whether a discharge for medical rather than psychiatric reasons would have been more appropriate. The Army physician in charge of his case noted: "It seems inconceivable that a person with the number of malaria attacks that this soldier has had should be retained in the service or that he should be referred for psychiatric disposition. In my opinion he should be separated on a medical basis."

On leaving military service J.J.M. almost immediately secured a position with a music store in the Midwest. He worked about two months repairing juke boxes before he was laid off. Shortly thereafter he was hospitalized by the Veterans Administration for another attack of malaria. During early 1946 he worked as a bartender before entering on-the-job training as a circulation manager for a local newspaper. Although he did quite well at this work he shifted in December 1946 to a job with a circulating library. Here too he received on-the-job training through the Veterans Administration. Throughout this period he had suffered a number of minor recurrences of his malaria. Whenever these attacks occurred he became increasingly anxious and upset. By August of 1947 his condition was so poor that he was unable to work at all and his training was terminated by reason of physical and psychiatric disabilities.

From mid-1947 until early 1949 he continued to live in the Midwest supporting his family largely on his pension. He held jobs as a restaurant doorman and a bus boy, but most of the time he was unable to do any work. Since his income during the two years between discharge from the service and his almost complete collapse in August 1947 had been small, due primarily to time lost from work, the family was in rather dire financial circumstances by January 1949. These problems were further complicated by the birth of a son toward the latter part of 1948.

Finally in early 1949 the family moved to Florida. However, the malaria attacks which had plagued J.J.M. throughout 1948 continued and in mid-1949 he was again hospitalized by the Veterans Administration. After returning to his family, J.J.M. took a job making up salads in a restaurant. The work required long hours and the pay was quite meager. Nevertheless, his condition improved and although he had a slight recurrence of malaria in February 1950 he has remained free of the disease since that time. By March he felt much better. He was less anxious and was sufficiently sure of himself to apply for further V.A. training as a household equipment salesman with a lighting studio.

Once free of his malaria the veteran has done very well. In October he transferred from the lighting studio to an electrical supply company and continued his training as a salesman. At about the same time a daughter was born and shortly after that his income was sufficient to permit him to bring his daughter by his first marriage, now eleven years old, to live with him in Florida. Throughout 1951 he made excellent progress in his training and by March 1952 he was advanced to a full-fledged salesman's position. He attained this in spite of the fact that he had not been scheduled to complete training until May of that year. At that time he was receiving a salary of $3,600 per year plus bonus and commissions. He was supporting a family of five and his psychoneurotic difficulties which had begun to clear up after the malaria attacks ceased in early 1950 had almost disappeared.

This case illustrates clearly the close connection between physical well-being and effective performance. J.J.M.'s early Army record was good, as was evidenced by his promotions. But after contracting malaria he became ineffective. Until his malaria, which had precipitated, as it almost always does, emotional complications, was brought under effective control J.J.M. remained ineffective. Once his physical condition improved, he was able to support himself and his family in a satisfactory manner.

GOOD INTELLIGENCE

The range of jobs open to a man depends more on his intellectual ability and his training than on any other factors. This is one of the most important advantages that men with high intelligence have over others who are less well endowed. They are able to explore a greater number of alternatives in seeking a satisfactory occupational adjustment. Moreover, they are able to qualify for the more difficult types of training and can more readily master what they are taught. In our society most of the good jobs are available only to those who have been well trained. But the advantages of superior intelligence are by no means limited to a man's occupational adjustment. An intelligent man is less likely to get himself into difficulty, and more able to extricate himself if he does.

G.T.F. was the second of six children born to a very poor family in a small Northeastern town. The father was an automobile mechanic, but because of his heavy drinking he worked only intermittently. What money he did make went for liquor. During the depression there were times when the family actually went hungry and the children were always shabbily dressed. There was considerable dissension in the home, primarily as a result of quarreling between the parents. At one time the father attempted to kill himself.

G.T.F. was quite fearful as a child and in school tended to avoid the other children, partly because he was ashamed of the poverty in which he lived. A good student, he obtained extremely high marks and graduated from high school at the age of seventeen. While still in school he worked as an usher in a movie theater. Although he would have liked to go to college, this was completely out of the question in view of the financial status of the family.

He worked for a while as a caddy on a golf course and then joined the Civilian Conservation Corps. He became bored with this work and went into the management of a service station with his father. The business failed within six months. A job as a lathe hand

in a factory followed, but before a year was over he again became
bored with the work. After several months in Florida he returned
home and went to work as a machine operator in another plant.
After a year in this position he was drafted for military service.
He was then twenty years old. Throughout this period of employment he found that a few months after learning a job he would
become bored and dissatisfied. The work did not seem to demand
enough of him to make it interesting.

At induction he scored in the top 10 percent of all draftees on
the intelligence test and did even better on the mechanical aptitude
test. He was assigned to the Air Corps and after basic training went
to the Midwest for schooling as a radio operator and mechanic.
There he met the girl who later became his wife. In August 1943,
just before going overseas, he was married. Almost a year as a radio
operator in India followed during which he was promoted to corporal. He flew 151 missions "over the Hump" into China. Although
there was little real combat, weather conditions were extremely
hazardous and the men were in constant danger.

Toward the end Corporal F. became very nervous, so much so
that he could neither read nor write. Sometimes he would awaken
at night convinced that someone was standing beside the bed in
the dark. He was too scared to move, but when he finally did turn
on his flashlight no one was there. Nevertheless, he did not report
to the doctor for fear he would be grounded and be forced to remain in India for a long time. Under the Air Corps policy then in
effect the best way to assure an early return to the United States
was to complete the required number of missions.

Once back in this country after completing his tour of duty,
he improved considerably. After a furlough he flew a mission to
Europe in connection with a ferrying operation. On his return
he became quite anxious again, could not sleep, and suffered from
headaches whenever he was ordered around. He was often nauseated after meals and became acutely disturbed when riding on
buses or trains at night because he could not see the road ahead
clearly. After a brief hospitalization he was returned to duty, but

soon caught scarlet fever and was back in the hospital again. On being released a second time he went to work teaching radio operation and repair. He did very well at this and enjoyed the work. However, he became increasingly irritable, and was particularly upset at not getting a higher rank, and in June of 1945 he was back in the hospital. He was discharged for psychoneurosis in July.

On returning home the veteran considered his years of military service as an overly long period filled with frustration, fear, and extremely unrewarding work. Nevertheless, it had presented him with an opportunity that had not existed before. Even though married and with a family to support he could now, with the aid of the Veterans Administration, go to college. He applied for admission to the engineering school of a university near his home—one of the top universities in the country. At the time of submitting his application he did not believe he would be accepted. However, his high-school marks had been very good and with his high intelligence he was able to do well on the entrance examinations. He started classes in the fall of 1945.

For the first time in his life he found himself faced with a task that was intellectually demanding for him. The work was hard, but he liked it and with his intelligence and marked aptitude for engineering subject matter he was able to get good marks. By the end of the first year he began to believe that he might become an engineer. As he gained confidence his fears diminished. The V.A. doctors found him greatly improved when he was examined in 1946 and recommended that his compensation be reduced. However, G.T.F. asked that it be continued at the same level because if it were reduced he would have to take a part-time job. He did not feel that he was able to do that. The V.A. concurred and he continued to devote all his efforts to his studies. A child was born in 1948.

G.T.F. continued to get good marks and achieved a feeling of satisfaction from his success. After graduating with a degree in mechanical engineering he took a job with an aircraft company in the West. His compensation was reduced since his neurosis had almost disappeared. However, he found the rather routine work quite unrewarding. In many ways it seemed little different from the jobs he had held before military service and in the Army. He did not feel that he had a chance to use his intelligence and did not attain any real satisfaction from his work. Gradually his anxiety and insomnia and headaches returned. He began to lose time from work. Finally he decided to return to the university where he had previously studied for graduate training.

In 1952 G.T.F. started his work toward a Ph.D. in engineering. Again he did very well. The work was even more gratifying than it had been when he was an undergraduate. He began to teach and in 1954 became a full-time instructor on the faculty. He had a feeling of real accomplishment and became much less nervous. By 1956 he had received his Ph.D. at the age of thirty-three and had been promoted to assistant professor.

G.T.F.'s high native intelligence and special mechanical aptitudes provided the basis for his successful postwar adjustment, and there is strong evidence in his record that his mediocre work record before the war was in large measure the result of unchallenging jobs. Whether a man performs effectively or not frequently depends on whether he finds an opportunity to make use of his strengths.

EMOTIONAL RESILIENCE

We know that serious emotional disturbance may make it impossible for an individual to perform effectively. But it is the character of the illness which will largely determine the prognosis and the possibility of the man's again performing effectively. Many who broke down in the Army were basically sound: they were simply overwhelmed by the pressures they faced. Others, however, afflicted from childhood with an emotionally unstable structure were more permanently weakened by their Army experience.

A man whose emotional energies are drained by internal conflict is very vulnerable if his difficulties become such that he cannot perform effectively. For unless he can support himself and discharge his responsibilities towards his family, he will become even further upset because of this failure. In contrast, if a man who has been emotionally upset to a point where he could not perform effectively recovers, his progress will be speeded by the fact that he can work again and otherwise discharge his responsibilities.

L.N.N. was born in rural New England but he and his family later moved to the West Coast. His father managed grocery stores for a national chain and was able to provide a very good living for his wife and four children. L.N.N. was a very active child and as a result had a number of accidents which resulted in, at various times, a concussion, a broken jaw, a broken shoulder, and a broken leg. However, he recovered from all of these and was in general quite healthy. In school he received slightly above average grades and was very popular. He left high school three weeks before graduation because his family moved, and therefore never received his diploma. At about this same time his mother died of cancer. He worked first as a salesman for a radio and television supply company, and then shifted to a job as assistant manager of a grocery store. He was considered a very good worker. When he was twenty-one his father died. Although initially upset at the death of his parents he adjusted well. Before entering military service at the age of twenty-two he married a girl he had known for some time.

Assigned to the Infantry for basic training he performed very well and was selected for further training in order to become a noncommissioned officer. Five months after induction he was promoted to corporal and became an instructor at the camp where he had received basic training. Later he assumed similar duties at a large replacement depot on the East Coast. Throughout this period Corporal N. was considered an excellent soldier and was in very good health, the only untoward incident was a sprained ankle which he received while playing football.

In July 1944 when the need for infantry replacements in Europe became acute, he was sent to England where he spent over a month at another replacement depot. Later he was assigned to an Infantry glider group as a squad leader and in December was flown with his unit to a point deep in France. This trip followed by only one day his release from a ten-day hospitalization for bronchitis. By early January the outfit had been placed on the line of battle with the mission of containing the German breakthrough.

Although Corporal N.'s regiment was initially in reserve, they were soon involved in heavy fighting over a frozen, snow-covered terrain. After five days of battle he came down with pneumonia and was also suffering severely from trench foot. By the time he returned from the hospital in mid-February the division had been pulled back into France for reorganization. Not long afterwards the soldier made his first glider landing behind enemy lines. This was followed by a month of intensive fighting which terminated with the total elimination of enemy resistance in the Ruhr industrial area. Throughout this period the corporal was very effective both as a leader and a fighter. Four days before the Germans capitulated completely he was wounded slightly in the shoulder. He did not require hospitalization.

For the ensuing two months the division remained to perform occupation duties. Later it was returned to France to prepare for return to the United States. But Corporal N. did not return home with his unit. During the period following his combat experiences he had had his first extra-marital intercourse and caught gonorrhea. Although he had weathered situations objectively much more serious, including severe injuries, the death of his parents, and extremely arduous combat, without developing even a mild mental disorder he now became very depressed and guilty. He was preoccupied with thoughts of suicide, was sure everyone was talking about him, and was quite confused.

He was hospitalized but became progressively worse. By the time he reached the States in September 1945 he was spending the whole day in bed picking at the bed covers and mumbling, "I want to die."

He refused food and water, would not shave or bathe. Once he jumped out of bed and kicked down a door for no apparent reason. Although cured of gonorrhea, he remained convinced that he still had a venereal disease. Both electric and insulin shock treatment were tried and at first had no effect. Later, however, he began to improve. By December he was sufficiently recovered to be discharged from the service as not requiring further hospitalization.

After a few months' rest L.N.N. was employed as the advertising manager of a small firm on the West Coast and continued to work for the same company for about two years. During this period he received several raises and in general did very well. His married life was happy, and he and his wife led an active social life. They have had no children. In 1948 he took a position with a radio and electronic supply house as a salesman. This job, although paying only slightly more than he had been receiving, seemed to offer a much greater opportunity. By 1953 the veteran was in fact making almost twice the salary he had started at in 1946. As a salesman he was considered outstanding and he had an excellent reputation among the people with whom he worked.

Although he is generally much better off than he was prior to military service, some residuals of his severe depression remain. He is still plagued with occasional feelings of guilt. Any mention of venereal disease upsets him and sometimes he still feels that he has not completely recovered from his gonorrhea. His emotional health is not as good as it was prior to the end of the war in Europe, but as the V.A. doctors note, it is far superior to that of most people who have suffered as severe an emotional disturbance as he did.

S.A.S. was the seventh of sixteen children born to a Negro family in the deep South. As a child he was healthy and spent much of his time helping his mother and brothers and sisters work the farm. His father rarely helped, was often away, and drank rather heavily. S.A.S. attended a country school for two years and then went to school in town where he completed the ninth grade at the age of seventeen. Actually he did quite well considering the fact that his education was frequently interrupted by demands for his help at home. At about the time he left school his father left his family for good. S.A.S. worked for about six months as a laborer in a dairy and then joined the Civilian Conservation Corps where he spent over a year. Several months as a laborer in a brick yard followed and then he went to work as a stock boy in a large department store. After about a year on this job he was drafted into the military service.

Private S. was assigned to the medical detachment at an air base in the South for his basic training. The soldier did well at first, but quickly developed a thorough distaste for military routine.

Quite suddenly after a month of training he began to behave very peculiarly. He walked over to another soldier's bed in the middle of the night and asked: "What is 6 over 3 and 3 over 6? What is alert? Why does a siren blow?" His talk became incoherent at times and he seemed to be in a daze. During classes he stared into space and apparently heard nothing. Sometimes he walked around with a perpetual grin while proclaiming: "I am a son of a living God." Later he refused to eat and began to do exactly the opposite of what he was told to do. He complained, "I can't figure out what's going on around here."

Within a week he was in the hospital. There his speech was so silly and confused that it was impossible to take a case history. The doctors felt, in spite of the fact that they knew very little about him, that his behavior was so consistent with the pattern commonly found in schizophrenic patients of the hebephrenic type that there was almost no chance of error in this diagnosis.

Accordingly, five days after entering the hospital Private S. went before a disposition board and was approved for separation from the service because of psychosis. Almost immediately he began to improve and soon was transferred from the locked ward to the open ward. By the time he was discharged just before Christmas 1942 with eighty-nine days of service he appeared to be very much improved. Nevertheless, he was turned over to the sheriff of his home county and after a jury trial to establish insanity was committed to the state hospital.

On his arrival, there did not appear to be anything wrong with him at all. He was quiet, cooperative, and exhibited no signs of confusion. He seemed to be well-informed for a man of his socioeconomic background and education. For a while the doctors were thoroughly mystified. Then the veteran began to talk to the ward attendants about the Army and how much he detested it. He indicated that he never had been really sick, but had put on an act to obtain a discharge. He was rather proud of his success. After a brief stay, S.A.S. was released and returned to his job as a stock boy.

At the store his supervisors were quite surprised to learn that he had been in a mental institution. He appeared to be quite normal and was a very satisfactory employee. Although his mother applied to the Veterans Administration for a disability pension while he was in the hospital the application was turned down because there was apparently nothing wrong with him. The veteran himself did not push his claim, and his mother later stated that she did not want her son to receive compensation as long as he could support himself.

After about a year he left the department store and worked first for a furniture store and later for a garage. In 1945 he was married. In late 1946 he applied for schooling under the G.I. Bill but was turned down because he lacked by one day the mandatory ninety days of military service. Shortly after this he began work as a mail room assistant and truck driver for a daily newspaper, a job which he still holds.

In 1954 he was supporting a rapidly growing family of five children. He was in very good health and had had no difficulties of an emotional nature. Observing him, one would never believe that he had suffered a severe psychotic breakdown but despite his statements to the attendants at the state hospital it is likely that he had suffered one.

Both L.N.N. and S.A.S. were at some point in their military careers so seriously disturbed that they were unable to take care of themselves, and certainly could not perform effectively as soldiers. But as their emotional disturbances receded, they had no difficulty in again functioning effectively.

GOOD MOTIVATION

We noted earlier that many soldiers hesitated to do their best in the Army because, among other reasons, they felt they had nothing to look forward to in the Army except injury or death. In civilian life a man is much more likely to put forth a special effort to advance.

J.K. was born and raised in a small city surrounded by the Rocky Mountains. In school he obtained good marks and finished high school before going to work. His father died of pneumonia at the age of sixty. After completing his education J.K. secured a job as a truck driver for a wholesale grocery firm while continuing to live with his mother. Two years later he enlisted for service with the Air Corps. Although he had never lived away from home for any period of time and enjoyed his job as a truck driver, he felt strongly that it was his duty to serve his country. He was then twenty years old.

Following induction he was sent to a camp in the Southwest for training as an aerial gunner. Assignments in the South and West followed during which he worked hard and performed well. In September 1943 after completing his training he was promoted to sergeant. In January he left for England as a replacement ball turret gunner. By late February 1944 he had been assigned to a B-17 crew and was flying missions over Germany. Although the flak was often heavy and Sergeant K. was afraid at times, he obtained a good deal of satisfaction from the feeling that he was doing his duty. He was considered a very good gunner and in April was promoted to staff sergeant. Two weeks later while on his ninth mission over Germany his plane was shot down and he parachuted to safety. For the next thirteen months he remained a prisoner-of-war. Although he was shifted from camp to camp rather frequently toward the end of the war and was not finally liberated until V-E day, he was generally treated well.

Returning to the United States in June 1945, J.K. went home immediately on a sixty-day furlough. While at home he had difficulty sleeping and was tired all the time. He was rather anxious and jumped at any loud sounds. On occasion he vomited after meals. When his furlough ended he reported to a replacement center on the West Coast for reassignment. A week later after a series of sleepless nights he went on sick call and was hospitalized. He hated to go to the hospital, but was so upset and tired that he felt he had to do something. The following month he was discharged medically though still very nervous. At the time of leaving military service he was urged to apply for disability compensation and did so.

However, J.K. felt strongly that it was up to him to support himself and he did not want to live off of a pension. He went back to his old job as a truck driver with the wholesale grocery company almost immediately. In spite of the fact that he was considered 50 percent disabled by the Veterans Administration he wrote to them a month after his discharge saying, "My nervous condition is now satisfactory and I believe I have no reason to apply for compensation." Nevertheless, the V.A. people felt that he was still suffering from his neurosis and continued the payments. Within a year he shifted from truck driving to sales work with the same company. He had become interested in the sales end of the business and applied for a transfer. Considered a good and very responsible worker, the sales manager decided to try him out. As a result he received a sizable increase in salary. Although he lived at home with his mother, in his new job he spent a large portion of his time traveling.

Examined by the V.A. doctors about a year after discharge he at first claimed that his neurosis had completely disappeared. Only after some urging did he reveal that he was still quite nervous. At the same time he said that he felt it was up to him to make his own way in the world. He had hesitated to mention his nervousness because he did not want the V.A. to feel any responsibility for his readjustment. He said that that was *his* problem and he would have to work it out for himself. As a result of this examination his compensation payments were reduced but not discontinued.

Over the next three years, J.K. continued to work as a salesman and live with his mother in a house which she owned. He paid all his own expenses and in actual fact spent over half his time on the road covering his territory. He found this work very enjoyable. When examined by the Veterans Administration in late 1949, he appeared to be doing well and to have recovered from his psycho-neurosis. He himself brought up the subject of his disability compensation saying, "I am still receiving $13.80 a month. That's fine and I appreciate it very much, but I really don't think it's something that is due me. Someone else who needs it more than I do might as well have it. As long as my condition is as good as it is, you might as well take it away." Since it was quite apparent that the veteran had in fact achieved a very good adjustment, his payments were discontinued. He has since continued to work as a salesman and has exhibited no signs of his prior symptoms.

D.E.W. lived throughout his early life on a farm in the deep South. There were nine children in the family and all but the very youngest contributed in some way to the farm's operation. D.E.W. attended school periodically, but he had to interrupt his education in the spring and fall to plant and harvest crops. In all he completed nine grades by the time he entered military service at the age of twenty-one. He liked school, but found the work very hard. It seemed to take him much longer to learn than the other children. For a while before entering the Army he worked as a clerk in a local store.

After induction he was sent to a port in the South for training with an armored regiment. Here, too, he found it difficult to learn.

However, he tried very hard and was able to keep up with the training, although his officers felt that he just barely met minimum standards in this respect. As time went on he began to have difficulty on marches and finally would fall out whenever the group had to run for any distance. On being questioned he complained of pains in his back which also occurred when he had to ride any distance in a truck. At about this same time it became known to the commanding officer that he had been wetting his bed several times a week since entering service. Consequently, in early March 1943, Private W. was sent to the hospital for further evaluation.

Interviews and tests showed that he was highly motivated, but of below-average intelligence. Further questioning about his enuresis brought out the fact that he had been wetting his bed ever since he was a child. Although he had tried to stop, he had been unsuccessful. He did not wake up and only realized what he had done when he found the sheets wet in the morning. This had created difficulties with his barracks mates ever since he entered the Army, but it had not been brought to the attention of his officers until recently. In April after serving for approximately six months, Private W. was discharged as unadaptable for service in the United States Army because of enuresis.

Returning to live with his parents, the veteran continued to have difficulty with his back which made it almost impossible for him to do farm work. For several months he did practically nothing and his parents began to fear that he would be a continuing burden on them. However, D.E.W. finally decided that the only way he could support himself and achieve the things he wanted in life was by continuing his education. He knew from past experience that he would have to work harder than the others, but felt it would be worth trying. Since his service had been very brief and he wanted to take courses at the college level later, he decided not to use his limited G.I. Bill benefits while completing high school. In mid-1943 he started school. After four years of very hard work he received his high school diploma. During this period he worked part-time as a store clerk.

In early 1947 he was married and approximately a year later a
child was born. He was then working in a textile mill. In 1948
D.E.W. decided to continue with his plans for advanced education. He was able to enroll in a small business college in his home
state under the G.I. Bill. For over a year he studied accounting
while working as a bookkeeper to support his family. After completing this course, he was unemployed for several months while
looking for a better-paying job. Then in June 1950 he got into
rather serious trouble over a personality problem that had plagued
him for many years. He was arrested for exposing himself in public.
Under questioning he revealed that since he was in his 'teens he
had occasionally had an uncontrollable urge to expose himself.
Although he attempted to obtain treatment from the Veterans Administration at this time he was turned down because this condition
was not connected with his military service.

In early 1951 D.E.W. began work as a salesman for a furniture
company. At first his earnings were small, but within three years
his salary had been raised 50 percent. For a few months in 1951
he took a course at another commercial school which he felt would
help him in his work. At the present time he is supporting a family
of four, he is making a comfortable living at a job he likes, and is
very happy with the position he has been able to achieve in life.

Both cases demonstrate quite clearly that often the course of a
man's life depends in considerable measure on his aims and the effort
he is willing to invest in their accomplishment. J.K. was determined
to get back on his own feet as quickly as possible after he was
discharged. He did not want to have the Veterans Administration
support him. In fact, he took the initiative in recommending that
his compensation payments cease.

D.E.W. was also determined to improve himself by his own
efforts. He worked and studied at the same time and, with few
advantages other than his determination, was able to make a satisfactory life for himself. As both cases demonstrate, it is hard to
overstate the role of motivation in performance.

Chapter Ten: FAMILY SUPPORTS

WE NOTED earlier that certain soldiers could not tolerate separation from their families and broke down as a consequence. This chapter seeks to illustrate the constructive role that families frequently played in helping men who had become ineffective in the military to rehabilitate themselves after their return to civilian life.

For some men, it was their parents who were most helpful; most married men were supported by their wives though sometimes a veteran was helped by both his parents and his wife. Although we do not have specific cases of an engaged man being aided by his fiancée at a time when he was still disturbed by his wartime experiences, it is likely that many benefited from such emotional support. Some veterans were aided in their readjustment by rejoining "the gang" with whom they had grown up, worked, and played before being drafted. Here was the counterpart to the Army's buddy system.

As we read the cases of veterans who had a hard time adjusting after the war, we were struck repeatedly with those who were able to pull themselves together only after a child was born. Apparently this event propelled them into action. One explanation may be that the veteran did not feel that it was necessary for him to hold a steady job as long as his wife could work and he had a pension. With a baby, however, it was no longer practical for many women to keep on working. Faced with a direct challenge to assume his responsibilities as head of the household, a veteran was often able to find the strength to perform with renewed vigor and efficiency.

The kind of help that veterans received from their parents or wives covered a wide range. First and most important was emotional support. They found warmth and understanding which helped them to forget, however slowly, the distressing experiences that they had encountered during the war. Many were given financial aid in amounts that were sufficient, together with whatever other resources they had, to enable them to stay out of the labor market until they could achieve a greater degree of emotional stability. Others were helped to pursue further education or a special training course. Still others were enabled to start their own farm or business. While it is true that some parents or wives by their solicitude probably delayed the full recovery of their loved ones, most families undoubtedly contributed much to the readjustment process.

PARENTAL FAMILY

Many veterans were started on the way to recovery just by being able to come back to their parents or wives. Such was the case of D.U. who had an extremely dependent relationship with his mother. Others had need for a respite in the early months after their separation so that they could evaluate themselves, their experiences, their future. Often they found this in their parent's home.

P.E.F. was brought up in the farm country of the Midwest. He was an only child and attended a rural school near his home. At the age of eleven he was rather severely injured in an automobile accident and was unconscious for seven hours. Although after six weeks in bed he had apparently recovered completely from his injuries, he began at that time to suffer from occasional headaches. Later when he went to work on his father's farm, after completing the eighth grade at school, these headaches continued to plague him and he often had to rest until they passed. Some time before entering the Army at the age of twenty-two, he married and his first child was born just before he was inducted. Prior to military service he had always worked as a farm laborer.

Although Private F.'s headaches were noted at the time he entered service they were not considered severe enough or frequent enough to bar him from full duty. He was first assigned to infantry training, but after six weeks was transferred to a quartermaster regiment, with which he remained throughout the remainder of his period of active service. By the time the regiment left for the Asiatic Theater of Operations in early 1943, he was working as a cook and in March was promoted to technician fifth grade. He continued to serve in a satisfactory manner until the fall of the year, when his headaches rather suddenly became much more severe. He experienced a dull ache which would not go away. It was there when he went to bed at night and still there when he awoke in the morning. When he walked his head seemed to throb. He could not concentrate on his work and often felt very depressed.

Finally P.E.F. went to the hospital. At first the doctors thought he was suffering from a head injury possibly related to the automobile accident of his childhood. He was sent back to the States for further studies. About a month after the patient reached this country, however, one of the doctors found that he could stop the headaches just by insisting that they go away. This did not always work, but it did sometimes. When medical tests failed to reveal any evidence of physical disease or injury, the diagnosis was changed to psychoneurosis and in the early spring of 1944 the soldier was discharged.

The return to his home and family did not, however, help P.E.F. He remained depressed and at times became very tense. The pain in his forehead, which had been only temporarily relieved by the Army doctor's suggestions, was almost continuous. He did not feel like working and even the birth of his second child about a year after his discharge did not seem to affect him.

Nevertheless soon after returning home he did begin to do some work, although at first it was very little. His father owned two farms close together, both of them on very good land. At the father's suggestion P.E.F. and his family moved into the house on the smaller farm. There was some discussion about rent, but the father did not make much of a point of it. In fact practically all of the costs involved in getting the son started on his own farm were borne by his father. At first P.E.F. did not do very well. He could not seem to get the work done and his father had to help him out frequently. Gradually, however, he began to feel better. By 1948, he was beginning to show some real progress with the farm and the following year entered institutional on-the-farm training with the Veterans Administration. This would have been impossible without the assistance his father had given him, since one of the requirements for such training was that the veteran have a farm of his own and the equipment to operate it. About this same time he began paying his father a nominal rent for the use of the smaller farm.

By the time he completed his training in 1952 P.E.F. was making an adequate living for himself and his family and had begun to pay off the debt which he had accumulated during the years when he was unable to work steadily. His father was still far from insistent about this and in all probability the whole debt will never be paid. Nevertheless, the veteran now feels an obligation to repay his parents for the help they gave him in overcoming his emotional difficulties and in getting him started as a farmer.

As a child D.U. was tense and high-strung, prone to temper tantrums and occasional sleepwalking. His family had been rather prosperous until they lost their money in the depression. After that the father began to drink heavily and the parents were separated when D.U. was nine. His mother took a job at a private boarding school in the deep South and her four boys went with her.

D.U attended school there until he graduated at the age of seventeen. His marks were not particularly good because he frequently became upset during examinations. He thoroughly disliked the military training which was part of the school curriculum. His particular interests were listening to jazz records and woodworking in his own shop. He did not care for social activities, but preferred to stay home with his mother and engage in his hobbies. After leaving school he went to work as a clerk in his mother's store with special responsibility for the soda fountain. He continued at this job until drafted for military service soon after his twentieth birthday.

In the Army D.U. did extremely well initially, primarily because he had already been exposed to much of the drill and military subject matter covered in basic training. For fourteen months he served with an infantry division at various camps in the South. Toward the end of this period they were given special training in mountain and amphibious fighting and then in early 1944 embarked for the Pacific Theater of Operations. After one and a half months at sea they landed in New Guinea in an area which had already been cleared of enemy resistance. Three months of intensive jungle training followed. They then landed at another point in New Guinea to take over a beachhead that had already been established by another division.

Here D.U. saw his first combat and also received the nickname, "Bundle of Nerves," from his fellow soldiers. For a month and a half he participated in patrol action against the heavily fortified Japanese positions. The fighting never became very heavy, however, and no attempt was made to expand the beachhead. In September, they were placed on ships again, disembarking several days later to capture an island to the north. At first there was no resistance, but as they moved on into the hills scattered firing occurred. Once the perimeter was established extensive patrol activity was initiated.

Two weeks after this invasion Private U. came down with malaria. Although this condition cleared rapidly in the hospital the doctors realized he was not suited for further combat. He was tremulous and given to acute panics. At times he felt very weak and suffered from severe headaches. He had difficulty sleeping and when he did sleep he had terrifying dreams of battle. Back in the States, he remained severely upset in spite of several furloughs. The soldier felt that he had done all he could in the Army and that he should be sent home to take care of his mother. He wanted very much to be able to support her so that she would not have to work. After almost a year in various hospitals during which he improved only slightly, the soldier was discharged because of psychoneurosis.

Returning home he rested for several months and then was employed by his mother at the school store. For five years he continued to work as a clerk. During this time he lost an average of three months a year from work because of his emotional difficulties. He was able to keep his job only because his mother ran the store. Not only was he frequently absent, but because of his impatience and belligerence he was thoroughly disliked by the students. During his time at the boarding school he took several courses as a nonmatriculated student.

When his mother became too old to continue running the store there was some question as to what D.U. would do. He was not psychologically fit to take over the store himself and wanted very much to remain with his mother. Finally it was decided that the mother would buy him a farm with part of her savings. This was done in late 1950 and D.U. entered on-the-farm training with the Veterans Administration at the same time. The mother invested a sizable amount of money in the farm over the next year. D.U., however, did very little work, restricting his efforts primarily to the supervision of men hired with his mother's funds. Nevertheless, the farm progressed quite well.

As of 1951 he remained restless, impatient, and easily upset. Occasionally he became dizzy and felt weak all over. In spite of his anxiety state, however, he was, with the emotional and financial support of his mother, making a living and maintaining some semblance of effective performance. He had not married.

In both of these cases the presence of family assets, together with good will on the part of parents, made it possible for these seriously upset veterans to adjust to civilian life. P.E.F. is well on the way to performing effectively, being able by his farming to support his family and himself; and D.U., who is much less stable, has a position in life, if only by virtue of the continued support of his mother.

CONNUBIAL FAMILY

Among the major deprivations of military service was the enforced separation of a man from his wife and children. Since most men derive a great deal of satisfaction from their relationship with their immediate family, they felt keenly this loss which the war inflicted on them. Hence, their return home was a boon on two scores: they no longer had to endure the hardship of military service; and they could enjoy the warmth and happiness which derive from close family ties.

Many single men also received an emotional boost on their return to civilian life. Some were able to renew friendships with young women which soon ripened into engagements and marriages. This often helped the veteran to have a better understanding of what he wanted to do with his life, now that he could again control it.

But it was the married veteran who was most frequently helped. Many married women had entered the labor market for the first time during the war and they gained confidence in their ability to carry added responsibilities. An understanding and supportive wife was thus in a better position to help her husband if he needed help after his discharge.

W.E.K. was the son of a successful electrical contractor in a small Northeastern city. As a child he frequently helped his father with electrical work and after graduating from high school he decided to make this his full-time vocation, although his four sisters had gone on to college. He was in part influenced by the fact that his father had had a heart attack two years before and could not work as hard as previously. In school W.E.K. did relatively well although he lost one year because of rheumatic fever and was actually much more interested in sports than in his studies. He played semi-professional hockey after completing his education.

When he was twenty-two his father suffered another heart

attack and died. The son subsequently went to work as a foreman on highway construction jobs. At about this same time he began to develop pains in his chest similar to those his father had experienced and had to stop playing hockey because of shortness of breath. When war broke out he tried to enlist but was turned down on several different occasions because of high blood pressure. In late 1942 he was finally drafted at the age of twenty-five.

As a soldier he was assigned to a medical battalion in the South for basic training, but almost immediately got into difficulty. Unable to obtain a furlough for the Christmas holidays, he went home anyway and was absent from duty for six days. On his return he was court-martialed and spent most of the month of January in the stockade. After release he rejoined his outfit, but had some difficulty with the training because of pains in his chest and dizziness whenever he had to run any distance. He was hospitalized for over three weeks, but was able to return to duty. For over a year, until sent to England in June 1944, Private K. worked as an ambulance and truck driver at various camps in the South, performing quite effectively. Once overseas, he was briefly assigned to an airborne division as a gliderman but was found medically unfit and reclassified as eligible for noncombat duty only.

A series of assignments at various replacement depots in England, France, and Belgium followed. While in Belgium he was under bombardment several times and his chest pains which had never disappeared for any appreciable period, became severe. Finally, while running up a hill during a training exercise, the pain became so intense that he decided to report to the hospital. He was evacuated through Paris to England and there was found to be suffering from a severe psychoneurosis as well as pneumonia. Although he soon recovered from the latter, he remained emotionally upset and was returned to the United States. In July 1945 he was discharged.

After leaving the service W.E.K. went to work as a painter but missed a good deal of time partly because of his chest pains and difficulty in breathing and partly because he began to drink rather heavily to relieve his anxiety. In April 1946 he had to stop work entirely because he became dizzy every time he got on a ladder. Later he managed a riding stable and did some carpentry work, but by the spring of 1947 he had given up any attempt at employment and was frequently drunk. His difficulties were further complicated by the fact that he visited a number of doctors some of whom told him that he was suffering from an organic heart condition. Extensive tests by the V.A. doctors, however, failed to substantiate this diagnosis and it was eventually established that the Army doctors had been correct in ascribing his difficulties to an emotional origin.

In early 1948 W.E.K. married a former Army nurse. She insisted that he give up his drinking and in actual fact he did. Furthermore, as a result of his marriage and the increased obligations involved, he was faced with the necessity of going to work. Although he remained emotionally upset and continued to suffer from chest pains, dizziness, and difficulty in breathing, he was able with the support of his wife to apply for and obtain a job at an ordnance depot in his home town. Later he began taking a course in electronics at a technical high school in order to prepare himself for a return to the occupation that he knew most about—that of electrician. Although he discontinued this training after several months, he did turn to electrical work and was still employed in that field in 1953.

His symptoms have continued to bother him, but since most of his employment has been as an independent contractor, he is able to adjust his work accordingly. Whenever he has an anxiety attack, which is usually about once a week, he takes it easy for that day and arranges his work so that he can make it up later. He has found that when he avoids contracting on a job that may involve delays in payment for his services and consequent emotional turmoil, he gets along much better. In this way he has been able to support his family, which now includes a young daughter, and thus carry out the resolutions made at the time of his marriage. Furthermore, he has been able to comply with his wife's request and no longer drinks excessively.

B.A.F. was born and raised in a rural area of the deep South. As a child he was nervous and high-strung, prone to temper tantrums and occasional sleepwalking. In school he had some difficulty but was able to complete high school at the age of twenty. During these years in school he had had gonorrhea and was once unconscious for several hours after being in an automobile accident. Other than this he was in good physical health. In the nine years between graduation from high school and induction into military service B.A.F. held a number of jobs none of which paid very well. He worked on his father's farm for a while and then, after getting married at the age of twenty-two, took a job as a truck driver for a construction firm working on the state highways. Later he held a position as sales clerk in a local store for several years. Although a heavy drinker, he never had any difficulty with the law.

In the Army he was assigned initially to a camp near his home where he was trained as a member of a field artillery battery. Later he worked as an ammunition handler and a driver. He was considered a good soldier by his officers and went overseas with his outfit in early 1944. Landing in New Guinea they received further training in jungle warfare before being sent to another section of the island to provide artillery support for infantry patrols. Although Private F. was rarely in any real danger during the ensuing month, his performance became increasingly poor. He did not do his share of the work and seemed to be preoccupied with thoughts of his wife. On one occasion he was very nervous for several days and was unable to eat or sleep. However, he appeared to recover and went with his unit when they invaded an island to the north in September 1944. Here they were subjected to some bombing and the soldier was frequently unable to perform his duties. About a month after the landing he was sent back from a forward detail by the lieutenant in charge because he was having hallucinations and had threatened to shoot himself.

Once in the hospital he complained that a group of soldiers in his outfit "had it in for him" and called him a "goldbrick." He saw visions of his wife's face frequently and wanted desperately to go home to her. Sometimes she spoke to him. At other times male voices kept calling, "Come here, take it, take it." He complained of peculiar sensations in his eyes, ears, and back. Transferred back to the States he became less confused. On one occasion he told the doctor: "Things have changed for me. I've got a different opinion about folks. Your money and your folks are your only friends. My whole outfit had it in for me. They talked about me and called me names. Too much damned politics in the whole outfit." Again: "Some fellow here in the States insulted my wife. I must be getting old. I am worried. Overseas I almost took my life once." He often mentioned that he wanted to go home to his wife, but he was too sick for a furlough. Later when he had improved sufficiently he was discharged. That was in February 1945.

For the first few months after his discharge, B.A.F. remained at home with his wife. He was bothered by loud noises and crowds and tried to avoid them. Occasionally he had rather disturbing dreams of combat. By August 1, 1945 he felt well enough to start on-the-job training under the G.I. Bill and with the encouragement of his wife entered a course for refrigerator service men, but after one day he turned in his resignation. He felt that he was too nervous. For a long time after that he was unwilling even to think of employment. His wife supported the family working as a clerk and he spent most of his time riding around with friends who had jobs as truck drivers.

In 1947 the veteran made several attempts to work, but his wife continued to provide the major portion of their income. Either he quit a job after a short period of time or was fired. If left to himself he would have preferred to remain unemployed. Work always seemed to upset him. But his wife kept urging him to work and so after leaving one job and resting for a while he would try another. There were some financial problems but these were not severe at first. For several years after his discharge he received disability compensation from the government, and even more important, Mrs. F. had a steady income. His condition was improving and as time went on he became less and less nervous. He enjoyed the company of his wife and she gave him a feeling of confidence in himself.

In late 1948 he worked for a while as a service station attendant, but he soon was fired. At about this time his pension was reduced considerably and his wife became quite insistent that he try to obtain another position. Finally in the spring of 1949 he went back to the store where he had worked before the war. He was hired and has been working there ever since. He is rarely troubled by nervousness now and although far from ambitious he has been able with the constant encouragement and support of Mrs. F. to earn the major part of the family's income.

Both cases point up the extent to which self-reliant and capable women can help emotionally upset men regain their confidence and find a place for themselves in the world of work. It is questionable whether these men would have been able to perform effectively in civilian life had it not been for this support at home.

Chapter Eleven: THE WORLD OF WORK

THE ARMY required of a soldier at a minimum that he perform effectively in his specific assignment. When, because of inaptitude, emotional disability, or any other reason, he could not meet this requirement he was discharged, for he was of no use to the Army.

Many soldiers became ineffective for reasons other than their failure in their duty assignments. But once back in civilian life, the ease or difficulty with which they readjusted was largely determined by their success or failure in reestablishing themselves in the world of work. In our society a man is expected to support himself and his dependents, and this is usually possible only if he works.

Moreover, work is a major outlet for a man's emotions. It is very difficult for most men, and for some it is impossible, to remain emotionally balanced unless they have an opportunity to work regularly, and to work at a meaningful job. Without such work opportunities, their emotions, instead of finding an outlet in constructive activity, turn back on themselves with destructive results. This is the great tragedy of unemployment—as we learned in two earlier investigations: *Grass on the Slag Heaps: The Story of The Welsh Miners* (Harpers, 1942), and *The Unemployed* (Harpers, 1943).

Many soldiers did not, however, immediately upon discharge take a job. They did not feel up to the challenge of regular work with its many demands: punctuality, the acceptance of authority, effective integration in the work group, meeting performance standards, and the host of other requirements. There was public understanding of their need for time to adjust and Congress provided for a modest readjustment allowance for up to fifty-two weeks to help tide the returning veteran over this initial period.

As we shall see from the following cases, some men went to work almost immediately, frequently at their old jobs to which, according to the law, they had a claim. Some started in their old jobs only to shift quickly when they discovered that they no longer wanted to do the same type of work as they had before the war. Others waited six months or a year before they even attempted to go back to work. Many who took a job found that they did not like it or could not cope with it and quit to take another—only to repeat the pattern. Sometimes it was two or three years before a man's work life became regularized.

The variability in veterans' reemployment reflected in large measure the differences prevailing among them at the time of separation from the service. Some were emotionally disturbed at the time of discharge—so ill that they had to be sent in the custody of attendants to a mental hospital in the vicinity of their homes. At the other extreme were men who were in good health, free of almost any type of disability. Many were in between—somewhat disturbed and upset by their military experience but basically sound. Moreover, there were marked differences in the conditions that the veterans encountered when they arrived home. Some had relatives who were able and willing to help; others found themselves largely on their own; still others came back to a situation that required their support or action—such as an ill parent or a wife who had become emotionally upset.

The occupational readjustment of these veterans was often affected by the impact of their Army service on their occupational skills and goals. Many farm boys who had grown up without any knowledge of the world of industrial work were first introduced to it during their Army experience. Frequently their first taste of urban life was while they were in uniform. As a result of these new experiences and exposures they had an opportunity to consider an alternative way of life to the only one which they had previously known.

In addition to broadening their horizons, military service provided many of them with the education and training that placed new choices within their reach. An illiterate may have previously hesitated to leave the confines of his backwater agricultural community. But once he had been taught to read and write in the Army, he might have acquired sufficient self-confidence to relocate in an urban center after his discharge. Many soldiers acquired specific skills that they could use in civilian work, so that frequently they were able to obtain a better job than the one they had had before the war.

The postwar economic readjustment of the veteran was also aided by the continuing strong demand for labor. The postwar depression which had been generally anticipated did not materialize. A seller's market for labor made employers willing to make adjustments and concessions if they wanted to attract and retain an adequate work force.

The contribution of the Veterans Administration to the veteran's adjustment was important. Many veterans took advantage of personal and occupational counseling, enrolled in educational programs or pursued special training on or off the job, and in other ways availed themselves of the help proffered by the Veterans Administration.

THE OLD JOB

No one could foretell the postwar level of the economy. But it was reasonable to anticipate that jobs would be scarce when millions of men were suddenly demobilized. The fact that the Government required an employer to offer a veteran his old job was a source of comfort to many soldiers when they thought ahead to the problems that they would face after discharge. Some knew that they would never return to their former jobs because they had never liked them and now that they were older and more experienced they would like them even less. Others, especially the younger men, had no job to go back to since they had entered the

Army directly from school or from the ranks of the unemployed. Some had liked their former jobs and looked forward to returning to them. Others returned to an old job only after a quick look at the market failed to reveal anything better—at least as a place to start.

The return to the old, familiar job was in many ways parallel to the return to one's family. It was not a new situation for the veteran. He knew the customers; he knew the boss; he had friends among the other workers. Even when the old job failed to come up to his expectations, it gave the veteran a breather so that he could look around before deciding on another.

Brought up in a small town in the middle of a prosperous Northeastern farming area, A.T.I. had a normal boyhood. He did average work at the local schools and graduated from high school at the age of seventeen. Although somewhat shy and bashful, he was popular and enjoyed the company of girls. After leaving school he worked on neighboring farms for several months and then returned to live with his parents while working as a body and fender repairman in a local garage. He enjoyed this job very much and learned rapidly. He spent eighteen months at the garage before he was drafted and he was sorry to leave it. The work fascinated him and he felt confident in his ability to do it well. He was popular with his fellow workers and frequently went out to drink beer with them on weekends. Sometimes he drank a little too much, but he never got into any trouble.

In the Army he was shipped to Texas and trained as an infantryman. After only three months of service, however, he was shifted to duty as a mechanic and promoted to technician fifth grade. Three months later he was made a clerk in the same regiment and served in this capacity while the division was on maneuvers in late 1943. In general he liked the Army and at that time seriously considered staying in service after the war ended.

Shortly after the turn of the year he began to spend increasing amounts of time at the post exchange drinking beer—usually ten to twelve bottles a night. He had rather suddenly begun to feel nervous and weak. By mid-February he was so emotionally upset that he went to the dispensary. After three visits on successive days during which he became increasingly nervous he was sent to the hospital.

There he was restless and refused to sit in a chair while the psychiatrist talked to him. He said: "You are just trying to knock me out. I know you are going to hit me and then I'll be done for. Just turn off the lights, and I'll be all right when I see my girl in the morning." Offered some medication he threw it on the floor shouting: "Don't you think I know when you're trying to poison me?" He had frequent outbursts of senseless laughter and he was convinced the ward attendants were German spies who were plotting against him. He had both visual and auditory hallucinations. After admission he improved somewhat, but a week later he became convinced that he was being controlled by a woman who had a steel plate in her neck. In April he was discharged and taken to a V.A. hospital near his home by a medical officer and two enlisted attendants.

A month later he had improved sufficiently to be sent home on a trial visit. At that time he remained convinced that people were talking about him and he was quite sullen and aloof. Nevertheless, he talked about getting his old job back and wanting to go to work. The doctors decided to permit this. Almost immediately after arriving home he went down to the garage and was rehired at a salary well above what he had received before entering service. His employer was very happy to have him back, not only because he considered A.T.I. a good worker and liked him, but because almost all his good men had been drafted and he was quite shorthanded. Within very few days A.T.I. began to join in social activities with the other men. His aloofness disappeared and he no longer felt persecuted. He felt that it was good to be back on the job. This was the kind of work that he could do. Gradually he started doing some work as a mechanic, getting help from more skilled men whenever he needed it, although his main interest remained body and fender repair. He no longer felt a need to drink large quantities of beer.

In early 1946 A.T.I. married. He continued to work at his old job for several years and received several raises. However, when he had an offer to do the same type of work for more money at a garage in a nearby city, he decided to take it. His family was growing and although he made a good income the money seemed to disappear at an ever-increasing rate. In addition, during his stay at the garage in his home town his emotional difficulties had almost completely disappeared. He felt quite competent to accept a new position.

In 1954 the veteran returned to his home town to operate his own body and fender repair shop. Almost from the start the business did well. He is making a good income, supporting a family which now includes three children, and is free of any trace of his former mental disorder.

This veteran is a striking illustration of the fact that work can be a great stabilizer. The satisfactions that men are able to derive from work which they like and can do frequently give them, as it did A.T.I., the strength they need to make the many other adjustments required for effective living in a modern complex society.

USE OF MILITARY EXPERIENCE

Many men, especially those who had completed a professional education, considered their military experience a loss—the lawyer who was turned into a company clerk, the engineer who became a lieutenant in an infantry division, the chemist who was assigned as a supply sergeant. Some of these assignments were faulty; others were the result of military exigency. In making its assignments, the Army was in no position to insure that a man could advance occupationally as a result of his military experience. But many were lucky enough to secure assignments which enabled them to grow. They learned a skill which was of direct value to civilian employers or one on which they could build after discharge.

C.O.R. was the only boy in a family of six children. His father was a farmer in the Midwest. As a child he was the favorite of his mother but he felt rejected by his father. After graduating from high school at the age of sixteen he worked on the farm until inducted into military service a little over three years later. During this period the father suffered from severe headaches and was unable to work much of the time. There was a good deal of conflict between the two and C.O.R. enlisted in the Army partly at least to escape from an intolerable home situation.

Very shortly after becoming a soldier he was selected for training as a radio operator and mechanic in the Air Corps. For a year he attended various schools in the South and Midwest. His work was excellent and for the first time he found himself engaged in work that really fascinated him. Immediately after completing his training he was sent to North Africa and then to India. During the long boat trip the convoy was bombed, and on one occasion a ship was sunk.

Arriving in India he spent two and a half months working as a latrine orderly at a replacement depot because the theater was oversupplied with radio men. Finally he was assigned to work as a radio operator at an airdrome. After two months he volunteered for flight duty in order to get home more quickly. During the next ten months he spent almost 600 hours in the air over Burma and China. He was considered an exceptionally competent radio man and was rapidly promoted to the rank of sergeant. Although he never engaged in actual combat there were frequent alerts and on one occasion the soldier was in a plane which nosed over while landing. He was unhurt. On his first missions he was quite anxious and had difficulty sleeping afterwards but these symptoms soon subsided only to return just prior to his shipment home in early 1945.

He continued to be upset while home on furlough and reported to the hospital on his return. There he was very restless and jittery. At times he became quite depressed and suffered from painful headaches. Although he wanted to get out of the Army and felt he had done his share, he wanted most of all to avoid flying. He was frankly afraid of airplanes. He felt that ground duty as a radio operator would not be too bad. In discussing his plans for civilian life with the doctors he told them that he was torn between a desire to get further training as a radio engineer and a feeling that he ought to work on the family's farm. He felt that in being introduced to radio work in the Army, he had found something that really interested him. At times he became quite enthusiastic as he discussed the career possibilities in the field. Certainly he had received valuable training and experience. He more or less welcomed the opportunity to return to civilian life. In May 1945 he was discharged for psychoneurosis.

Returning home the veteran found the situation even more intolerable than before he left. There were many arguments with his father, but his mother tried to make life easy for him. He felt restricted and at times almost helpless. His nervousness increased and he was plagued by headaches, indigestion, and insomnia. His parents wanted him to take over the operation of the farm and even offered to build another house on the place for him if he would stay. But C.O.R. did not want to live near his parents. He became more anxious when he was with them and he was sure he would never recover from his psychoneurosis as long as he remained at home. Moreover, as a result of his Army experience he now had an alternative. He could continue with his radio work.

In November he married a girl whom he had known for many years and at about the same time applied for admission to a radio school located in a city 200 miles away from home. His application was accepted and in January 1946 he started his training. Although his nervousness continued to bother him he was able to draw heavily on his Army training. He was upset before examinations and found it difficult to study as hard as he should. Nevertheless, he was frequently able to answer questions on the basis of his prior experience. After ten months of schooling he obtained his federal license as a radio operator and also a license as a radio telegrapher. In addition he was authorized to enter an advanced course in radio communication and maintenance that would qualify him as a radio repairman. This he completed successfully in the spring of 1947.

For the next few months he looked for a job, but without success. However, by late summer he obtained a position as a radio operator at a commercial station located in a city about 25 miles from his home town. This was a good job and paid well, but after three months the veteran had to quit because the work made him very anxious. He then went to work at a much lower salary with a company that manufactured radio broadcasting equipment. He found his radio experience and training very valuable in carrying out his duties as a transmitter wirer and radio assembler and in spite of the fact that he was qualified for a better job was happy in this work.

By 1951 he had received a number of raises and was being paid almost as much as the radio station had paid him four years before. Early in the year he started psychotherapy with the aid of the Veterans Administration and, although the treatment was continued for only six months, he improved rapidly. By the summer he was actively looking for a new job that would permit him to use his extensive experience in radio. He liked his job at the plant, but realized he could do better elsewhere. He and his wife had one child and had a very happy home life.

A.E.E.'s parents were divorced when he was two years old and at that time he went to live with neighbors in the Northeastern city where he was born. Later, at the age of nine, he returned to live with his mother who had just remarried. Shy and self-conscious, he considered himself inferior to his schoolmates. Nevertheless, he did very well in his studies although he left high school at the end of his sophomore year. His scholastic success seemed to make it easier for him to bear his general feeling of inadequacy.

At first he worked with his stepfather as a mason's helper, but after a year and a half entered the Civilian Conservation Corps. A year later he became an attendant in a state mental hospital. After several months, he left the hospital during an evening when he was supposed to be on duty and was subsequently fired. A job as a truck driver followed, but again he got in trouble, this time over a minor accident, and had to leave. His last position before entering military service at the age of twenty was as an apprentice boilermaker repairing steam locomotives.

After induction he was assigned to an infantry division that was just being formed at a Southern camp. Here he did very well although he remained rather aloof from the other men and adopted an attitude of superiority. Since the division had practically no noncommissioned officers at its inception there were many opportunities for promotion and Private E. was made a corporal within three months of the time he entered service. This promotion later proved to be unwarranted and he was reduced to private. At first the soldier would say practically nothing about his prior life. He felt that he had not accomplished very much and had been pretty much of a failure. Nevertheless, he did not want to admit this and remembering his scholastic success he gradually fabricated a rather detailed—if mythical—story about his job as a high-school teacher. Many of his fellow soldiers believed him and by the time the division left for Hawaii in the spring of 1944 he had established himself as the leader of a group of malcontents in the outfit. His advice on methods of outwitting the officers was frequently sought and he found this very satisfying. He felt that his accepted status as an ex-school teacher was the basic reason for this popularity.

In June of 1945 while still in Hawaii he was hospitalized for appendicitis and while in the hospital he went to see a psychiatrist and complained of periods of anxiety and depression. After being returned to duty he continued to be upset and within five days was back in the hospital. Here he was sullen and belligerent and wanted only to be left alone. He said everyone was against him and that he could not trust anyone. Although there was some question as to the severity of his illness, he was diagnosed as psychotic, returned to the States, and discharged in late 1945.

Back home he continued to be irritable and tense. Nevertheless, he soon married and after three months of unemployment returned to his apprentice training as a boilermaker. This lasted less than nine months. His performance was generally poor because of his nervousness and whenever he was reprimanded for a mistake he became upset. When the training force had to be reduced, A.E.E. was one of the first to go. Once again he felt himself a failure, and decided to try to obtain more education in the hope that he could again attain the feeling of satisfaction he had experienced in the Army when he was known as an educated man, a school teacher. Maybe, he felt, he could really live out his story.

Accordingly he applied for admission to a small college near his home and was accepted after he made an extremely high score on tests of general educational development in spite of the fact that he had completed only two years of high school. Taking courses in education, liberal arts, and business he progressed rapidly and received a degree after less than three years of study. As he worked toward his goal he became much less nervous and at the time of graduation was considered practically cured by the V.A. psychiatrists. However, he had not been able to obtain enough training in the field of education to qualify as a teacher. Although he had a college degree, he needed further schooling to obtain his objective.

Several months of work as a construction laborer followed during which A.E.E. attempted to pay off some of the debts he had accumulated while trying to support his rapidly growing family. In addition he tried to make arrangements to continue his education. During this period his nervousness increased but it rapidly subsided after he entered a state teachers college in January 1950.

By 1953 the veteran had obtained a master's degree in education as well as some special training in public school administration during the summer at the state university. He was teaching and also acting as principal of a small school and doing very well at it. His home life was happy and he and his wife had three children. A.E.E. felt that he had more than attained the realization of a dream which had had its inception when he was a very insecure soldier at a Southern camp. He no longer felt inadequate.

The crucial part that a man's work plays in his overall emotional adjustment is underscored by the preceding two cases. Effective performance in adulthood is often determined by the opportunities that a man has to realize his occupational goals. The war contributed to broadening these opportunities for many.

Military service gave C.O.R. an opportunity to learn a skill which provided him with an alternative to living on his family's farm with its severe drawbacks because of conflict with his parents. The fact that A.E.E. found support in the Army for passing off his fantasy as reality undoubtedly reinforced it and made it that much easier for him to realize after his return. But he would never have been able to turn his fantasy into reality had it not been for the substantial help which he received from the Veterans Administration as a consequence of his military service.

LOW LEVEL WORK

An important advantage of a rapidly expanding economy is the ease with which individuals with handicaps can find work. In periods of poor business the employer can pick and choose, with the result that the more disabilities a person has, the less likely he is to find or keep a job. The extent to which employers were willing to help veterans adjust is suggested by the following two cases. Had it not been for a public sense of responsibility towards

men who had served in the Armed Forces and many employers'
knowledge that the civilian labor market was thin, it is doubtful
that these veterans could have adjusted.

A.P.T. was the eighth of nine children and was born
in this country to parents of Italian origin. Brought up in a Northeastern city, he attended schools there and did satisfactory work
until he reached the third grade. At that time his father, a shoe-
maker, suffered a stroke which partially incapacitated him and
A.P.T.'s work then became so poor that he had to repeat a grade.
He left school at the age of seventeen after completing his junior
year of high school.

Except for his early difficulties his marks were good and he had
many friends among his classmates. While in school and for a year
afterwards he worked as a clerk in his brother-in-law's grocery
store and received some training as a butcher. Later after being
turned down for enlistment in both the Navy and Marines he took
a better paying job at a shipyard. In late 1942 he was drafted at
the age of twenty.

Private T. received his basic training in the Medical Corps at a
camp in the South. Although his initial duty was as a litter bearer,
he was soon shifted to the kitchen where he worked as a cook's
helper. In all, he spent nearly two years in this country before
being sent overseas with an army headquarters to the South Pacific.
Arriving in New Guinea he was rapidly promoted to the rank
of technician fourth grade in early February 1945. In early July,
shortly after the headquarters was shifted to the Philippines, the
soldier received word that his father, whose health had become
increasingly worse over the last few years, had suffered another
stroke and was completely bed-ridden. There was some question
as to whether he would live very long.

A.P.T. became rather depressed over this news and ate very little
with the result that he lost almost twenty pounds in a few weeks.
His energy seemed to evaporate and he was often nauseated. In
late July he went on sick call and after being treated in his quarters

for several days was hospitalized. Although seen by a psychiatrist he was not considered to be severely emotionally disturbed, but when he was about to be returned to duty in early September he was discovered one morning hanging from a rafter with a tent rope around his neck. Cut down immediately, he survived his suicide attempt although with rather severe neck injuries. Following this episode he was returned to the States in a markedly depressed state. With electroshock treatment he improved somewhat and was discharged just before Christmas 1945.

Back at home he remained depressed and anxious and was unable to work at all for over a year. Finally, he returned to his former job at the grocery, but became so excited and upset during rush hours that he had to quit after a few months. Again, he was unable to work for a period of time. In the summer of 1947 he took a job with a soft-drink manufacturing company as a laborer, but again had to stop work because he was too nervous.

In early 1948 he entered on-the-job training under the Veterans Administration as a meat cutter with a chain grocery store. He completed his training there in late 1950 and was hired as a regular employee in the meat department. He was married in mid-1949 and shortly after that began to attend courses in meat cutting at a trade school to supplement the training he was getting at the store.

Although A.P.T.'s work was considered satisfactory by his employer, this was primarily the result, at least initially, of his great popularity with the store's clients. Friendly and always helpful, he rapidly accumulated a group of personal customers who always asked for him when they came in to buy meat. Because of this his employer made only limited demands of him and permitted him to take time off whenever he became upset. Often when this happened the veteran would go to the back of the store and spend two or three hours by himself before returning to serve customers. On other occasions he was too depressed and disturbed to work at all and as a result was away from work for six or seven weeks out of the year.

He considered himself somehow inferior to others and tended to avoid social activities. These feelings of inferiority became almost overwhelming at times and it was then that he would remain home for periods of time until he was able to bring his emotional upset under control. But his employer was extremely sympathetic and, realizing, in addition, the value of his popularity with the customers, made every effort to adjust the job to A.P.T.'s emotional state. Gradually, his periods of depression became less frequent and the veteran began to perform more effectively. At times he actually enjoyed his work although as of 1951 he still had to spend a good deal of time alone in the back of the store attempting to get his emotions under control.

B.I.H., the oldest of seven children, was brought up in a large Midwestern city. His education was marked by almost constant difficulties largely because of his lack of interest in school work. He finally left school at the age of twenty when he completed the freshman year of high school, having had to repeat several grades. There were numerous occasions when he was almost expelled from school. Sometimes it was because of truancy, as it was when he ran away from home for a week after an argument with his father when he was sixteen. Sometimes he got in trouble over fighting. His worst difficulties came when he was caught having sexual relations with a girl in the school cloakroom at the age of thirteen and when he was caught participating in sexual activities with several other boys in the washroom. But somehow he stayed in school.

At the age of twelve B.I.H. began to experience a great deal of anxiety coupled with almost constant sexual preoccupation. When riding in the car he worried that the brakes might fail and everyone would be killed. He was caught masturbating several times by his father, who beat him severely. Although very upset over this he continued to masturbate several times a day. His sexual activities with women were frequent and often perverted. He had incestuous relations with two of his sisters until they were married. Although frequently worried about this constant sexual preoccupation, he was never able to control himself. At fifteen B.I.H. was fired from a job selling fruit from door to door after he withheld money from his employer. A job in a market was terminated after two days when he propositioned a woman customer. Later he worked in a machine shop, but was dismissed after breaking the machine. He was also fired after three months from a position in a paint shop. When drafted for military service he was employed as a stockroom worker in an aircraft plant.

As a soldier Private H. performed quite well from his induction in late 1942 until the time he broke down in early 1945. He served for a year in the United States working as a laborer at various air bases in the Northeast. Shipped to England, he continued at the same type of work until February of 1945 when he was transferred to an infantry replacement depot preparatory to assignment as a combat rifleman. At this time his fears began to mount. He had dizzy spells and pain around his heart. He was afraid he would be killed in combat. Later he talked of his conviction that the sun was coming closer to the earth and would burn everyone to death. At other times he was afraid the ocean would sweep over the land and drown many people including himself. He claimed the other men picked on him and, once in the hospital, would sit for hours describing his lurid sexual behavior, dwelling on the details. He would end up by saying: "I'm bad clear through. I wonder what you must think of me." He was returned to the States and discharged in June.

B.I.H. returned to live with his parents and after about a month obtained a very good job in the molding department of a rubber manufacturing company. He was paid at a base rate of $1.80 an hour —much more than he had ever made before. The work, however, was too demanding for him. The noise bothered him and he became panicky on the rare occasions when he was producing at a high enough rate to earn a bonus. He lost a good deal of time from the job only because he could not bring himself to go to the factory and face all the noise and confusion. When he was working he was so nervous he could hardly stay on the job. He was very worried about how he would support himself since he felt sure that he would soon either lose his job or be seriously injured. He was still sure the sun was too close to the earth and expected that at any moment he might catch fire and burn to death.

As time went by his state became quite obvious to his foreman, who was afraid that B.I.H. would collapse completely if he remained in the mold department. In addition his production record was so poor that it was not feasible to pay him at his former rate. In fact the choice was between firing him outright and giving him a trial at a lower level job. The company chose the latter course largely because he was a disabled veteran, and finally, he was shifted to another position at the same factory which the company considered less stressful. As a laborer assigned to loading tires he was able to work in a noise free area under much less pressure. His pay was changed to a day rate basis and, after a period of what amounted to probation in this position, the decision was made to retain him.

B.I.H. has continued to work as a laborer at the same factory. His fears have largely disappeared and although his work is not considered very good, it is at least satisfactory. He is absent from the job rather frequently, but the company does not feel that this is an adequate basis for firing him. For the first time in his life he has been able to hold a job over a sizable period of time and perform in an acceptable manner. He continues to live at home, although his mother died in 1950. At the time of his last examination for pension purposes, the V.A. doctors considered the veteran almost completely recovered and noted that in actual fact he was doing much better than he had before military service.

As these cases demonstrate, an economy which is sustaining a high level of employment can contribute substantially to the successful adjustment of men whose working capacity is little more than acceptable. In a tight labor market employers are much more willing to tolerate men with handicaps, especially if their disabilities are presumed to be connected with their war service. From the employer's point of view he can keep handicapped people such as A.P.T. or B.I.H. on his payroll as long as they can contribute in useful work at least the equivalent of their pay. Since both of these men held relatively unskilled jobs, they were easy to retain. There was also the hope that with time they would lose most of their disabilities and become better workers.

THE RIGHT JOB

The average person can adjust to any one of a rather large number of jobs, although he may find some which are better and some which are less well suited to his interests and capacities. But some people can perform effectively only if they can find the "right" job. If their emotional needs can be safely met in the work situation, they gain strength and balance. But if the reverse occurs, they may become upset, for their internal difficulties are reinforced by the pressures which they encounter at work.

S.T.'s father was a farmer in the deep South who also operated a small crossroads grocery store. The son had a relatively normal and uneventful childhood although he wet his bed until he was sixteen years old. In school he had some difficulty with the work but finally completed twelve grades at the age of twenty. He enjoyed sports and played on the high-school basketball team. After graduation he worked with his father on the farm for several years and then as the shipbuilding industry in his area began to expand, shifted to a job as a rigger. After about eighteen months at the shipyard and very shortly after his marriage to a local girl, S.T. was drafted for military service. He was then twenty-six years old.

Four days after induction Private T. was assigned to a newly organized artillery battalion and began basic training. Initially he was trained as a radio operator, but later was shifted to duty as an ammunition handler and gun crewman on one of the large field pieces. For almost two years he remained in the South, during which time his first child was born. Then in July 1944 his battalion was sent to England, and, after a brief stay, on to France.

Initially assigned to guarding German prisoners of war, Private T. saw little combat except for one terrifying night during which the battalion was bombed and strafed steadily for over two hours. A number of prisoners were killed, but American losses were not heavy. In October they took up firing positions for the first time, although it was not until the German counteroffensive in December that the battalion was actually under fire itself. During late December and early January 1945, however, S.T. was frequently very close to the lines and in real danger. He was afraid, not just occasionally, but constantly. Then one night while on guard duty in Luxembourg his carbine went off and the bullet pierced his left foot and shattered his big toe. He himself hardly knew how it had happened.

Hospitalized, his wound proved to be not too severe and healed rapidly. An investigation was initiated to determine whether Private T. should be court-martialed for deliberately maiming himself, but there was no evidence to indicate that the shot had not been fired accidentally. Then rather suddenly, about a month after entering the hospital, the soldier became severely agitated and made every effort to avoid other people. During interviews he would alternately sit down and pace the floor. He constantly twisted his hands and sobbed intermittently. He was extremely guilty over having shot himself. Once or twice he mentioned that he had been on the verge of killing himself. Gradually his agitation subsided and his depressive ruminations were broken by an occasional smile. Nevertheless, he remained severely guilt-ridden and could relax only when away from other people. He could not stand crowds and seemed to shrink away when other people were in the room. Returned to the States he was discharged in June.

At first S.T. and his family lived with his parents. Although still emotionally upset he soon secured a job with an oil company and was able to continue working for several months before the company moved to another state. He attempted to find a home for his family near the new location, but was unsuccessful—largely because talking to people about renting a place upset him so much that he gave up after only a minimal effort. On returning home he was unemployed for several months, but had to start looking for work again when his wife became pregnant with their second child.

He finally went back to the shipyard where he had worked before entering military service and was hired. His job required him to assist the crane operators by fixing the load in place and directing them as it was moved into position. There were always other workers around and their very presence upset him. He developed a shield of apathy and indifference as if to pretend to himself that he was working alone and thus need not be nervous. To the other workers he seemed rather dull and they tended to ignore him. He seemed to prefer it that way. Often he was absent from work.

After several years the shipyard cut production and S.T. lost his job. In a way he was relieved. The work upset him so, especially the constant contact with other workers, that he was on the verge of quitting anyway. A long series of odd jobs followed. Sometimes he worked on a farm, sometimes he drove a truck. But always it seemed he had to be around other people and then he became tense and tremulous. He wanted to work alone, but he could not find that kind of a job.

Finally, in the spring of 1951 S.T. began working as a driver for a dairy company. His job was to deliver milk to a receiving station, frequently during the night and early morning hours. Most of the time he worked alone. Free of the intolerable stress of having other people around he did very well, working seven days a week and missing hardly any time. He enjoyed his work for the first time since the war and also began to extricate himself from the financial difficulties that had plagued him during his long period of intermittent employment. He and his wife, who by 1952 had four children, began to participate a little more in local social activities. Although still far from free of the anxiety and depression that had been his almost constant companions ever since his Army days, S.T. felt very much better.

M.M.B. was born and raised in a Midwestern mining community. His parents were immigrants from Hungary. In high school he took a vocational program with primary emphasis on auto mechanics while working part-time in a garage. After graduating at the age of nineteen he took a job as a mechanic's helper and for a while attended a special course in welding. Then as the defense industries began to expand he moved to a nearby city and went to work on the assembly line of a small-arms manufacturing plant. Shortly after his twenty-first birthday he enlisted in the reserves and was called to active duty two months later with the rank of private first class. As he later put it: "I just had a feeling that I wanted to get in and do my duty."

At the time of induction his experience as an automobile mechanic was noted and he was assigned to an ordnance company for work in this capacity. For over ten months he served with the same unit at various camps in the South. During this period he received over a month of special training in his specialty. His performance was considered quite satisfactory by his commanding officer, and to the casual observer he seemed quite happy with his work.

In his own mind, however, the soldier was far from happy. He became increasingly angry with his officers and became convinced that he was being mistreated. Finally, in October 1943 he went on sick call and told the doctors that he was afraid he would kill his captain. Later in the hospital he described his complaints in detail: "I wasn't feeling good for some time and stayed away from the fellows and I got to dreaming up things, got scared of the officers. The captain is always bothering me. I don't like him. He is not a square fellow, I dreamt that I was going to kill him. I also dreamt that I was going to get even with the First Sergeant. He was always talking about me and razzing me. I get mad easily and then I do things. When it happens, my dreams, I get up and want to do things. I talk to them all the time and try to tell them to leave me alone."

Later, he further discussed his inability to get along with his superiors: "I liked the captain in a way, but I didn't like the way he was doing things and it got to preying on my mind and I couldn't get rid of it. When I was away from him I was all right, but when I got around him or even heard his voice I would get sore and cuss him to myself. When I went and asked for a transfer to the paratroopers he wouldn't accept the transfer. I just don't like the fellow. I get a nervous feeling where I shake and it comes from inside so that I can't speak or anything." For two and a half months he remained a very sullen, irritable, and impulsive hospital patient. He was then discharged and sent to a V.A. hospital near his home.

There he became somewhat more cheerful and, after his mother requested his release, he was permitted to return home. His V.A. hospital stay totaled ten days. He rested for about five weeks and then took a job as a laborer on the railroad. He found this work extremely distasteful. He again had difficulties with his employer because he felt that he was neglected and poorly treated. He developed a rash in the rectal area which persisted in spite of a great variety of medical remedies. Later he became convinced that an ill-smelling fluid exuded constantly from his rectum and that he must wash it away by taking frequent showers. No amount of reasoning would convince him that he did not emit an odor. Unable to bathe during his working hours, he was acutely uncomfortable. Finally, in order to escape his employer and to be free to take showers at the three-hour intervals which he felt were necessary, he left his job. He had worked for just six months.

Since that time M.M.B. has operated an automobile body and paint shop of his own. He works entirely alone and, although he does not have many jobs, he is able to make between $150 and $200 dollars a month—enough to support himself. He feels much relieved at being free to do as he pleases. There is no longer a company commander or a first sergeant or a boss around to mistreat him. He is able to bathe as frequently as he wishes and in actual fact usually takes a shower every three hours. His conviction about his odor remains. In addition he continues to visit doctors frequently for treatment of his rash. Nevertheless, he does good work as an automobile body repairman and with the exception of these symptoms and a certain seclusiveness, is considered by the V.A. doctors to have made a satisfactory social and occupational adjustment. He has never married.

Both S.T. and M.M.B. were under great tension as long as they had military assignments or held jobs which forced them into situations with which they could not cope because of their deep-seated emotional difficulties. However, both have made a passable adjustment once they were able to find the type of work which suited their needs. The fact that M.M.B. still has the delusion about his "smell" is proof of his continuing psychiatric disability. Yet he is able to meet at least minimum performance standards since he has found work which is congenial to him.

Chapter Twelve: REHABILITATION

AN INDIVIDUAL changes sometimes from day to day, and surely from one year to the next. Changes take place within himself and within the environment to which he must adjust. Many of the soldiers who broke down because they could no longer cope with the demands that the military situation made on them were on their way to recovery as of the moment they received their discharge papers. The Army found that its elaborate efforts to rehabilitate soldiers prior to discharge were frequently ineffective because many men remained depressed and despondent as long as they continued to be in uniform.

While many men were able to make a quick recovery after their discharge, others were so disturbed by their military experience that they were not able to adjust quickly to civilian life. While time usually proved to be a major rehabilitative agent, it did not always have a beneficial influence. If a man was very disturbed and if his civilian environment was oppressive, time might find him sinking even deeper into a depression. But in general, time was a constructive influence primarily because the innate drive towards health is especially strong among young people.

Nevertheless the American public early recognized that special assistance would probably increase the number of veterans who could be rehabilitated. Hence the Veterans Administration was empowered to make available a wide range of services, including medical care, educational and training opportunities, and outright grants of money to assist soldiers who had been honorably discharged in their adjustment to civilian life. Special benefits were provided for those who had been seriously injured in the service of their country.

Since the Veterans Administration was an agency of the federal government, since its sole function was to aid the veteran, and since it was provided by the Congress with liberal funds, it was able to play a dominant role in the rehabilitative efforts of the post-war period.

State and local governmental agencies as well as voluntary organizations also made significant contributions to the readjustment of the veteran. But the Veterans Administration was unique not only because of the scale of its program, but because veterans considered that their war service entitled them to benefits.

A depressed person may not know why he cannot function effectively or what he can do about it. Frequently he has more need for a sympathetic ear than for money or other material assistance. The more at ease he feels with those he consults, the more likely he is to profit from the relationship. The fact that the Veterans Administration had been set up to help him and others like him was a source of considerable support to many a disturbed veteran.

Ex-servicemen also received help from various veterans' organizations which, in seeking new members, provided many valuable services free of charge. Here, too, the bond between the veteran in need and the organizational representative was close—for both had served in the Armed Forces of their country.

Even though the Veterans Administration tried to simplify its procedures as much as possible, many veterans found the paper work burdensome. Some men did not ask for the benefits to which they were entitled because they were overwhelmed by the forms. Many others, especially those whose claims were not clear-cut, could not have submitted their papers without the help of an intermediary—usually a veterans' organization.

Veterans' organizations helped many ex-servicemen in other ways, especially by finding them jobs and by referring them to local agencies for particular services. The relative availability of a wide range of services, especially in the larger urban centers, undoubtedly speeded the readjustment of many veterans. Many were able to secure hospital or out-patient care without cost. Often this helped them attain sufficient emotional stability so that they could look for or hold a job.

Many others needed time—just time—but often they would not have had it without the $20 a week for fifty-two weeks that they could receive under the G.I. Bill to sustain themselves during initial adjustment. This was a small sum but together with their savings from their service it enabled many to take a year off to find themselves.

Others profited from the opportunity of going back to school or entering vocational training. The Veterans Administration not only provided tuition for eligible veterans but also contributed a modest amount toward their living expenses. If a veteran had a wife and children, his maintenance grant was correspondingly increased. Many who had not had adequate education or training during the difficult 1930s when jobs were few and family incomes lean had a second chance now that they were entitled to G.I. benefits. Some who had dreamed of a profession but who never had any hopes of realizing their ambition suddenly found the goal within reach. A man is likely to be strengthened when given a second chance to shape his life.

The significance of what the country set out to do for the veteran and how these efforts affected his readjustment are presented at length in *Patterns of Performance*. At this point we will limit our comments to two aspects of this comprehensive rehabilitation effort for the light that they can throw on the following cases.

The adjustment process tends to be cumulative. Consequently, there is considerable value in undertaking substantial rehabilitation efforts early in a period of readjustment. Secondly, in assessing the costs and gains from expenditures for rehabilitation services, it is essential that the accounting recognize not only the contribution made directly but also the aid received therefrom by the family and other members of the community at large. A veteran whose mental illness is ignored may deteriorate to a point where he seriously disturbs other members of the family and may have to be permanently institutionalized.

MEDICAL TREATMENT

Despite the major efforts that were made at the end of World
War II to expand psychiatric resources rapidly, the number of
veterans requiring help continued to exceed the available personnel. Nevertheless many were helped by being admitted to a V.A.
hospital for shock treatment or for other types of therapy, and
even larger numbers received some supportive help by attending
an outpatient clinic or from consulting a private physician who
was reimbursed by the Veterans Administration.

R.L.O. spent his early life in a large Midwestern city.
His mother died of tuberculosis when he was very young and he
was raised by his father. After graduating from high school with
above average grades, he worked briefly as a mechanic's helper
and then worked for a year in a defense plant operating a drill
press. He was then drafted for military service at the age of
twenty-one.

After infantry basic training, Private O. was transferred to the
headquarters of his regiment and assigned to repairing and taking
care of various weapons. He was promoted to technician fifth
grade after seven months of service. In the fall of 1943 he was sent
as a rifleman to another infantry division which was preparing to
go overseas. He reached England shortly after the end of the
year. Intensive training in invasion tactics followed and on D-Day
he landed with his unit on the beaches of Normandy.

By the end of the first day his division had a firm "toe-hold" on
French soil. Two weeks of continuous fighting followed during
which the beachhead was widened, but at a heavy cost. Then after
several days of rest the division was thrown into the Battle of
the Hedgerows, one of the most difficult campaigns of World War
II. Finally, in late July came the breakthrough on the road to Paris.
For the next month the men advanced rapidly until resistance stiffened along the Seine just outside the city. The fighting became
very heavy before the division finally broke through into the

streets of the French capital. But R.L.O. did not enter Paris with his outfit. He was hit in the right leg by a rifle bullet during the river crossing and evacuated from the front lines for treatment.

R.L.O. spent two and a half months in the hospital while the wound healed, and it was early December before he rejoined his outfit. The company had just completed a series of attacks along the Luxembourg border during which it had suffered heavy casualties especially among the noncommissioned officers. Within three days of his return R.L.O. had been promoted to sergeant and placed in charge of company communications. Soon they were on the attack again, this time to relieve a company that had been surrounded by enemy units. Successful, they set up defensive positions only to be ordered forward again, in an all-out effort to break through the Siegfried Line into Germany proper. The objective was achieved after nine days of extremely heavy fighting, but again Sergeant O. did not complete the operation with his outfit. On the fourth day of the attack he was hit by a rocket shell. His right leg was mangled again and several fragments shattered his skull and penetrated his brain. He lost consciousness briefly, but was conscious by the time he reached the hospital.

Although his wounds healed it was not possible to remove all of the shell fragments from his leg and brain. He still carries them today. In England his leg became seriously infected, but it healed completely. For several months he was somewhat confused, but this condition cleared and only severe headaches remained. Then, in July after returning to the States, he became increasingly withdrawn and depressed. He felt that people were watching him and saying behind his back that he was crazy. A man's voice seemed to be calling him, but he did not know where it came from. He was aware that something new and strange was happening to him and requested treatment. Insulin shock therapy was prescribed and after ten treatments he improved sufficiently to be returned to civilian life in October 1945.

By December R.L.O. had obtained a job as an automobile repairman at a garage in his home city. However, he remained quite depressed and nervous. Shy and retiring, he rarely smiled. He was frequently so upset that he could not work and in fact put in only about half the usual number of hours. By late summer he was so disturbed that he could not work at all. Occasionally he looked for a position, but he was always turned down because he could not pass the physical examinations.

In mid-1947 he married and his wife soon became pregnant. Faced with new responsibilities the veteran decided that he was completely unable to handle his emotional problems by himself and applied to the Veterans Administration for treatment. Arrangements were made for him to see Dr. G., a psychiatrist who lived near his home, and the Veterans Administration assumed responsibility for the payments. In the remainder of 1947 he had four hours of psychotherapy during which he discussed his difficulties with Dr. G.; here he first began to acquire some understanding of the emotional problems which had made it impossible for him to work. Gaining some confidence from this relationship almost immediately, he applied for admission to a local university and was accepted.

After starting school under the G.I. Bill he stopped seeing the psychiatrist for a while. A child was born soon after the first of the year. R.L.O. did satisfactory work in a business course during the first year, but as summer approached he could not even bring himself to look for a job. He was quite nervous and when examined by the V.A. doctors toward the end of the summer was found to be still suffering from a rather severe depression. The doctors suggested that he continue with his psychotherapy. After returning to school he got in touch with Dr. G. and saw him on four occasions before the end of the year. Although Dr. G. felt that his patient's sufferings were attributable to rather deep-lying personality conflicts, he did not attempt to give R.L.O. an understanding of these deep forces. That would have required almost daily visits over four or five years, a commitment which the veteran was not willing or able to undertake. Rather, an attempt was made to build up his self-confidence and support him through periods of difficulty.

During 1949 the veteran continued his education, but was still unable to work during the summer. He saw Dr. G. irregularly—whenever his nervousness became particularly disturbing. These visits became more frequent in 1950 and 1951, when they averaged about once a month. Gradually his condition began to improve and by the time he received his degree in June 1951, he felt capable of holding a regular job. However, he had some difficulty obtaining a position at first and was unemployed for several months. By September he had started work as a civilian employee at a government air base and was doing quite well. He worked steadily and enjoyed his job. At that time Dr. G. decided to discontinue treatment. His patient had achieved a measure of self confidence, was much less nervous, and was well employed. Dr. G. felt that although there was a possibility that under adverse circumstances he might become emotionally disturbed again, he was now functioning adequately and did not need psychiatric help in dealing with his day-to-day problems.

N.T.H., an only child, was born in a large Midwestern city, but moved frequently with his parents as his father, a crane operator, shifted from one construction job to another. The family had an adequate income and always lived in apartments situated in relatively good neighborhoods. Their son's schooling was frequently interrupted, however, and he stopped entirely to enter the Civilian Conservation Corps after completing the ninth grade at the age of sixteen. There he began to drink rather heavily and was frequently in fights with other men.

Soon he began to ride freight trains from town to town, working only enough to buy a few meals before he moved on. In all, he held some fifteen or twenty jobs during the next two years, the longest was for six months as a machinist's helper on the railroad just before he entered military service. Once he was arrested by the railroad police when he was found asleep in an empty boxcar. At the age of seventeen he tried to enter the Navy, but could not obtain his parents' permission. A year later he enlisted in the Army shortly after marrying a girl of sixteen whom he had known for slightly less than a year.

During the first six months of his service Private H. received training as an aerial gunner at four different air bases. On completion of this training he was promoted to sergeant and four months later to staff sergeant. However, a week after this second promotion he was picked up in town without a pass and demoted one grade to sergeant. When he sailed for Europe in September 1943, his first child, a son, was only a few months old.

Assigned to a bomber squadron in Italy, Sergeant H. almost immediately began flying missions over Germany and Italy as a tail gunner on a B-17. On his fifth mission his right leg was scratched by flak but he did not report for treatment because he wanted to keep flying. Three missions later he was hit again in almost the same place and this time the wound was sufficiently severe to require hospitalization. A promotion to staff sergeant came through while he was still in the hospital. In all, the soldier flew 50 missions before returning to the United States in June 1944. In a way he enjoyed the fighting although toward the end he began to suffer rather severe headaches. He received a number of decorations and awards including the Silver Star for gallantry in action.

Home on furlough he drank almost constantly and was in a number of fights. This behavior continued on his return to duty and he was finally hospitalized for alcoholism and extreme nervousness. Two weeks later he was released only to turn up the next day in the local jail thoroughly drunk and with a badly cut wrist. After another brief hospitalization he was again returned to duty. For a while he served adequately, but his heavy drinking continued. He had frequent headaches and was quite jittery.

Remembering his success in combat, he applied for another tour of overseas duty. In connection with this application he underwent a psychiatric examination following which he was sent to a convalescent hospital for further treatment. His application was turned down. In this new setting he began to drink almost constantly. He was always in trouble and finally after smashing several windows in a drunken rage and subsequently being knocked out in a fight with another soldier, he was reduced to the grade of private. After a month in the hospital, he was returned to duty. However, that night, he swallowed a number of sleeping pills and was rehospitalized while still in a coma. When he awoke after eight hours he was so violent that he had to be placed under restraint. Ten days later he was discharged from the service with a diagnosis of severe psychoneurosis.

After leaving the Army in March 1945 the veteran returned to live with his wife and young son. During the next two years he held five different jobs. Each time he quit because he became too nervous to work. Actually his periods of employment were very brief and he was not able to provide adequately for his family. Without his disability compensation and the income his wife was able to earn, they would have been in serious economic straits. He continued to drink heavily. His home life was consequently in almost constant turmoil and once he was arrested for disorderly conduct. Throughout 1947, N.T.H. worked intermittently and drank heavily. Most of his rather small earned income was derived from work he did as a mechanic repairing the cars of his friends.

In early 1948 he was admitted to a V.A. hospital in an acute alcoholic state and remained there for over a month. At that time he had three children. No extensive treatment of his emotional disorder was attempted. Following his release he remained anxious and at times depressed. Over the next three years his condition became steadily worse. He worked only occasionally at odd jobs and his wife had to provide the major part of the family income. He wrecked his car several times and only narrowly escaped serious injury. Sometimes when drunk he would break up chairs and tables in the house. On four different occasions he was in jail for short periods of time. He threatened to kill himself several times and in the summer of 1950 attacked his wife while intoxicated, apparently intending to kill her. She escaped, however, and went to the police. While efforts were being made to get a court order committing N.T.H. to a state mental hospital, he himself voluntarily entered the institution thus circumventing the authorities and avoiding a possible long period of hospitalization. Five days later his wife signed him out and he returned home.

At the end of 1951 the veteran returned to the V.A. hospital. At that time he was very tense and was considered both suicidal and homicidal. His hands trembled at the slightest unexpected noise and he stuttered when he talked. He was diagnosed as psychotic. Insulin shock was prescribed and over the next four months he received thirty-four treatments. At first the insulin treatments seemed to have little value. He remained anxious and depressed. The outbursts of rage continued. Gradually his condition improved, however, and by the time it was decided to terminate the insulin injections, his anxiety had subsided considerably. The diagnosis of psychosis was changed to psychoneurosis and he was released on a trial visit to his home in June 1952.

Almost immediately N.T.H. started looking for a job. He soon obtained a position at a service station and within three weeks had been made manager of the station supervising the work of several other men. As of late 1953 he still held this position and was doing very well at it. In addition he had his own stock car which he drove in races throughout the state. He has obtained a G.I. loan and is building his own house. Much of the work he does himself in spite of the fact that he works long hours at the service station. He and his wife still have rather frequent arguments, but these no longer terminate in furniture-breaking outbursts. Mrs. H. has recently started receiving psychotherapy and, in the therapist's opinion, much of the present difficulty at home is attributable to her immaturity, not the veteran's.

Both men performed well in military service until they were disabled. Both found readjustment to civilian life quite difficult. However, the thirty-odd visits that R.L.O. had with a psychiatrist helped him over the rough spots so that by the time he had completed his studies he was able to function effectively in the world of work and take care of his family.

N.T.H. had a much stormier time, reflecting his more seriously disturbed state. However, at last reports his course of insulin shock treatments had enabled him to make, at least for the time being, a satisfactory adjustment. No one can tell how much stress either man would be able to withstand before breaking down again. But the contribution of psychiatric treatment to their current effective performance is clear.

EDUCATION AND TRAINING

Veterans had a wide range of educational and training opportunities available to them. Some used their benefits to become literate or to raise themselves a notch or two above a minimum literacy. Others went on to colleges and universities and some even secured doctorates, financed largely or exclusively by the Veterans Administration. Some veterans, such as E.S.E., were entitled to more liberal benefits because they had a service-connected disability (Public Law 16); the vast majority were entitled to benefits that were related to their length of service (Public Law 346).

E.S.E. was brought up in a rather poor home on the outskirts of a Midwestern city. His father drank heavily and contributed little to the support of his wife and four children. The family kept chickens and rabbits to help eke out their meager income. E.S.E. attended the local schools and completed a college preparatory course in high school with above average grades. However, his family was unable to finance any further education and in fact was acutely in need of whatever income he could contribute. Accordingly he went to work as a laborer shoveling ore in an aluminum plant. Shy and timid, he never dated girls and in fact had very few friends. In the fall of 1942 he enlisted in the Army at the age of twenty.

As a soldier Private E. performed satisfactorily for some months. He remained rather withdrawn and was the kind of person who is likely to go completely unnoticed in a large organization. After completing infantry basic training, he was shipped to Australia and there became a rifleman in a division which had just returned from fighting in New Guinea. Over a year of intensive training in Australia followed. Here he began to get into some difficulty and was court-martialed once in the summer of 1943 for being absent without leave for· two days and again six months later for "straggling on a hike without just cause, feigning illness, and returning to camp without permission." In all, he spent about a month and a half at hard labor.

In February 1944 Private E. began to act rather peculiarly. He believed that people were talking about him and he heard their voices. He felt that he was no good any more and wanted to kill himself. He was convinced that he had syphilis. Hospitalized, he was returned almost immediately to the States. There tests were made which established clearly that he did not have syphilis. The soldier was unconvinced. He became increasingly depressed and on one occasion attempted suicide. While in the hospital he suffered several attacks of malaria. In June 1944 he was transferred to a V.A. hospital on the West Coast. At that time he was still severely psychotic.

As a civilian E.S.E.'s condition remained approximately the same. After about three months he was transferred to another V.A. hospital on the West Coast which was situated nearer his mother's home. She had separated from his father while E.S.E. had been in service and moved to a large city in the West. E.S.E. continued to have occasional recurrences of his malaria, but after about six months these ceased. His psychosis, however, did not abate. He was at times quite difficult to manage, striking other patients without apparent cause and breaking windows. In early 1945 he was given twenty-two electro-shock treatments and improved sufficiently so that he was permitted to leave the ward for walks around the hospital grounds. By July he seemed well enough to be released.

At home with his mother the veteran did little other than sleep. In part this was a result of the overprotective attitude his mother assumed. She vetoed immediately any display of initiative on his part. Consequently, he did nothing that went against her wishes. He did not even attempt to secure employment. His hallucinations, which had abated somewhat after the series of electro-shocks, returned. His speech was confused and the conviction that he had syphilis remained. Six months after returning home he was as sick as he had been on discharge from the Army, although his mother would not permit rehospitalization.

There was little change in his condition for several years. In late 1948 a vocational adviser from the Veterans Administration contacted E.S.E. and spent some time with him discussing possible training and employment prospects. The resulting report indicated clearly that the veteran was too emotionally disturbed to undertake any training or employment at that time, although he did appear to be interested and had inquired at some length about work in radio and television. Approximately a year later, however, he began to make some friends among men of his age and gradually spent more time away from home. Finally, in early 1950 he was able to bring himself to start courses under the G.I. Bill at a local trade school. Specializing in radio, television, and electronics, he did quite well and gradually developed more confidence in himself. The training forced him to think in terms of the future and also provided a much more stimulating and healthy environment than he had experienced during the long hours at home. He continued to be quite nervous and shy, his hallucinations remained, but he did feel that life was worth living, that the future might even be pleasurable. He looked forward to study and work in the radio-television field.

In June 1951 the veteran decided that he wanted more courses than the trade school could provide and transferred to a university near his home. This school had not been approved for rehabilitation training by the V.A. and therefore E.S.E. could not obtain the more extensive support usually granted to disabled veterans in training (P.L. 16). Nevertheless, with the aid of his disability compensation and the usual G.I. Bill benefits (P.L. 346), he was able to start his college education. He took courses in radio-television engineering and spent most of his time studying and did rather well. Later he began to make friends among his fellow students and for the first time in his life began to date a girl steadily. In early 1952 he married. However, the marriage ended in divorce after three months. By the fall of the year the veteran had exhausted G.I. benefits and since his university was not properly accredited could not obtain further funds for his education. However, the V.A. money had been sufficient to give him a good start on his education. He was now well enough to assume responsibility for further training himself.

Throughout 1953 E.S.E. attended classes from eight o'clock in the morning until one o'clock in the afternoon. He worked at a part-time job from four-thirty to eight-thirty in the evening. In spite of the added burden of his working he has maintained good grades including A's in such courses as calculus. He is somewhat nervous and he still occasionally hears the "voices." However, he cannot now understand what the "voices" say and has given up the conviction that he has syphilis. Although the V.A. doctors still consider him psychotic in a clinical sense, the improvement in his condition since beginning his education has been remarkable and his academic and occupational performance is considered very good.

One of seven children, J.J.D. was raised on a very poor farm in the deep South. He attended school intermittently, but completed ten years before his father took him out of school entirely to work on the farm. His grades had always been poor and his father finally decided there was little point in his continuing his education, especially since he was badly needed at home. Subsequently he worked on the family farm and occasionally in a nearby sawmill. He was generally in good health except for infrequent attacks of malaria throughout his early adulthood. These had ceased entirely by the time he was drafted for military duty in late 1942 at the age of twenty-seven.

During his first year of service, which was spent almost entirely in the western part of the United States, Private D. suffered from frequent colds and aching muscles. He was hospitalized three times and was often on sick call. His basic training was with a medical detachment at an air base, but he later was shifted to laboring duties and guard work. Shortly after arriving in Italy in November 1943 the soldier was again hospitalized for a severe cold. When first overseas he was assigned to a military police company, but was soon transferred to duty as a truck driver with a quartermaster unit at the same air base.

He performed quite satisfactorily until the early spring of 1945 when his aches and pains became so severe that he was again sent to a hospital. There he appeared to be very nervous and constantly complained of pain in various parts of his body, especially his legs and abdomen. In May he was returned to the United States and after extensive medical studies failed to reveal any organic basis for his discomfort, he was diagnosed as psychoneurotic. At the time of his discharge in July 1945 the soldier was still quite emotionally upset.

J.J.D went back to live with his parents after leaving the Army, but for some time was unable to do much work on the farm. He suffered frequent outbreaks of panic during which he was overcome with what he called an "awful fear." His legs and stomach gave him a good deal of pain which often made it necessary for him to stop working. In early 1948 his girl friend gave birth to a baby and J.J.D. acknowledged paternity.

Shortly afterwards, the veteran rented 200 acres of rather poor land from his father for $200 a year and started to farm it on his own. At the same time he enrolled in the institutional on-the-farm training program under the G.I. Bill. This provided him with subsistence money from the Veterans Administration as well as instruction in farm management. He attended classes at the local high school under the supervision of the County Agent and was visited periodically on his farm. At first J.J.D. had a great deal of difficulty with the courses. Since his intelligence was low and since he was suffering from a psychoneurosis as well, he found it very hard to absorb the training. Gradually, however, he began to improve his farm under the constant supervision of his instructor. As he progressed his nervousness subsided and he was able to work harder.

In the spring of 1950 he married the mother of his son and at Christmas a daughter was born. He was beginning to make some profit off his farm and his anxiety attacks had practically disappeared. In addition the pains in his legs and stomach occurred only rarely. By late 1951 he had amassed enough money, largely through his subsistence allowance, to buy a farm of his own. He purchased 123 acres of relatively good land and, relieved of the necessity of tilling almost barren soil, was able to put his training to real use.

Within a year he had doubled his corn yield per acre and almost doubled his cotton yield. He owned a tractor and some equipment as well as a new farm pick-up truck. In addition, he was making a good profit on the hogs he raised. His income was quite adequate to support his wife and two children. His psychoneurotic symptoms had almost disappeared. At the time his farm training was terminated in mid-1952, his instructor noted that J.J.D. was not only doing much better than he had after leaving the Army, but that his performance was also better than before the war.

At the time of their discharge from the Army, both of these soldiers were seriously disturbed and had little prospect of making a successful postwar adjustment. Yet the assistance which each received from the Veterans Administration enabled them to improve their education and skill and served as a catalyst to reverse the trend. J.J.D. is now well on the road to becoming a successful farmer; and E.S.E., although still far from emotionally stable, has shown sufficient strength in advancing towards his occupational goal that he may well succeed.

DISABILITY COMPENSATION

The American public has long acknowledged its responsibility to men who were seriously injured in the service of their country by liberally compensating them. But the same public has criticized the implementation of this policy. There seems to be a widespread belief that many veterans draw pensions for disabilities that were not incurred during their military service. Moreover, some critics have argued that liberal payments by the federal government, instead of helping a man readjust, hinder him by encouraging him to exaggerate his disability so as to continue to qualify for his pension.

Pension policy at the end of World War II can be summarized in these terms. If a man was separated from the Armed Services for some medical reason—either physical or psychiatric—the Veterans Administration accepted this fact as presumptive evidence that he was entitled to disability compensation which varied from 100 percent to a minimum of 10 percent. The initial award was usually liberal but as the Veterans Administration later evaluated the veteran's adjustment it frequently revised its initial determination, usually downward.

During P.L.Y.'s early years, his family was continuously plagued with financial worries. His father died when the boy was two years old and his mother had great difficulty in making enough to keep the family fed. During the depression they were often on relief. He left high school after two years and after several very low-paying jobs went to work as a machine operator in a lumber factory. His salary was $16 a week. At the age of twenty-one he was drafted.

Private Y. was assigned to a succession of camps in the South during the first fifteen months. Although his basic training was in the Field Artillery, he was soon transferred to Ordnance and remained in that type of work throughout the rest of his Army career. In the spring of 1943 he was in the hospital for over a month with a broken toe suffered while he was carrying out his duties as an automobile mechanic. Other than that he was in good health and performed very well throughout his period of service in this country.

In early 1944 the soldier went to Europe with an ordnance company that he had joined about six months previously. By late summer the outfit had established itself in France well behind the lines and was actively engaged in automotive assembly and repair work. Private Y. was doing very well. Then in early September a land mine suddenly blew up about 10 feet away from him. Fragments of shrapnel struck both his feet and made wide gashes. The shrapnel was removed in the hospital and the wounds gradually began to heal. However, he could not walk for many months and experienced a good deal of pain for some time. His feet were in casts until the time he returned to the United States in February 1945.

However, even after the wounds had healed, Private Y. continued to complain of pain and to limp around the ward. Whenever the doctors touched his feet to examine them he would pull away quickly. During these examinations he was tense and flushed. When he walked barefoot he would pick his way along gingerly holding his toes up so they would not touch the floor. In spite of his obvious pain, extensive medical studies failed to reveal any reason for it. The wounds had healed well and there were no broken bones in his feet. Finally he was referred for psychiatric examination. The psychiatrist concluded that the difficulties Private Y. was now experiencing with his feet were entirely attributable to emotional factors and that he was suffering from a severe hysteria. Discharge from the service was recommended.

Before returning home in late August 1945 the veteran filed an application for disability compensation alleging nervousness and disabilities associated with wounded feet. After an examination of his service records the Veterans Administration, concluding that P.L.Y. was at that time totally incapacitated for employment, awarded him 100 percent disability. This gave him an income of approximately $115 a month. The veteran went to live with his mother in a small apartment. Toward the latter part of 1945 he married and with his wife continued to live with his mother.

For the next two years he and wife were supported mainly by the income provided by the Veterans Administration. P.L.Y.'s feet continued to pain him so much that it was impossible for him to seek a job. Nevertheless, he was able to avoid accumulating many debts and he did not feel that he had to obtain work at any cost. As he saw it the compensation was his due for a condition arising directly from his military service. He deserved it and it provided him with an opportunity to rest and attempt to recover from his disability. Gradually the pain in his feet did subside. By late 1947 he felt considerably better and the improvement in his condition was noted by the V.A. doctors. Accordingly his pension payments were reduced by 50 percent. He still limped and was rather nervous, but he could stay on his feet for relatively long periods of time.

Shortly afterwards he rented a 73-acre farm from his father-in-law and began to cultivate a few acres. He was not able to work steadily and during the first year made less than a thousand dollars. With the disability compensation, however, he and his wife had enough to live on and P.L.Y. could continue to develop the farm. He did not feel capable of taking a full-time job that would provide a greater income. Early in 1949 he entered the institutional on-the-farm training program. His condition continued to improve and he was able to work longer and longer hours.

By 1953 his limp had almost entirely disappeared and the veteran was doing very well on his farm. Although he was still receiving some compensation from the Veterans Administration, it was no longer the most important factor in his income. He had turned to dairy farming primarily and had increased the value of his property. At that time the training director noted that P.L.Y. had taken good advantage of his instruction, had improved his status substantially, and was quite capable of making his own way as a fairly successful farmer.

P.L.Y. used his liberal compensation to support himself during the time it took him to regain his emotional balance. The fact that the Veterans Administration was sympathetic but not overindulgent—after two years it cut his payments in half—would have made it difficult for P.L.Y. to resign himself to the life of a pensioner. While some veterans lost their motivation to become self-supporting, most of them responded like P.L.Y. and used their disability payments only as a crutch while they were readjusting themselves to perform effectively in civilian life.

VETERANS' ORGANIZATIONS

Many veterans, especially those who were disturbed by their war experience, felt comfortable only with those who had shared their experiences in the Armed Forces. Hence many were drawn towards one of the veterans' organizations such as the American Legion or the Disabled American Veterans. These groups served a double purpose. They provided emotional support by enabling ex-servicemen to associate with one another and they also helped, as we shall see, by providing a wide range of technical services aimed at speeding the readjustment of their members. In particular, these organizations helped their members to secure their benefits from the Veterans Administration.

Shortly after T.A.G. was born his father died in a mining accident. The family was quite poor and he had to leave school at the age of sixteen after completing the second year of high school, in order to support himself and his mother. Always nervous and easily upset, he found it impossible to remain on any job very long. He drifted from one position to another, all within the Northeastern states where he had been born. For a while he worked as a carpenter's helper, but heights bothered him and he quit. Then he joined the Civilian Conservation Corps and worked up to the job of pastry cook, only to leave after six months because he was bored. Later came jobs as a factory worker and construction laborer. The only job he really enjoyed was one which involved cleaning snow off a skating pond. But, of course, with the coming of spring this job disappeared. At the age of twenty he was drafted.

Private G. was assigned to an anti-aircraft battalion soon after induction. His initial training was as a radio operator although he worked for some time as a messenger. After six months on maneuvers in the South his outfit went to England in early 1944. More training followed. In May the soldier was made a technician fifth grade. Within ten days of his promotion he was aboard ship waiting to go ashore in France with the invasion troops. His unit landed early on the second day of the assault and rapidly set up gun positions along the beach. For eight days T.A.G. was in heavy fighting and he did well. Then, as he was crawling from his foxhole a sniper's bullet crashed into his left leg and ended his combat career. The bone was shattered and his leg badly mangled. He spent eight months at various hospitals in England and the United States before his leg healed.

While in a military hospital near his home the soldier married a girl whom he had known for over four years. Later when he was released from the hospital and sent to a new unit in the South, his wife took a job as a waitress. Four days after his arrival at his new post, T.A.G. appeared at the dispensary in a very nervous state. He was sent to the hospital and was sobbing quietly by the time he saw a psychiatrist. Then he began to talk rapidly, jumping from subject to subject, but always coming back to his wife and his feeling of responsibility for her care and financial support. By the time the interview ended he was crying again.

Over the succeeding days his condition became progressively worse. He began to claim that he had not been hit by a sniper's bullet, but had shot himself because he was a liability to the unit and felt he could help the others most by removing himself from the scene. He felt extremely guilty. Later he changed the story to indicate that he had shot one of his officers thinking he was a German paratrooper and then on learning of his mistake had shot himself.

Later still he began to contend that it was not his fault that he did these things that there was a devil in him and he was really dead. He began to bang his head against the wall in order to kill the devil. He became convinced that his wife was dead. At times he stated that he could not be seen, that he was invisible and did not have a body, only a head, and that belonged to the devil. He would eat only if convinced that the food would help to drive out the devil. After ten electric shock treatments he improved slightly and was discharged to a V.A. hospital near his home. That was in June 1945.

A month later T.A.G. returned with his wife to the city where he was born. Much improved, he was considered only 60 percent disabled by the V.A. examiners. He took a job in a chain-store bakery, but quit after three weeks and went to work as a driver salesman selling coffee and tea. A year later when examined by the V.A. doctors he was still working at the same job, which he seemed to enjoy, and was considered practically recovered. His compensation payments were cut and his disability rated at 40 percent.

In September 1946 his first child was born. He continued as a coffee and tea salesman until late 1947, but throughout that last year found it increasingly difficult to handle money. He made mistakes, such as failing to pick up large bills after giving customers change and trying to collect from the wrong houses. By borrowing money from finance companies he was able to make up the arrears on his accounts, but he himself was going deeper and deeper into debt. Finally he had to leave the job entirely. He was very upset because he felt he was failing in his responsibility to his wife and child by not providing for them financially.

During 1948 T.A.G. went from one job to another trying in some way to keep up the payments to the finance company. Every time he heard of a position that might pay more than the one he had, he tried to get it. Most of his jobs were in some kind of sales activity where there was a possibility of getting a commission. To make matters worse, in mid-summer his disability compensation was reduced to very little. The V.A. psychiatrist felt he was in very good shape emotionally.

At this point he sought out the representatives of the Disabled American Veterans, a veterans' group which he had joined previously, asking them to help him get his compensation increased. The D.A.V. people gave T.A.G. the necessary papers to file an appeal and with their aid he filled them out and sent them to the Veterans Administration. As a result another examination was given him which indicated clearly that he was far from completely recovered. His speech was rapid and at times somewhat confused. He seemed to be convinced that the housewives with whom he dealt were in league against him. The previous examination was held to be in error and his 40 percent rating was reinstated. He was much relieved. Working at that time as a sewing-machine salesman, he was doing quite well and with the small additional amount of compensation from the Veterans Administration he now had some hope of paying off his debts and getting out from under the heavy strain his financial situation imposed on him.

Within a short time, however, the veteran was in even more serious trouble. One day after work, he stopped off at a tavern for a few drinks. On his way home he met his wife's thirteen-year-old sister. He offered to give her a ride home, and after she got into the car he raped her. He then drove west, abandoning his truck along the way, and finally arrived in Chicago. Four days after the incident he called his wife saying he was stranded without funds, clothing, or any knowledge of how he got to Chicago. He returned voluntarily and was held for Grand Jury action. However, because of his mental condition and because his mother-in-law refused to prosecute, the case was not pressed against him on condition that he get into a V.A. hospital immediately.

On admission to the hospital his disability rating was increased to 100 percent. His debt at that time stood at $1,200. He was quite confused and rambled on at some length about his financial problems. After a series of combined insulin and electric shock treatments, he improved somewhat and was released from the hospital in July of 1949. Unable to return to the city where he was born and had spent most of his life because of the rape incident, he settled in another Eastern city and took a job as a dishwasher. A month later he started working as an auto mechanic under the V.A. on-the-job training program, only to be fired after three weeks because his employer was convinced he had no aptitude for that kind of work. Next, he obtained a position as a semiskilled worker in cabinet making. The pay was not high and the hours quite long, but he had to do something.

Some three months after he started this job and just as he was beginning to start paying off his debt again, the Veterans Administration again reduced his disability compensation—from the 100 percent he had been receiving since entering the hospital to 50 percent. Again T.A.G. contacted the Disabled American Veterans in order to appeal the reduction in payments. They helped him secure affidavits dealing with his condition and when the case was finally carried through to the Board of Veterans Appeals in Washington the D.A.V. prepared an extensive brief in his behalf. This brief was presented by the Washington representative of the D.A.V. in person. As a result of these persistent efforts which the veteran could not have made without help, the disability rating was raised from 50 percent to 70 percent retroactive to the date of the original change. As a result all subsequent payments were increased by about $35 a month and T.A.G. also received almost $250 in back pay. The Board felt that although his emotional state was much improved his leg wound was still quite disabling and that therefore a 70 percent rating was justified.

In November of 1950, at about the same time the appeal of his case was being presented in Washington by the D.A.V., the veteran obtained a better paying job as a laborer on the railroad. He has since been promoted to brakeman and is doing quite well, although he still misses some time from work because of nervousness and various somatic complaints which the V.A. doctors feel have an emotional basis. His disability is still rated at 70 percent and with the additional income he receives from the V.A. he has been able to pay off the debts which he accumulated as a coffee and tea salesman in 1947. Free of the constant burden of his debts and secure in the knowledge that he can support his family, he is much less upset now than at any time since his breakdown.

This case illustrates the advantages of having a professional organization assist a handicapped individual in pushing a complex claim through a government bureau. Such support can frequently mean the difference between success or failure. Although T.A.G. is still disturbed emotionally, he was able to assimilate a number of reverses and has a reasonable chance of continuing to perform effectively because of the liberal help which he has received since his discharge from the service.

OTHER ORGANIZATIONS

Our democratic society is characterized by a large number of governmental and voluntary agencies whose sole or primary mission is to assist people in need of help. While many veterans sought help from various veterans organizations, others made use of established or newly constituted governmental or community agencies. The complexities of modern society are so great that one of the major contributions of communal organizations is to help individuals to contact the appropriate agencies.

M.P.R. was the youngest of three children. Born and raised in a large Northeastern metropolis, he spent much of his childhood on the city streets. He was always very nervous and for a while suffered severely from hives. In school he did quite well, but left high school after three years to play the drums in a dance band. In the daytime he worked as an apprentice diamond cutter, although his primary interest was in a musical career. Soon after joining the dance band, he began to smoke marijuana occasionally when he was particularly nervous before playing a date or when he was idling with his fellow musicians. He saw nothing particularly wrong in this. From an early age he had known people who used drugs and in fact had come to accept it as natural. Marijuana cigarettes were quite easy to obtain. Soon after his nineteenth birthday, he enlisted in the Army.

Entering the Air Corps, Private R. was sent to school for almost eight months to learn to be an airplane mechanic. Except for being absent without leave for five days for which he was not court-martialed, his performance was very good. The remainder of his period of service was spent at a field in the West where he worked briefly as a mechanic and later as a drummer in an Air Corps band. Again, for a while, he was an excellent soldier.

However, from mid-1943 on he became increasingly nervous. He was hospitalized for a few days in August of that year because of his anxiety and tenseness, and again in December. He went on sick call rather frequently complaining of headaches, a pain in his chest, and hives. In January 1944 he was hospitalized briefly again with the diagnosis of psychoneurosis but returned to duty. His hives became increasingly worse. Every morning when he woke up there were swellings all over his body. Frequently his lips and eyelids were swollen. By noon, however, the hives had usually disappeared. Throughout this period Private R. continued to smoke marijuana whenever he could obtain it. It seemed to calm his nerves.

In April 1944 he was hospitalized again for treatment of his hives and his anxiety state. Soon after admission he gave three marijuana cigarettes to one of the ward officers explaining that he did not want to use them in the hospital. Upon questioning he told of smoking marijuana for the last four years. He had never had any difficulties with civil authorities over this. At the post where he was then stationed he had not been able to obtain much of the drug, but had been able to buy it occasionally in a nearby city.

Actually, his use of drugs had been rather intermittent and he was not considered a true addict. Nevertheless his behavior was illegal and constituted grounds for a discharge "without honor." Private R. did not feel that the use of drugs was wrong and in fact said that it made him feel so much better that he did not want to stop permanently. The doctors felt that if he were returned to duty the soldier would continue to smoke marijuana whenever he could obtain it. Consequently they suggested he be discharged as possessing "habits and traits of character which render his retention in the service undesirable."

Shortly after returning home, M.P.R. applied for disability compensation because of psychoneurosis and drug addiction, but was turned down by the Veterans Administration. His disability was considered not to have been incurred during wartime service and to be a result of his own misconduct. Back in the city he went to work again as a musician and diamond cutter and between the two jobs made a very good income. However, he continued to be nervous and with marijuana readily available again he used it more and more to "quiet his nerves." Then after a year or so he started taking heroin. The injections were expensive, but he was making enough to afford it. He married, but when his wife found out he was a confirmed narcotics addict, they separated. Finally after three years on heroin he was picked up by the police.

When M.P.R. appeared in court it was apparent that he was a very emotionally disturbed individual who was badly in need of treatment for his drug addiction. However, the last thing he himself wanted was to be deprived of narcotics for any period of time. With the drugs he felt good; he was not anxious and he felt like a man. Without them he knew only too well that he would suffer "the tortures of the damned." Occasionally in the past he had decided to quit only to run for the heroin when the withdrawal symptoms became severe. He frankly did not want to face that kind of panic again and in fact never would have if he had not been taken into custody. Now, however, the decision was out of his hands. He was sent to the U.S. Public Health Service Hospital at Lexington, Kentucky for cure and was deprived of narcotics. The courts did what he himself was unable and unwilling to do.

He was confined at Lexington under court order for one and a half years. When he emerged in 1950 he was cured. He continued to work as a diamond cutter for several years. In 1954 he returned to high school and easily obtained a diploma. That fall he applied to the Veterans Administration for G.I. Bill benefits in order to enter college. Again he was turned down because of the character of his discharge from service. Nevertheless, he decided to continue his education on his own and completed the first year successfully. At the present time he is still in college majoring in psychology and has recently married again. He works part time as a jewelry salesman. He has not returned to narcotics since leaving Lexington.

Although born in a small town in the Midwest, D.A.J. later moved with his family, which eventually included fourteen children, to a large city in the same part of the country. He completed grammar school at the age of fourteen and then went to work. At first his employment was rather irregular, but ten of the ensuing twenty years were spent with the same company as a driver of an oil truck. D.A.J. lost this job just prior to entering military service because of his heavy drinking.

At about the age of twenty he had begun to get intoxicated quite frequently although for a long time it did not interfere with his employment. It did, however, interfere with his marriage. Married at the age of twenty-five, he and his wife had two children before they were finally divorced nine years later. Throughout this period they had many quarrels and many reconciliations. The trouble always centered around his drinking. Just before he entered the Army at the age of thirty-five, D.A.J. remarried his former wife.

After receiving basic training with an anti-aircraft battalion on the West Coast, he was assigned to an infantry regiment which was preparing for overseas shipment. Early in July he landed on the island of Attu in the Aleutians which had only very recently been retaken from the Japanese after heavy fighting. In August his unit went ashore on the nearby island of Kiska fully prepared for equally strong resistance. But there was not a Japanese soldier on the island when the invasion forces landed. For nine more months, Private J. remained in the barren North. During this period he worked as a truck driver and for the first time in fifteen years had very little to drink. The only things available were Sterno and hair tonic, and these he drank mixed with lemonade. But the supply was limited and he was only drunk on a very few occasions. In the spring of 1944 the soldier was transferred to another regiment and shortly thereafter returned to the States.

For the next few months he was repeatedly transferred before being assigned as a truck driver at a camp in the South. Almost immediately after arriving in this country he began to drink heavily and by early fall landed in the hospital. After a month's stay he was returned to duty, but his drinking continued. During the day he was able to stay sober, although he was so nervous and shaky that he had to be taken off truck driving and assigned to work cleaning up the company area.

After duty hours, however, he would go to the PX or any place else he could get beer or liquor and become thoroughly intoxicated. Then he would return to the company area, often causing a good deal of trouble. Sometimes he would pass out in a ditch or in the barracks. More frequently, he would go to the day room and become quite belligerent—breaking beer bottles, throwing the mop bucket around the room, and trying to tip over the pool table. Once the other men got him in bed he usually quieted down, but that frequently required concerted effort by several people for as long as an hour. In April of 1945 his commanding officer decided to send him before a disposition board, and the following month the soldier returned home with a "blue" discharge (without honor).

Soon after arriving home the veteran applied to the state employment service for the $20 a week readjustment allowance normally paid to ex-servicemen who had not as yet obtained a job. The application was forwarded to the Veterans Administration for determination of eligibility. The decision was that D.A.J. should not obtain these benefits because he had received a discharge without honor due to his own misconduct, namely persistent drunkenness. Following this ruling he did find a job, but his drinking continued.

In early 1946 his wife divorced him for a second time and he started drifting from one rooming house to another. He worked intermittently but only long enough to obtain money to buy liquor. Sometimes he would find a position as a truck driver. More frequently he worked as a dishwasher, janitor, or laborer. He was arrested so many times for drunkenness that he hardly cared any more whether he spent the night in jail or not. In late 1947 he spent some time in a state mental hospital, but this did not help him.

In early 1948 after he had been drinking steadily for nine days he appeared at a shelter operated by a Catholic priest. The priest talked him into going to the County Psychopathic Hospital where he spent about a month. His condition was considered serious since there was some evidence of brain deterioration as a result of his heavy drinking over some twenty years. After leaving the hospital he returned to the shelter and there came in contact with a representative of Alcoholics Anonymous.

At first he was not impressed with the group and considered it a "sissy" organization. He consented to attend some meetings, however, and gradually was drawn into the activities. He had been brought up as a Catholic, although he had not attended church in some time, and the religious approach to his problem appealed to him. So did the fact that here he was dealing with men who had suffered as he had, who were not merely condemning him out of their own self-righteousness. As he listened to man after man tell about his past, he felt a common bond with these people. He saw himself over and over again. These men had been through the same experiences he had, had felt the same insatiable need to quell that pervasive, constant fear with just one little drink and then one more. But they had stopped. They had been saved. Maybe he was capable of salvation, too. Gradually, the idea began to grow on him that he could possibly live without alcohol. During the summer of 1948 he decided to try.

He has not touched a drink since. As he says, "I thank God that I found A.A." Several months later he obtained a job as a plant protection guard at a steel factory, a job which he still holds. In 1950 he applied to the Army Discharge Review Board to have his discharge changed from "without honor" to "honorable." Although this request was denied and D.A.J. was upset, he did not resort to liquor to relieve his concern. In 1951 he remarried his former wife—their third marriage in twenty years—and they have been much happier together than at any previous time.

Both cases illustrate how difficult it is for a man to perform effectively if his difficulties lead him to engage in behavior that cannot be tolerated by his wife, his employer, or society at large, such as the excessive use of alcohol or drugs. Similarly, the two cases suggest that if such destructive behavior can be brought under control, the individual may be able to make use of his strengths so that he can perform effectively. No one can be sure that M.P.R. and D.A.J. will be able to sustain the satisfactory levels of performance which they have been helped to reach, but the prospect is that they will.

Chapter Thirteen: FREEDOM TO CHOOSE

THE VALUES men live by may be only dimly perceived but their power and influence are pervading because they are so deeply imbedded. As long as a man's life proceeds on a more or less even keel, a substantial congruence is likely to exist between his values and the demands of his environment. One of the great advantages of a democratic society is that everybody does not have to conform to a single norm. As long as people do not break the law or otherwise engage in public behavior that is overtly disapproved by the dominant majority, they have considerable latitude.

Although there is a great sameness in the cultural pattern of the United States from the Atlantic to the Pacific, significant regional variations persist—as between North and South, between rural and urban, between ethnic minorities such as the French Canadians or the Latin Americans and the native population among whom they live. The range of differences was greater in the past, for accelerating industrialization and urbanization are taking a steady toll of the different and the unique.

Among the most pervasive of all American values is a belief in equity. As a man sows, so shall he reap. Not parentage nor social influence but his own efforts and performance should determine his rewards. Although the gap between theory and fact has been large, there has always been considerable evidence in support of the doctrine—poor men did rise to the top; the boy who worked days and studied nights became a leader in his profession, the wastrel son of the rich occasionally ended his life on the Bowery.

Business organizations, trade unions, universities, government agencies have all sought to gear their promotion policies to the quality of a man's work and contribution. It is true that the son of the founder advances more rapidly, and good connections pay off—but there has been a widespread respect for equity. As we have seen, even a military organization in the midst of a war could not afford to ignore this value, although it was forced by exigencies to ride roughshod over it on many occasions.

Some soldiers could not reconcile themselves to the arbitrary and what appeared to them to be discriminatory actions of the Army, especially during a war being fought in the name of freedom and democracy. They broke under the strain. They could not continue to perform effectively because of conflict between their cherished values and beliefs and the situations which mocked and violated them. The freedom which they gained on being discharged frequently enabled them to bring about a new alignment between their values and their environment. The Negro who could no longer tolerate the oppressive segregation of the South was not forced to live there. He could move to another part of the country where he felt more at ease. The soldier who felt abused by his sergeant had no effective recourse; if his foreman behaved badly, he could get himself another job.

In addition to their respect for equity, Americans have long placed freedom of choice high in their scale of values. A man is master of his own fate and as long as he does nothing to harm others, he has the right to do what he wants, when he wants, and where he wants. But all this is changed when a man is called up for military service. Instead of relying on himself, he must henceforth acknowledge the authority of his superiors even if they are younger, know less, or are otherwise inferior to him. Most men were able to make this very radical transition under the overwhelming pressure of war. But some could not. The conflict between their need for freedom and the severe restrictions on their freedom in the Army led them to break down. In the absence of complications their recovery was likely to be rapid once they were discharged and regained their freedom.

Although most Americans believe in God and many go to church on Sunday, their daily life is not directly influenced by religion.

But the conduct of a small minority is dictated by their religious beliefs and convictions. Some of these men, not being able in the Army to adhere to their religious beliefs, developed severe conflicts and became ineffective. Many of them on their return to civilian life were able to bring their beliefs and actions into alignment, with the result that they could again function effectively.

The individual who runs into conflict with the moral code may become ineffective, especially if society acts to punish him. Among the principal deviations from the sexual code is homosexuality. In the Army the homosexual is in an extremely difficult situation. In addition to being constantly tempted, he knows that he runs the risk of bodily harm if his barracks mates find him out. A discharge without honor was mandatory if the authorities became aware of his deviation. Such were the pressures with which a homosexual had to cope while in uniform. Many did so successfully but only by paying a high price of constant vigilance and control. Others failed or were denounced. Once out of the Army, however, they could usually work out a tolerable adjustment.

EQUITY

Among the most serious blights on American democracy has been the belief that if a man's skin is not white or if he was born abroad and cannot speak English properly, the standards of equity do not necessarily apply. If men are not equal in capacity, if they are unable to assume the same order of responsibility, there is no need to treat them as equals. So the segregationists and the super-patriots have argued.

Violations of equity are found not only in the area of race relations but usually wherever gross inequality of power exists in our society—in business, labor, and voluntary organizations.

T.I.V., a Negro, was born and raised in the deep South. Subjected to discrimination from the time of his birth, he came to accept it. As he later put it: "I thought the country belonged to the whites because they had found it and fought for it." In school he did quite well and completed the third year of high school before leaving to go to work. He was employed as a butcher and as a bartender prior to entering the Army as a draftee at the age of twenty.

For almost ten months Private V. was stationed at one camp in the heart of the South. There he served as an aidman and surgical technician in the medical detachment of an anti-aircraft battalion. His unit contained only Negroes. On the way across the Pacific he was promoted to technician fifth grade and assigned to duty as a surgical technician. The outfit spent several months in Australia before being given a combat assignment.

During this period the soldier had many opportunities to meet the people of that country. He found them initially quite unfriendly, but later, getting to know them better, learned the reason for this attitude. Apparently white soldiers previously stationed in the area had told them that Negroes would rape and murder them. As a result the local population was so frightened that they would have nothing to do with the Negroes. Over time this fear disappeared and T.I.V. made many good friends among the Australian people. But he retained a feeling of resentment and bitterness toward white Americans in general and especially toward the unknown soldiers who had made it so difficult for him and his fellow soldiers even in a foreign land.

This feeling continued to bother him as he entered combat with his outfit, first in New Guinea and later on the islands to the north. He could not see much sense in dying for his country if at the end of the war members of his race would be treated as badly as before. The fact that he was now fighting for his country indicated that he was just as much an American as anyone else and yet here he was in a segregated unit expecting to return to his former life, characterized by discrimination and prejudice. Nevertheless, he performed very well under severe combat conditions and in June 1944 was promoted to technician fourth grade. Finally, however, in early 1945 he became extremely nervous and was sent to

the hospital. There he appeared very tense, trembled all over, and
sobbed intermittently. His breakdown was attributed to the stress
of prolonged combat duty.

Two months later he was back in the States assigned to a convalescent hospital in the Rocky Mountain area. Free of the combat
situation he felt better and his condition improved at first, but then
remained relatively static. A furlough at home did not help him.
He was irritable and sometimes rather confused throughout his
stay. The discrimination against members of his race now bothered
him severely.

The inequities were not confined to the South. On returning to
camp he found many similar evidences of prejudice. At the post
exchange waitresses waited on all the white soldiers first. White
soldiers made comments about "niggers" and "coons" when he was
around. Negroes were not permitted in the swimming pool at the
same time as whites. Even in town there were many places where he
was refused admittance because of his race. All this made him both
bitter and anxious. He complained to the social workers: "If only
the other people would realize that I am just as much an American
as they are."

As he mulled over these inequities, he began to think of leaving
the United States after the war ended. More than anything else he
wanted to go to a place "where a man is gauged by what he is
worth and not what his color is." Only then could he escape from
boiling anger and the fear which was intertwined with it. He had
almost decided to seek refuge in the one country where he felt he
would be free of discrimination, the Soviet Union, when he met
a young Jewish social worker. In part because of his own sensitivity
to the realities of discrimination this social worker devoted considerable time and effort to talking T.I.V. out of going to Russia.
By the time of his discharge in June 1945, T.I.V. had given up the
idea.

Nevertheless, on returning to his home in the South he found the
situation intolerable. Every sign of prejudice against his race turned

his stomach into knots. He was constantly tense and anxious. He could not sleep at night. Within a short time he married a girl he had been dating since before the war. In August he and his bride moved north to a Midwestern city where they hoped to escape at least part of the inequities of their life at home. The veteran obtained a job as a bartender which paid no more than he had received before the war. Nevertheless, he felt freer almost from the day he stepped off the train. He began to feel that people here really would treat him as an American. True there was discrimination and occasionally he was refused a meal in a restaurant but he was not always faced with evidence to support his belief that he and his people had been relegated to second-class citizenship.

His rage and anxiety subsided rapidly as he became convinced that he would be treated fairly. Within a year his psychoneurosis had almost completely disappeared. Later he shifted to a better-paying job as a bartender, a job which he has held for over seven years. His wife had a child and shortly afterwards he bought a home for his family with the help of a G.I. loan. He no longer feels that every white man he meets wants to deprive him of his rights. He has met too many white men both at work and in his daily life who have treated him as an equal. In describing how he feels T.I.V. says: "I feel all right now, but there were a lot of things that existed in the Army that I didn't like—the way the Army permitted the states to apply their rules of descrimination, especially in the South, but also throughout the country as a whole. With due credit to President Eisenhower some of these things have been corrected."

D.D.D. was the second of two children born to a very poor farm family in the deep South. His mother died when he was still a child. He had pneumonia twice before the age of ten. Always rather sickly, he suffered from an almost constant ache in the joints of his legs. In school he had a great deal of difficulty and completed only eight grades by the age of eighteen. Subsequently he worked as a farm laborer and, for a year prior to entering military service, as a carpenter's helper in a shipyard. His father was killed in a grist mill accident.

On being drafted at the age of twenty-four he was assigned as a rifleman to an infantry regiment. Over a year and a half of training followed during which Private D. spent a number of months on maneuvers in the South and also on the desert. Just prior to leaving for Hawaii in June 1944 the outfit was given intensive amphibious training. Training continued in Hawaii, but was abruptly terminated in August when they boarded ship for the South Pacific. After rehearsing landing operations at an island en route, they finally reached their objective, a heavily fortified island off the Philippine coast, in mid-September.

The initial landing was not difficult thanks to a heavy pre-invasion artillery bombardment, but resistance soon stiffened. The heavy jungle growth, the almost complete lack of trails, and the cleverly concealed Japanese fortifications slowed the advance. After an enemy mortar shell landed near him Private D. became afraid. He could not sit still, sweat all the time, trembled, and felt as if there was a knot around his heart. Then, on the third day of the attack a fragment of shrapnel from a 75 mm gun penetrated his left foot. Evacuated, he did not reach a base hospital until twenty days later although during the 3,000 mile trip by water he received frequent medical attention. The wound was by then healing well, but the soldier remained upset emotionally. His joints ached constantly, and he had sharp pains in his chest. He was listless and at times had attacks of dizziness and trembling. Diagnosed as suffering from heart symptoms of emotional origin he was returned to the States.

For the next seven months D.D.D.'s condition remained much the same. His wound healed completely, but he was frequently in pain, anxious, and very easily tired. He attended courses in farm management under the hospital's reconditioning program, but seemed to learn little. It was apparent to the instructors that he knew little about the operation of a farm, and since he had low intelligence and was suffering from an emotional disorder which left him listless and apathetic he would require long-term training before he could hope to carry on a profitable farming operation. Such training was not within the scope of the Army rehabilitation program. In June 1945 he was discharged.

Returning to the South, D.D.D. obtained 18 acres of very poor land and began planting a variety of crops—corn, cotton, peas, potatoes, and sugar cane. His yield per acre was very low and he was barely able to support himself. Nevertheless, in March 1946 he got married and toward the end of the year a son was born. Throughout 1946 the Veterans Administration wrote to the veteran a number of times informing him of his opportunity to obtain further farm training under the G.I. Bill. These letters continued into 1947 and finally toward the end of the year he did enter the institutional on-the-farm training program. In debt and unable to operate his farm efficiently, he realized by then that he needed help if he was ever to make a steady living at farming.

After a month of training at one high school he was transferred to another. Then, two months later, just as he was beginning to understand what the program was all about an incident occurred which nearly destroyed his hopes of ever readjusting.

Still anxious and suffering from a variety of bodily symptoms of emotional origin, he had begun to take a few drinks whenever he was faced with a situation which particularly disturbed him. The classes at the high school were upsetting because he found it difficult to understand much that was said and realized he was not doing as well as most of the others.

Inevitably he appeared for class one evening in a slightly intoxicated state. He had been drinking with a young Negro couple and brought them along with him. Although none of the three was really drunk, the instructor was so outraged that he ordered D.D.D. and his friends out of the classroom. Subsequently this same instructor went around to all the citizens of note in the community and obtained affidavits to the effect that the veteran was so uncooperative that he should not receive further training. His major argument in talking with these people was that by associating with Negroes and bringing them to a white school, D.D.D. was upsetting the traditions of the community. The fact that he had been drinking was not a major concern. As a result of the affidavits and the instructor's strong condemnation of his behavior, the veteran was dropped from the V.A. training program.

Shortly afterward D.D.D. appeared at a nearby V.A. clinic in a very disturbed state. He ached all over, especially his back, could not sleep, and was extremely tense. He was very resentful over having been deprived of what he considered his right to farm training. After two weeks in the hospital he calmed down somewhat and was discharged. The doctors felt at that time that there was very little hope of his ever making a satisfactory readjustment. For the next year he moved around from farm to farm and kept applying for reinstatement in the training program. Farming was the only life he knew and yet it was clear to him that, if he could not obtain further training, he would probably continue to be a failure even at that. In July of 1948 another child was born. Finally, in June 1949 he was reinstated by the Veterans Administration, but the farm which he then had was so poor that training on it was not considered feasible.

By September he had obtained 14 acres in another community and was approved for four years of institutional on-the-farm training. At that time the veteran had approximately $1,000 worth of land, buildings, and equipment on which he owed between $600 and $700. Under the training program, however, he began to make some real progress, although he continued to suffer from his emotional difficulty and had to take time off from work quite frequently. In mid-1950 a third child was born. By 1951 the value of the farm had increased to over $3,000 and D.D.D. had paid off part of his debt. In early 1952 he leased an additional 30 acres to put into crops. When training was terminated in 1953, the instructor felt that progress had been quite satisfactory and that the veteran would be able to make a satisfactory living for himself and his family on his farm. A report by the V.A. doctors at about the same time indicated that despite his low intelligence and the fact that he still suffered to some extent from his emotional disturbance, he had improved considerably since his hospitalization in 1948. He appeared to enjoy his work and felt quite confident of his ability to make a success of it. He no longer was troubled about having been dismissed from the farm training program. That wrong had been rectified.

Men are sometimes forced to make their peace with the arbitrary behavior of their superiors. Serious difficulties arise when the behavior they are subjected to conflicts with what they have been led to expect. When this happens their energies are likely to be dissipated in rage or resentment and they are likely to lose the sense of direction and hope which men need in order to perform effectively.

T.I.V. was in constant turmoil until he moved North where the relations between the races had improved at least to a point where he felt he was being accepted as a human being, most, if not all, of the time. D.D.D. would probably have gone steadily downhill had the Veterans Administration not reinstated him in the farm training program from which he had been unjustly excluded and without which he could probably never have made a proper living for his wife and children. Lack of equity not only wounds a man in his soul but it may deprive him of his livelihood.

SELF-DETERMINATION

Most visitors to these shores have been impressed with the self-confidence of the average citizen. Even the child is not frightened to speak up and fight for his point of view. Our culture has deliberately strengthened this respect for freedom. The young person growing up in the United States is encouraged to believe that he can lead whatever kind of life he prefers, so long as he stays within the law. He is under no compulsion to follow the educational program or occupational plans designed by his parents, and there is no agency of society that can order him around. The only exception is in time of war if he is in uniform.

Many men found the restrictions on their freedom in the Army so crippling that they were unable to perform effectively. From many points of view getting out from under military discipline and being able once again to make one's own decisions—to plan one's life and work—did more to contribute to the successful readjustment of many veterans than any other single development.

Both of H.A.B.'s parents were born in Germany. On coming to this country they settled in a Midwestern farming community and with hard work became quite prosperous. H.A.B. was the youngest of nine children. As a child he had frequent nightmares of falling or people chasing him and would awake screaming. He also fainted easily especially at the sight of blood. In school he did quite well in his studies, but he did not participate in sports because of shortness of breath. From a young age he was taught the values of thrift and individual initiative. He came to feel that he should do everything for himself, free of any domination or assistance from others. Freedom and independence of action were very important to him. Freedom was his birthright; independence, his code of behavior.

When he was fourteen his father became emotionally upset, threatened suicide, and was sent to a mental institution. Although he returned to the farm after several months he continued to be somewhat disturbed. As a result of this illness and the economic depression, the family income fell off rather sharply. H.A.B. finally decided that it was his duty to leave school and help out at home. He was then eighteen and in his junior year of high school. During the ensuing two years father and son were in frequent conflict. The father wanted to run the farm the way he had always run it. H.A.B. had his own ideas and had no hesitation in making them known. After one particularly heated argument he left home and went to work as a beer truck driver. Later he worked for a while at an ice plant and then at the age of twenty-two moved to a city several hundred miles west where he obtained a position as a construction laborer.

Two years later his father died of meningitis and H.A.B. immediately returned home to help work the farm. Soon afterwards, he married a local girl whom he had known for many years. In late 1942 he received his draft notice and was inducted into the Army. He was very unhappy over this. His wife was pregnant and he considered it his duty to stay home and support her. Furthermore he felt that he could contribute more to the war effort as a farmer than as a soldier. At that time he was running the farm himself and doing very well at it. He felt that in forcing him to serve in the Armed Forces, the United States government was depriving him of his right to shape his life.

In spite of his resentment at being deprived of his freedom, Private B. served well. He felt that it was his duty to take orders and to do the best he could. But every time he was ordered to do something he did not want to do, he boiled inside. Just the thought of being told to do something made him angry. When he received orders for shipment to Hawaii within a month of his induction, he was so upset he could hardly talk. He hated to go overseas, even to Hawaii, since his wife was about to have a baby. He thought of going AWOL, but he was not that kind of person. He went to Hawaii and said nothing.

For almost seven months Private B. did as he was told, feeling as he did so that he had given up his basic freedom, that he was an automaton guided by others. He completed basic training in the Coast Artillery and went to work as a searchlight operator. His wife gave birth to twins. Secretive and retiring, H.A.B. was nevertheless considered an excellent soldier. Then in June 1943 he became increasingly fatigued. He felt unable to keep up with the other soldiers, began to develop headaches, and suffered from dizziness. Sometimes it seemed as if there were a belt around his chest and he could hardly breathe. His back ached and at times he felt as if he were going insane. He was hospitalized for several weeks and then returned to duty. His symptoms continued and he was hospitalized again in September. After several months he was returned to the States. In January 1944 he received a discharge for psychoneurosis.

Back in his home town, H.A.B.'s condition began to improve. It felt good to be able to do what he wanted again. He played with the twins, went out with his wife, and began to plan for the future. Soon he started in farming for himself. Although he did not have the equipment and stock that he had before the war, he did have the feeling that he was now doing something on his own. Being able to plan his work for himself was in itself satisfying. As the farm progressed he had the feeling that *he* was doing it. Gradually the memories of being bossed around and kept from doing what he wanted faded from his mind. His Army life did not really seem a part of him anymore.

This did not come all at once. In the year immediately following his discharge he often felt depressed. He felt that the Army owed him compensation for having deprived him of his rights. When the payments were discontinued a little over a year after his discharge, he was quite angry. For a while whenever anyone mentioned the fact that he had been discharged before the war ended he felt rather ashamed but then he launched into a story about how easy it had been for him to fool the doctors and get out of the Army.

By 1949, however, he no longer felt upset about his treatment at the hands of the military. At that time he and his wife had four children and were doing well. He started farm training under the G.I. Bill and by the time he completed it two years later had built his farm into a fairly large operation. He was grossing about $12,000 and had a net profit of almost $3,000.

Although most men were able to accept orders in the Army, there were many who like H.A.B. resented being told what to do. So much of their emotional energy was devoted to controlling themselves that they developed various somatic symptoms or disturbances. On being released from such an acutely frustrating environment and again free to follow their own initiative, they frequently were able to perform very effectively.

OPPORTUNITY

Many children grow up with only a slight religious and moral indoctrination. But those who are reared in deeply religious homes will always be influenced by their early training, even if they eventually rebel against it, as often happens. When placed into an environment such as the Army where much that happens is in direct conflict with their deep-seated values, they frequently develop high orders of emotional stress. Discharge provides them with an escape from such a stressful situation and as they are able to establish a greater harmony between their values and actions, they usually are again able to perform effectively.

A.T.T.'s father was a farmer and part-time Baptist minister in the deep South. He died when his son was twelve years old. The family which included ten children was always poor. The father as the religious leader of the local Negro congregation received practically no pay although there were occasional gifts of food and clothing. A.T.T. attended school through the eighth grade before quitting to join the Civilian Conservation Corps. At the age of fourteen he was very sick for some time. As he later described it: "I had some kind of spasms. They said I liked to died. I had fever and chills, just growing fever and chills." Shortly before entering military service at the age of twenty-one, he married a girl of nineteen.

Following his induction Private T. served for ten months as a machine gunner with an anti-aircraft battalion. Although initially his performance was quite satisfactory, he began to get into difficulty toward the end of this period. In August 1943 he went home on furlough prior to going overseas with his unit and returned six days late. He was court-martialed and spent most of the month of September in the stockade. Several weeks later he was found to be suffering from a venereal disease and spent a month in the hospital undergoing treatment. By this time his outfit had left for the Pacific, and he was attached to a replacement group at the port of embarkation to await reassignment to another unit. However, before this could be accomplished he was picked up in town with a pass made out to another soldier and sentenced to another month in the stockade. He finally left for the South Pacific with a signal construction battalion in early January 1944.

Throughout his overseas tour Private T. worked at various air bases on and around New Guinea. Although never in combat, he was exposed to frequent air attacks. Toward the middle of 1944 he spent a good deal of time in the hospital—two weeks with a cold, two separate hospitalizations totaling over a month for venereal conditions, a week with malaria. After returning to duty following the malaria attack, he seemed at times to be unable to remember things. He went on guard duty without his rifle and became quite confused while doing K.P. Sensations of something crawling on his flesh began to bother him. In the morning on awakening he would feel as if he were drunk.

Later came periods, lasting from a few minutes to several days, during which everything seemed cloudy and unreal. He had visions and voices spoke to him. The voice of God seemed to come to him and told him to go about helping others. He felt the power of God in his body. It was the power to preach and be good. He was convinced that he had received a commission from God to preach the gospels. But no one would listen to him. Some of the men laughed at his attempts to preach and the officers began to consider him insane.

Finally, in December 1944 he was again sent to the hospital and shortly afterwards returned to the United States. Although his periods of confusion and unreality became less frequent, he continued to believe that he had been chosen by God. As the doctors put it: "He lacks insight into the nature of his hallucinatory experiences." He remained convinced that the voices and visions were real, not just products of his own vivid imagination. In fact he was rather upset and angry when people refused to believe him.

By March he had improved sufficiently to warrant discharge. The psychiatric opinion at that time was that he had suffered a series of psychotic episodes characterized by a belief in his divine mission and supernatural powers as well as by auditory and visual hallucinations.

The veteran's wife returned from the city where she had been working and they went to live in a two-room cabin in the rural area where they had been born and raised. The veteran began to tell people about how God had visited him and given him a mission to preach the gospel. Gradually the word got around the community. The people believed him. Hadn't his father been a religious man and a minister? Wasn't it natural that God would pick the son of a preacher to continue his work? It seemed only right that a man such as A.T.T. should be visited by God and guided in his work. The veteran had further visitations which he described in church. Everyone seemed to accept him as a minister. Now it was quite different from his Army days when the men laughed at him and considered him "crazy." Here he was a leader of his people, a man close to God. He felt an intense satisfaction, a new confidence in himself.

For a while A.T.T. did little to support himself and his wife other than preach at various churches in the surrounding area. Each sermon brought in two or three dollars. In September he worked for a couple of weeks in a saw mill at five dollars a day. However, he developed a pain in his back and had to stop. Two years later he started a course in carpentry and cabinetmaking at a trade school under the G.I. Bill which he completed in early 1951. During this period his wife gave birth to three children.

Since completing his carpentry training, the veteran has worked intermittently at odd jobs while continuing to preach. He considers his primary occupation that of minister. The periods of confusion, the visions, and the voices have almost completely disappeared, but he remains convinced that he has received a call to preach the gospel. Although he is occasionally quite anxious and suffers from severe headaches as well as stomach pain, he continues to support himself and his family. Sometimes it is very hard to keep going, but he feels that it is his duty as a man chosen by God, to continue to minister to the needs of his congregation. To do this he must somehow support himself. And when he sees how the people respond to his preaching, the good it does them, the faith they have in his divine power, he feels revived and has the strength to keep going.

L.B.F., a Negro, was one of sixteen children, although nine of his brothers and sisters died in childhood. He was born in a small town in the rural South and lived there until he left home to go to a nearby city at the age of fourteen. His schooling was frequently interrupted and he only went as far as the third grade.

Once in the city on his own he soon became associated with a group of homosexuals and participated frequently in homosexual activities. Women never held any attraction for him. Among the men with whom he associated this kind of behavior was accepted. It was only on rare occasions that anyone condemned him for his sexual activity, and he was never particularly concerned at these times because he had so many friends who were also homosexuals. The people who mattered in his life accepted his behavior.

During his stay in the city he worked at a variety of jobs— delivery boy, mill worker, porter, store clerk. Whenever he got tired of one job he changed to another. For the seven years preceding his military service he worked as a bootblack at a newsstand. His income of $10 a week was quite sufficient to cover his needs. He was thirty-four years old when he was drafted.

Private F. spent slightly over seven months in the United States before being sent overseas. All of his service was with an engineer regiment. Initially he was given some training as a general electrician, but because of his low intelligence he learned very slowly and finally had to be transferred to laboring duties. These he performed in a quite satisfactory manner.

For four months after induction he was unable to obtain a pass and since he did not want to take the risk of making advances to another soldier, he abstained completely from homosexual activity. Later he did have relations with men on several occasions in town, but always with civilians. Nevertheless, he became quite upset because he was afraid someone would find out about him. The Army was not like his home environment, where almost everyone he knew accepted homosexuals. Here the men talked about beating homosexuals and he understood he would be punished severely if the officers ever found out. He was frankly afraid. After a while he developed a numbness in his left side and went on sick call several times. Although the numbness was considered emotional in origin and his condition was found to be sufficiently severe to warrant a diagnosis of psychoneurosis, he left soon afterwards for England with his outfit.

On arrival the unit was restricted to camp for three months and again Private F.'s homosexual activities were interrupted. However, after the restriction ended, passes were easy to obtain and he had sexual relations with a number of civilian men. Then he became very apprehensive. He thought the men suspected he was a homosexual and expected that at any time they would either beat him themselves or turn him over to the officers for punishment. Finally, in desperation he went to the chaplain for protection and poured out his story. The chaplain referred him to the medical officer and he was hospitalized in late December 1944. After several more months in England he was shipped to the United States and in the spring of 1945 was sent before a board of officers to determine whether he should be returned to duty or discharged. The decision was to discharge him under "other than honorable" conditions.

The veteran applied for disability compensation alleging that he had become very nervous during his period of military service. His application was turned down because of the condition for which he was discharged. Nevertheless, his anxiety rapidly subsided. Back among his friends, among people who did not consider homosexuals evil and who did not punish them, he felt secure. Here in the city where he had spent a large part of his life there was nothing to be feared. He was of course a homosexual, but so were his associates. He went back to work as a bootblack. It was just like before although now he made more money.

He has continued to work at shining shoes since his discharge. As we might expect he has not married. Whenever anyone asks him what happened to him when he was in the Army he tells them he had a slight stroke. The panic and the guilt are almost forgotten. He is among people who feel as he does, who understand and accept homosexuality.

A.T.T. was able to perform much better at home among people who knew and respected him than in the strange and unsympathetic military environment. Despite suggestions of continuing emotional instability, civilian life was sufficiently supportive to enable him to make a tolerable adjustment. The same was true of L.B.F. who managed his problem in a flexible civilian society but who became tense and anxious in the more restrictive military environment. Whether men with markedly deviating characteristics such as A.T.T. and L.B.F. succeed or fail frequently depends on the degree of freedom that the environment offers them to make the special adjustments that they require in order to perform at their best level. The ability of people to perform always depends in part on the presence or absence of the opportunity which they have to realize special values or special needs.

Chapter Fourteen: A FAVORABLE
ENVIRONMENT

THE INFLUENCE of the environment on performance is pointed up by the many soldiers who broke during the war because they could not tolerate a situation where they were constantly exposed to injury or death. They were not able to muster the emotional resources required to endure such a basic threat. But it is not surprising that many of these men, once they were discharged, made a speedy and complete recovery from their anxiety states. Freed from the intense pressure of combat—or the threat of combat— they had no special difficulty in coping with the ordinary stresses and strains of civilian life.

The fact that American society offers the citizen a wide range of options as to where he may live and at what he may work often contributed to the successful readjustment of many veterans who had broken down in the Army. The burgeoning economy was helpful to the veterans, for they had an opportunity to try out a large number of different jobs if they wanted to, and they were usually able to hold on to a job even if their performance was less than satisfactory. The labor market was sufficiently tight that employers were willing to tolerate performance standards considerably below what they otherwise would have accepted.

LOCATION

Since few men, especially among those who have passed their youth, are ever in perfect health, a favorable or unfavorable climate can frequently exercise a determining influence on how well they are able to perform. And climate is important for more than purely physical reasons. Many men find it emotionally difficult, if not impossible, to live in an extreme climate, such as the tropics or the arctic. Many veterans were well on the way to a successful readjustment once they were freed from having to live in a climate which was not to their liking.

Some men have very specific goals not only about the work they prefer to do, but where they want to do it—in a large city, on the farm, at sea. While in the Army these men were unable to work toward their specific goals, but once back in civilian life they were usually free to realize their ambitions.

A.S.Q. was born in the Midwest. He completed high school before going to work and, in 1927, at the age of twenty, he enlisted in the Army for three years. His service, all in the grade of private, was considered excellent. During the year following his discharge he married. Shortly afterwards he experienced the first of several periods of extreme nervousness during which, as he put it, "I go all to pieces." In addition he suffered intermittently from sinus trouble and began to develop an arthritic condition for which his teeth were removed. In spite of his many physical and emotional difficulties he was able to work relatively steadily throughout the next twelve years. He was employed in various capacities, primarily at a skilled level including positions as a mechanic, carpenter, and electrician. In late 1942 at the age of thirty-five he again enlisted for military service. He was then residing in a small village in the Northeast.

Since he had high intelligence, Private Q. was assigned to the Air Corps and sent to school for training as an airplane mechanic. His wife obtained an apartment near the field and he was able to see her frequently. Almost from the beginning he suffered severely from sinus trouble. He went on sick call several times and was hospitalized for three weeks in early 1943. Within a month he was again hospitalized for the same condition and missed four weeks of training. He also suffered periodically from severe arthritic pains.

Nevertheless, the soldier was able to keep up with his training at first and in March during his second period of hospitalization was promoted to private first class. However, he was not doing nearly as well as he could in his courses, largely because of the time spent in the hospital, but also because he felt so miserable.

Under constant pressure to keep up with his training and worried about his ability to do as well as the younger men, he began to get increasingly nervous. He felt that if he could get free of the sinus trouble and arthritis, he would do all right. He began to suffer from nausea, and often vomited after meals. By May he was back in the hospital for another three weeks. On his release he "went all to pieces." His stomach continued to bother him. He had headaches and periods of dizziness. He could not sleep. During duty hours he was extremely anxious. Within ten days he was back in the hospital, this time for a long stay. In August 1943 he received a discharge for psychoneurosis; his condition had not improved.

The veteran and his wife returned to the Northeastern village where they had lived before he entered military service. There he soon obtained a job as a carpenter. Still nervous and suffering from many bodily symptoms of emotional origin, he found the work very difficult. Nevertheless, he was able to keep going until the early winter when his sinus condition returned. At about the same time he began to have a recurrence of his arthritis. He now found it almost impossible to work and finally had to quit his job. For the next year he worked on his own at electrical and carpentry jobs whenever he could find them. During the winter months he was almost a complete invalid, but in the summer when his sinus condition and arthritis bothered him less he was able to work. Even in the summer, however, he was nervous and tense.

Finally in early 1945 he decided to go to Florida, hoping that the climate there would give him some relief. After he and his wife had moved South, A.S.Q. obtained a job at a resort hotel. Almost miraculously his sinus condition cleared up and he was much less troubled with the arthritis. For the first time in several years he was able to work during the winter months. He enjoyed the warm sunshine and felt better than he had in a long time. Even his nervousness subsided.

Since that time the veteran and his wife have spent most of their winters in Florida and their summers in the North. For a while he tried to continue with carpentry work, but finally shifted to work at resort hotels—sometimes as a cook or steward, but more recently as a butcher. At the present time he is alternating between a hotel near his former home in the Northeast and another in Florida. He actually works somewhat less than ten months a year due to the nature of the resort seasons in the two places, but he makes a good income and receives room and board for his wife and himself in addition. They have no children.

Occasionally he has attempted to spend a winter in the North, but the cold weather invariably brings with it a severe sinus attack and he begins to yearn for the relief he knows he can obtain in the South. Although still troubled by occasional nervousness, headaches, and sleeplessness, he is able to support himself and his wife quite comfortably. His sinuses bother him once in a while, especially when the weather gets cold and damp, but this is not a problem as long as he goes to Florida for the winter. He is still troubled by arthritis and as a result tries to spend as much time in a warm, dry climate as he can.

W.W.N. was the only boy in a family of eight children. His father, an immigrant, settled in the Rocky Mountain area and reared his family there. W.W.N. completed high school at the age of nineteen although he was often truant. He was generally healthy, except for a period when he was sixteen, when he suffered from severe stomach pains and occasional vomiting. This condition cleared up after a few months and he himself attributed it to drinking a bottle of wine and some catsup.

After finishing high school, W.W.N. held a variety of jobs. For a while he worked for a brewery, but left to go to the West Coast. There he joined the Coast Guard in late 1940. His performance was quite satisfactory until he went to sea. There he became violently seasick and was quite incapable of any work aboard ship. Every time he was on the water for any length of time he would become nauseated and feel very weak. He was discharged after just five months of service because of chronic seasickness.

He continued to work on the West Coast for several months, but returned home when his mother died. His nausea and vomiting almost completely disappeared when he started working on land again. Back in the Rocky Mountain area he worked briefly as a laborer on a construction job. However, in spite of his unpleasant experiences, he was still attracted to the sea. He both wanted and did not want to be a sailor. The life of adventure appealed to him and yet it made him nervous and sick. He started out for the West Coast again, intending to join the Merchant Marine, but ended up working as a laborer. He got as far as the Coast, but never as far as a ship. Four months later he was drafted at the age of twenty-two.

He was sent immediately to Air Mechanics School. Two days before graduation he received orders to leave his class and report to an East Coast port for training as a crewman on Air Corps crash boats. There he was taught how to operate the small boats and all about rescuing pilots and crew members from planes which had crashed in the water. As long as the training was conducted on land he performed very well, but as soon as they got out on the water in any kind of rough weather, he became seasick and also very nervous. He went on sick call several times, but the nausea and vomiting continued. Finally in August 1943 the training ended, and five days later W.W.N. was on board ship crossing the ocean. He was sick most of the way across and spent a large part of the time in his bunk.

For almost eighteen months the soldier worked on crash boats out of various ports in the Mediterranean area. Much of his duty was quite safe since his boat was operating from North African ports either towing targets or performing rescue operations in the coastal waters. However, for one four-month period they worked in the area north of Corsica and there were subjected to frequent bombing and strafing. This was W.W.N.'s first and only taste of severe combat. In general he performed quite well, although constantly plagued with seasickness. His condition was no worse during his period of combat duty than before and after. It was being on the water that bothered him, not the fighting.

It was during a prolonged period of relatively safe duty in the waters off the coast of Morocco that the soldier's sickness began to have a pronounced effect on his performance. He was nauseated all the time and began to lose weight quite rapidly. It was difficult for him to sleep and he started getting anxious as soon as they were alerted for sea duty. Finally in early January 1945 he was hospitalized for three weeks. On returning to duty he felt just as bad as ever and was soon back in the hospital. He was then seen for the first time by a psychiatrist. The diagnosis was psychoneurosis. His promotion to corporal came through shortly before he was flown to the United States.

Except for an attempt at duty which lasted slightly over a month, Corporal N. spent the remainder of his military service in various hospitals. His anxiety condition improved somewhat on his initial removal from sea duty, but then remained relatively static. Tense and anxious he nevertheless still planned to join the Merchant Marine after leaving the Army. Even though the very thought of being on a boat made his stomach hurt and his palms sweat, he felt he had to go back. He was discharged in the fall of 1945.

W.W.N. returned to his home town and after several weeks took a job in a clay mine. He still planned to go back to sea, but decided to wait a while. In the spring of 1946 he married a war widow with a young child. Gradually he gave up his plans for a career at sea. Although still somewhat emotionally upset and occasionally nauseated, his condition improved steadily. He missed practically no time from work. As time went on he forgot all about the idea of joining the Merchant Marine. He was happily married, he was supporting his family and was much less anxious. He thought that there was little point in precipitating all his troubles again by returning to the water and he decided to stay on land where he felt better.

In mid-1949 the veteran left the clay mines to look for a better job. His wife was pregnant and they needed more money. Moreover, his wife and he both felt that he should try to find an occupation which offered a better future. For a few months he worked as a welder for a stone company, but this job terminated when the company's project was completed. Next he became a service station attendant, but left after three months to take a position as a bartender in an American Legion club. This job was terminated over a year later when the business did not justify his employment. Then in mid-1951 W.W.N. went to work for a paint manufacturer at a salary well above those he had been receiving.

He has remained at the same job since, doing extremely good work and receiving several raises. He likes this work and wants to stay with the company. Recently he has started tending bar in a tavern during the evening hours to supplement his income. Free of the neurotic need to go to sea, he is doing very well and with the exception of occasional headaches and a tendency to become irritable with the children is practically free of neurotic symptoms.

A man's ability to perform effectively depends in considerable measure on whether he is in good health. In turn his freedom from disabling symptoms depends on whether he can locate himself in areas conducive to his health, including emotional well-being. A.S.Q. got considerable relief from his crippling conditions once he could winter in Florida. In the warm climate, he was able to work, as he had been unable to do in the wet and cold north. W.W.N. represents a more unusual case in that he was for a long time drawn to a type of work—on the water—to which he could not satisfactorily adjust. After he became free of this compelling, but destructive, drive, and was able to find work on land, he was able to make a satisfactory adjustment.

PEACE

Many men broke down in the Army because of the mounting tension that accompanied their fears of injury or death. Although initially able to keep their anxiety under control, more and more men collapsed as the war lengthened, as they got closer to the front, as they saw more of combat, as they encountered death more frequently. As might be anticipated, once they were out of the Army and free of the dangers that had threatened them, they were once more able to function effectively.

E.S. was born in a medium-sized city in the Northeast. He attended the local schools until shortly after his sixteenth birthday, by which time he was in the eighth grade. His marks were not good and he was glad to be able to leave his studies behind and enter the world of work. For five years he operated a reeling machine in a rope factory. Later he held a variety of laboring jobs but he never worked long in any one place. Prior to induction into military service he spent a year and a half with a drug store as a delivery boy. He was twenty-six years old when he entered the Army.

Assigned to the medical detachment of an infantry regiment, he served for almost two years in the southern part of the United States. During this period the unit underwent intensive training including several months on maneuvers. Private S. was given special training as a surgical technician and did very well. Later he was assigned to one of the rifle companies as an aidman. He was promoted to technician fifth grade after ten months of service. He married in March 1944 and went overseas with his unit six months later.

Landing in France the division received further training and was finally sent into combat in early November 1944. The sector to which they were assigned was quiet and there was little contact with the enemy for several weeks. Each company was placed on the line for several days in order to season the green troops and then withdrawn to permit another company to gain experience. Under these circumstances E.S. saw practically no fighting until the latter part of the month. Then the whole regiment went on the offensive. Although their attack was successful, supporting units on either flank were unable to advance and after two days in an extremely exposed position the troops had to withdraw. During this period they were under heavy fire constantly and the aidmen were kept very busy tending the wounded. E.S. did not have time to think about his own dangerous position.

However, after the unit was pulled back, he spent the night in a cellar and following breakfast, with little to do but await new orders, he began to feel very upset. All of a sudden the dangers of his situation became real. He began to shake all over and soon was sobbing. He was too scared to move. He felt that at any moment he might die. He experienced a sharp pain in his chest and vomited. One of his buddies helped him to the aid station and shortly afterwards he entered the hospital.

Although the acute panic subsided as soon as he got well away from the front lines, he continued to be nervous and shaky. His stomach remained upset and he had difficulty sleeping at night. Even after returning to the United States, he felt anxious and sick. The military environment, with its guns and military vehicles and barracks and uniforms, made him think of war—and death. His mind kept going back to his brief combat experience and the morning in the cellar. His surroundings continuously reminded him of those few days. He was discharged in June 1945, a month after the war ended in Europe.

One week after leaving the Army, E.S. started in again at his job with the drugstore. His anxiety subsided rapidly. Back at home with his wife and in his old job, he no longer felt that he lived in a world at war where death could strike suddenly. This was a peacetime environment—no uniforms, no barracks, no military vehicles, no guns, no constant reminders of war. All that had been left behind him. He was a civilian in a world at peace. By the time the war in the Pacific ended, he had practically recovered from his neurosis.

E.S. has continued to live with his wife in a small rented house in the city where he was born. He goes to work each day, gathers together the drugs and other supplies for delivery, and drives his truck from point to point about town. He and his wife have many friends and participate in a variety of social activities. They do not have much money and the veteran has often considered getting another job that would pay more. But he likes his job and finds it hard to leave. It is a simple, peaceful life very different from the one E.S. experienced as a company aidman in Europe.

V.S.C. was the youngest of six children and the favorite of his mother. As a child he had violent temper tantrums and walked in his sleep until he was fourteen. He had many fears. Darkness, mice, and snakes in particular bothered him. He attended schools in the Midwestern town where he was born, but received very poor marks. After failing several grades, he finally discontinued his education two months prior to the time he would have graduated from high school.

After working for a short time, he enlisted in the Regular Army. About a year later he received a dishonorable discharge as the result of a general court-martial for stealing a pair of G.I. shoes. This discharge was subsequently set aside in order to permit V.S.C. to enter the Army during World War II. But at the time he was quite upset and began suffering from the intermittent attacks of diarrhea which plagued him for a number of years. Nevertheless, he soon obtained a job which he held for two and a half years as a switchman on the railroad. In 1941 he was arrested for participating in a robbery and was on probation until drafted for military service. He was married in early 1942 to a nurse several years older than himself.

Private C. was sent to Hawaii shortly after induction and received his basic training there. He had not expected to be sent overseas so soon. It seemed to him as if he had suddenly been up-rooted from the relative safety of his home and placed in a position very close to the fighting. He often thought of the Japanese attack on Pearl Harbor and trembled since he felt it could happen again. He was suddenly very aware of the fact that although some men became heroes in combat, others died there.

Shortly after starting his training he began to have fainting spells and as a result was frequently excused from drill. Nevertheless, in early 1943 he was assigned to a Regular Army division as an in-fantry rifleman. This scared him even more than coming to Hawaii. It meant that he would sooner or later be expected to fight. He be-gan to have periods of extreme panic and his diarrhea troubled him more and more. By April he was in the hospital, but after ten days was returned to duty. Rumors of a move were rife on his return. In July he spent another two weeks in the hospital with severe diarrhea.

By now the rumors of impending shipment to the South Pacific had taken on some substance. Equipment was packed and last minute personnel changes made. Private C. was shifted to work in the kitchen. He felt somewhat relieved in the knowledge that at least he would not be one of the first to enter the fighting. Still, the threat of death hung over him. When it developed that his unit was being sent to Australia for further training, he felt as if a stay of execution had been granted. At least he would be safe from the enemy a while longer.

A month or so after his arrival in Australia however, an incident occurred which brought his fear to fever pitch. While riding a horse for pleasure through the countryside he wandered onto a mortar firing range and several shells landed very close to him. He began to shake all over and continued to tremble for the remainder of the day. That night he was unable to sleep at all and in the morning came down with one of the worst cases of diarrhea he had ever experienced. Occasionally he fainted. He constantly thought about fighting and death and mutilated bodies. Stories of Japanese tortures filled his mind. He was quite sure that he would be unable to control himself under combat conditions and would collapse.

He finally entered the hospital again in late October 1943. He told the doctors, "I can't control it. If I get scared, I just get scared." It was quite obvious that the soldier was in no shape to enter combat. The very thought of fighting was enough to throw him into a panic that lasted for hours and usually ended in a fainting spell. Since his outfit was definitely slated for combat duty (it later was engaged in heavy fighting on New Guinea and in the Philippines), the decision was made to return him to the United States. There he improved slightly, but he seemed unable to overcome the fear that he would be sent back to duty and returned to the Pacific. Less than two months after his return he was discharged.

Convinced at last by his discharge in February 1944 that he was safe from combat, V.S.C. improved rapidly. The fears of death and mutilation seemed almost to evaporate from his mind. He returned to the city where his wife had been living during his period of wartime service and very shortly went back to work at his former job as a switchman on the railroad. His diarrhea recurred intermittently for several months, but disappeared entirely after treatment by the company physician. His recovery was effected at this time although similar treatment by Army doctors had had no effect whatsoever. Now, however, he was free of the constant threat of death. It made all the difference in the world. He did not have to worry about each little sign that he was being moved closer and closer to the enemy.

In late 1946 V.S.C. left his job with the railroad to enter on-the-job training as a salesman with a chemical company. Four months later he quit that company to join another concern, again as a salesman. Although he had worked hard and done satisfactory work, he did not have the technical background for work in the chemical field. Consequently he decided to transfer to a company where his lack of education would place him at less of a disadvantage. He and his wife have remained happily married and have two children. The veteran is considered by the V.A. doctors to be completely cured. The mere fact of discharge from the Army, and all that the

Army meant in terms of fighting and death, coupled with the return to a peaceful environment free of impending disaster, seemed to have accomplished what no amount of treatment could in a military setting.

Some men cannot endure even the idea of being threatened by injury or death, while others can steel themselves to being exposed to danger for a period of time. When their anxiety swamps them, they become ineffective; but out of danger and away even from reminders of danger they can make a speedy and total recovery. This is what happened to both E.S. and V.S.C.

FULL EMPLOYMENT

Often, whether a man can perform satisfactorily depends on the standards which he has to meet. The veterans of World War II were indeed fortunate that the expansion of business forced many employers to adjust their standards downward. The fact that many jobs were readily available redounded to the benefit of many veterans; if they found one too difficult, they were usually able to get another more geared to their capacity.

Among the important differences between the demands of an assignment within the Army and those encountered by the ex-serviceman in a civilian job was that the military organization had to insist that a man meet its performance standards not only while on duty but during the entire twenty-four hours of the day. A civilian employer generally need not be concerned with the private lives of his work force as long as they meet the requirments of the job. This means that many men who are suffering from tension or other emotional disabilities may be able to work out a tolerable balance for themselves in civilian life because of the special adjustments that they can make off the job. This is denied them within a controlled military environment.

The full employment situation which characterized the United States in the postwar period had the additional advantage of making it possible for wives of veterans to hold the jobs which so many had taken during the war. This meant that the family would not be without all income if the veteran occasionally could not report for work.

T.L.M. and his seven brothers and sisters were raised on a farm in the Midwest. He was educated in a nearby town and, except for one year when he was unable to attend because of eye trouble, progressed normally. Throughout most of his childhood and adolescence he spent considerable time working on the family farm. After graduation from high school, however, he obtained a job as a truck driver with a large meat packing company. He continued at the job until inducted into military service at the age of twenty-two.

He spent his first ten months of service with an infantry division in the United States. Then, in October 1943 an order was issued which stripped the division of many of its trained personnel in order to meet replacement needs in Europe. Private M. was one of the men put on orders. He was shipped to a port of embarkation on the East Coast and, within a month of leaving one infantry division, had joined another in England.

A series of pre-invasion training exercises followed and on D-Day the division landed in France in the first wave. Bitter fighting continued until the end of July. Then suddenly the resistance crumbled. The division raced across France covering almost 20 miles a day. In early September they entered Belgium. Here they caught up with long columns of retreating German troops and took thousands of prisoners. Pushing on, the division reached the Siegfried Line and breached it. But enemy resistance began to stiffen. Counterattacks became more and more frequent. By the end of September the advance had slowed to a crawl.

Private M. was in the thick of the fighting throughout and served well. However, shortly after they crossed the Belgian border, he became increasingly irritable, tremulous, and fatigued. It was as if his energy had evaporated. By late September he developed a severe skin rash and had to be hospitalized for almost two weeks. On his return, his company was on the offensive after having repulsed a strong enemy counterattack. For several days they inched forward slowly moving from ruin to ruin through what had once been a city of over 150,000 inhabitants. The weather was miserable. Just a week after his release from the hospital the soldier was hit in the right leg by a fragment from an exploding mortar shell. He went back to the aid station and there the wound was treated and bandaged. By nightfall he was back in the line. Three days later the city fell, but there was no time for rest. Patrols were constantly out probing toward the enemy lines. During this action Private M.'s leg gave him more and more trouble. It began to throb and then a swelling developed. Finally he went to the aid station. Infection had set in.

Sent back to the hospital he seemed to collapse. It was as if in the heat of battle he had gone beyond his breaking point and then, in the hospital with ample time to think, disintegrated. He perspired constantly. His head jerked involuntarily and throbbed in synchrony with his wounded leg. A severe cold developed. Everytime he fell asleep he would start dreaming of combat and awaken terrified. A series of brief stays in various hospitals followed—two in Belgium, Paris, the Coast, and finally England. His physical wound healed, but the emotional one did not. By early March 1945 he was in the States. He was discharged in June and returned to his home town.

A month later he started working as a passenger bus driver. Required to meet specific schedules and unable to stop and rest when he became nervous, T.L.M. found his job difficult from the start. There were days when he could hardly bring himself to climb into the bus. And when his head started jerking as he was driving along the highways he became terrified. Finally in November he decided to quit. He did not care if he ever worked again. All he wanted was to get away from the bus. Consequently, he told his employer that he was leaving, that he needed a good rest at home—a good long rest and anyway he was a disabled veteran who had sacrificed everything for his country; he deserved a rest.

But his employer had other ideas. It was hard to get workers at any price. He had a lot of unfilled positions already and he did not want any more. The veteran might be in bad shape, but he could do something and they needed every man they could get—especially men with some experience around trucks and buses. Would T.L.M. be interested in a vacancy they had in the garage? It was not very difficult—just to help keep the buses in shape, and he would not have to take a cut in salary. True he deserved a rest, but still this job was pretty easy and the money would help.

Finally, T.L.M. agreed to keep working. And the job did turn out to be pretty easy. As a helper he did not have any specific work to be done by a specific time. There were no schedules to meet and if he felt too nervous he could just take the day off. Sometimes he lost as much as two weeks' time in a month. It was obvious they were shorthanded and some of the servicing was being delayed longer than it should be, but for that very reason there was no chance of his being fired. There just was no one around to replace him. After he had been working for a year and a half, the company developed an acute shortage of mechanics. The veteran had no formal training, but he had picked up a good deal of knowledge over the years. Somebody had to do the work and so he was promoted. For some time, however, he received no increase in salary. He was absent from work so much that a raise really did not seem justified.

Gradually he began to feel a little less nervous and the periods of sickness and headaches became less frequent. In early 1948 he got married. It made him feel better just to think he had been able to hold a job through all his difficulties—and now he was supporting his wife too. A year later their first child was born. Although he was still very nervous at times, he worked steadily. He even received several small raises. In 1952 he and his family moved to a large city not far from their home town and T.L.M. went to work

servicing trucks for a large trucking company at a wage well above
that he had been receiving. The trucking company was short of
mechanics, too, and was willing to pay to get them. The veteran
was very pleased. It made him feel stronger to think he was worth
that much money.

I.E.H. was brought up in a large Midwestern city. The
family always had a small income and in fact was on relief for a
period during the depression. Nevertheless, I.E.H. completed high
school before going to work. His grades were good, but he did
not get along well with his teachers and classmates. After graduation he was uncertain as to what he wanted to do and tried out
several different jobs before settling in a position as timekeeper in
a factory. He had been checking time cards and production records
for about a year and a half when he was drafted. Two months
prior to induction he was married.

During his period of training in the United States the soldier
performed in a satisfactory but not outstanding manner. He was
a litter bearer with the medical battalion of an infantry division.
He found the physical training rather difficult and during the
winter suffered from repeated colds. In the late summer of 1944
the division landed in England and then proceeded to the Conti-
nent. They entered combat along the coast in September and remained in that area for four months fighting a German force which
had been isolated by the drive across France.

Then in early January 1945 the division was rapidly shifted to
positions along the German border. The fighting which ensued
was extremely fierce. The division was on the offensive for almost
two weeks, but met heavy resistance. The ground was covered with
snow and the cold was intense. When Private H. had been called
on occasionally to bring wounded men in to the aid station during
the fighting on the coast, he had not experienced anything like this.
He no sooner had one man back than he had to go forward again
to pick up another. It was hard and emotionally trying work.
Sometimes the injured man died before they could get him to the

aid station. And it was often difficult to work through enemy fire to reach the wounded. But the soldier did his job well.

Finally the attack began to slacken as ammunition ran low and enemy resistance stiffened. Just before the order to pull back came through, Private H. brought a wounded man in from the front and then walked outside—the sight of the maimed men inside the station had depressed him. The chaplain came up and asked, "How is it up there?" Suddenly, the soldier went berserk. His mind went blank and he became violent.

He awoke later strapped to a hospital bed, completely unable to remember how he got there. He felt almost drunk. His vision was blurred and he was trembling. He cried easily and his speech was incoherent. Two months after his breakdown he was returned to the United States unimproved. During his subsequent hospitalization, he improved somewhat, but remained depressed and anxious —particularly when he was with other people. He found it very hard to forget about the wounded men he had seen and preferred not to talk about his experiences in combat. He was discharged in July 1945.

Back in the city, I.E.H. had no difficulty obtaining a job. The demand for people with clerical experience was, he found, great. However, it was difficult for him to work. On the job he experienced a variety of symptoms which he attributed to factors in his work environment. With so many people around he was almost constantly anxious. The noise of the talking and office machines gave him headaches. The food in the restaurants upset his stomach. He felt that his employer treated him unfairly and that made him feel weak and a little dizzy. He was irritable and could not sleep at night because of worry over problems which had come up at work. He wanted to get away from all the people, but could not get an office of his own.

As a result he held five different jobs in the two years following his discharge. He would become increasingly upset on one job until he could not stand it any more. Then he quit and started looking for another. Finding one was no problem. There were plenty of jobs available and the companies rarely asked many questions about his prior work experience. It rarely took more than a day or two to obtain a new position. After being hired the veteran would feel better for a while. It was encouraging just to know that these people thought enough of him to give him a job. Then the headaches and sleeplessness and anxiety would come back. He would move on in search of a place with less noise or nicer people or better restaurants. But in spite of his many shifts, he always kept working.

For a while in 1946 he took on-the-job training with the Veterans Administration as an accounting supervisor with a finance company. At about the same time he enrolled at a local university for courses under the G.I. Bill in the area of business administration. This lasted for less than six months. He quit both the job and the college courses, but soon obtained a new position. He felt strongly that he had to keep working to support his family. He felt that to be unable to obtain a job, as his father had been during the depression, was the lowest level to which a man could sink. In fact he felt that people like that were hardly to be considered men. But he did not have to worry about that. There always seemed to be another opening available. He never had to wait long enough between jobs to consider himself really unemployed.

He remained at the job he had taken after leaving college for less than three months. His next position was with a manufacturing concern doing general office work. He stayed for almost three years. The job paid well and he began to feel less anxious. At times he almost enjoyed the work. However, his employer felt that I.E.H. lacked any pep and initiative. He got the work done, but there were likely to be mistakes. Finally he was fired. This depressed and upset him a good deal. In fact he felt much worse at the time of losing this job than he had in several years. He feared that he might be incapable of working and supporting his family.

However, there were still plenty of jobs available and within a few days he was driving a taxi. Two months later he quit. Next came a job as a laundryman, but he did very poorly and was fired shortly after starting work. For several nights he could not sleep at all, his stomach bothered him and his head ached. He considered the job with the laundry as low-level work and to be fired from that was hard to take.

But as soon as he went to look for work, he felt reassured. Everyone seemed to want to hire him. He finally took a position doing general office work with an automobile manufacturer—a job which he still holds. Although he is still anxious, he is able to work pretty much alone. He feels that his employer is fair, the work is not too noisy, the food in the company cafeteria is all right, there are not too many problems that he has to take home with him. He feels a good deal better and thinks he will stay.

The heavy demand for labor in the postwar period contributed substantially to the readjustment of men like I.E.H. and T.L.M. If I.E.H. had not been able to find a new job soon after he left or got fired from his old job, he might have deteriorated rapidly. Now he has a good chance of making a fair adjustment.

A high level of employment meant many things to T.L.M.: an easy job when he wanted one; a chance to learn a skill when he felt better; an opportunity to capitalize on what he had learned when he wanted to earn more money following the birth of a child. The situation was so favorable that men with quite serious handicaps had relatively little difficulty in performing effectively.

Chapter Fifteen: PERSPECTIVES
ON PERFORMANCE

WE HAVE PRESENTED seventy-nine life histories of soldiers who broke down while in military service, most of whom recovered after their return to civilian life. What general conclusions can be drawn from these case materials? This concluding chapter seeks to provide new perspectives on the theory of performance based on this presentation.

One approach to new knowledge is through the use of analogy and comparison and this is the way we hope to clarify the concept of performance as we have developed it in the present volume as well as in the two related volumes. Some students of human behavior—psychologists, psychiatrists, psychoanalysts—conventionally deal with performance by considering the personality factors that can help to explain the individual's behavior or, as in therapy, the factors that are interfering with his effective performance. For the most part, then, they usually accept the environment in which the individual lives and the range of opportunities and limitations which it presents and concentrate on the internal forces, those which make up the individual's personality, in seeking to understand or change his performance.

While we include personality constellations within the scope of our inquiry, our approach to performance also includes the simultaneous consideration of the environment, that is, of organizational forces and situational pressures.

Our principal road of inquiry is to illuminate how factors in the environment can contribute to a more complete realization of the values and goals of our society as well as of the individuals who comprise it. This broad goal makes it necessary to establish a broad framework so that adequate consideration can be given to the several factors—individual, organizational, and situational—that determine performance.

For those who study performance from the point of view of the individual, the goals of inquiry and the framework of analysis are more narrowly defined. They focus usually on changes within the individual which can help to bring about a higher level of performance and personal satisfaction. These changes are usually the removal through therapy or education of barriers that have previously blocked accomplishment or the acquisition of new skills and competences.

As a result of our different approach and method, our findings will be different. Our conclusions about performance will be in terms of averages or probabilities relevant for a group, and will point in the direction of changes in policies that can affect the performance of large numbers. Understanding about the performance of an individual and how it can be altered can be acquired only through the individual approach with its concentration on the internal personality forces.

In developing our multidimensional framework for the study of performance, we have always been interested in what the resulting analysis might contribute to the more effective utilization of manpower. This has been our concern in this as in the accompanying volumes. We will now try to delineate some of the major findings that have emerged.

The individual's assets and deficiencies inevitably play a major role in determining the level of his performance, irrespective of the organization in which he finds himself or the situational pressures to which he is exposed. His physical, intellectual, and emotional qualities determine whether he can be effectively integrated into a going organization, and if he is, whether he can meet its minimum demands. Although a paralyzed man served with outstanding success as President of this country, he would have had no place in a military unit. An illiterate with a green thumb might make a good living as a farmer but he would have a hard time in a modern industrial organization which depends heavily on written communications.

Whether a man with minimum or even above minimum qualifications performs effectively frequently depends on his motivation and his values. He may possess all the specific requirements for a job except one, a willingness to perform. If the demands which are made are onerous and dangerous, as in a war, failure resulting from poor motivation is likely to be common. Or to reverse the situation: people with major handicaps frequently perform exceptionally well because they are dedicated to their task. Wrong results will accrue if in selecting personnel objective measurements are used alone. Motivation cannot be measured directly and in many instances it determines the difference between good and poor performance.

Another finding about how an individual's qualities affect his performance relates to the element of time. While adults are not likely to change their basic personality radically, no human being ever remains the same from one year to the next. Some change a lot, others little, but all change. Even if their environment remains substantially unaltered—which of course it does not—individuals still change as they get older. This means that any effort to predict on the basis of a current assessment how an individual will perform several years hence is fraught with uncertainty.

The multidimensional approach goes beyond the individual, his strengths and weaknesses, and includes a consideration of how the demands and pressures, the opportunities and supports in his environmental situation are likely to affect his performance. There is no way of assessing performance adequately except by making room for these situational forces. This lesson is imbedded in the many cases of breakdown in the Army. The pressure that war exerts on men is unique and sooner or later even the strongest may break under the strain. Fortunately most who succumb can reknit themselves once they are removed from the severe pressures, especially if they are fortunate enough to find supports in their new environment.

Since no man lives or works alone, his performance will be affected by the quality of his relationships with the individuals to whom he looks for support and leadership. Among the disturbing effects of war is the disruption in personal relationships, first when a man is separated from his family and friends, and later if he sees those with whom he has established new bonds injured or killed. Less drastic, but of the same type of disturbance, is that which takes place in an organization when the leadership is often changed. Without the security that comes from established relations to their superiors, many individuals perform poorly.

The same adverse effect on performance will result if individuals are suddenly unable to live in accordance with their values. Many young men who had been brought up in religious homes where killing for any reason was considered a sin could not adjust to being a part of an Army at war. Their performance became ineffective as a result of their conflict in values.

An analogous problem arises occasionally in business or other organizations where individuals with rigid values find it impossible to operate at maximum efficiency. They are unable to pursue their own self-interest as aggressively as many others who comply only nominally with the moral code. They prefer to lose a prized promotion or a valuable contract rather than to take advantage of another man.

While it is frequently possible to identify a particular situational factor which has a strategic impact on a man's performance, a broader perspective is required in order to reach a judgment about its significance. Human life is a continuum, and early occurrences are certain to influence later events. Many men who broke down in the Army became so seriously disturbed that it appeared unlikely that they could ever again function effectively.

But most of them did, if their earlier life had been free of pathology. When men were discharged from the Army, usually to an environment where they frequently had the help and support of their families, they were able to reknit their lives by building on their strengths. They did so slowly—a step at a time. As their military service faded into the background, their emotional stability improved; they were able to go back to school or undertake special training; they slowly gained confidence and after a while were able to find a job. Later, perhaps, they married or, if they were married, perhaps a baby was born and they had an added incentive to support themselves and their family. The process of adjustment is usually cumulative—and the pull towards health is powerful, especially in young people.

While the qualities that individuals possess and the pressures to which they are exposed will materially influence their performance, we have noted another set of determinants, those which we have subsumed under the heading of organizational policy. Good policy can facilitate successful performance just as bad policy frequently results in failure. While management is restricted in what it can and cannot do, it always has some margins of freedom and within these margins it can contribute to or retard effective performance by the policies it formulates and implements.

With the passage of time large organizations must alter their policies in order to meet the changes in people and situations. Most of the turbulent periods in American labor history reflect the failure of management to adjust its policies. Policies that contribute to effective performance at one period cannot be equally successful at another period if in the interim the situation or the individuals involved have materially changed. The proper balance between stability and change in policy remains a major challenge to every management.

Since every large organization has a large number of different tasks to perform and has a large number of different individuals under its direction, it must constantly seek to help people make use of all their capacities. Here lies the key to effective performance. If an organization's policies and procedures result in serious over- or under-assignment, the result will be a significantly lowered level of performance.

Every organization must, however, recognize that there are limits to the resources that it can afford to devote to helping people make use of all their capacities. Even an organization as large as the Army, which had to accept a large number of marginal individuals, was confronted with such limits. The Army, like all other large organizations, in fact like society itself, must always keep in sharp perspective the need to facilitate the work of those who can contribute the most while making efforts to increase the contribution of all others.

THE LESSON

WAR tries the souls of men and the spirits of nations as does no other experience. Each individual must stand up and be counted. He is expected to do things which he believes he cannot. Some can endure little; others a great deal. A nation's faith, its values and goals will largely determine its response to war.

When faced with the challenge, most young Americans performed well. Some could not because of handicapped background. Others because of errors in assignment made by the Army. Still others because they were overwhelmed by the military situation. Even a brave and patriotic man can be broken by the agonies of combat.

War took a heavy toll, but peace brought surcease. Most of those who had failed recovered. They were able to find new meaning and direction to their lives.

The lesson is a simple one. While every man has his weakness, he also has strengths. Even if he breaks down, he is likely to recover if he is aided by a loving family, a sympathetic government, and there is a place for him in an expanding economy.

SELECTED BIBLIOGRAPHY

Ahrenfeldt, Robert H. *Psychiatry in the British Army in the Second World War*. New York, Columbia University Press, 1958.

Allport, Gordon W. *The Use of Personal Documents in Psychological Science*. New York, Social Science Research Council, 1942.

Beebe, Gilbert W. and John W. Appel. *Variation in Psychological Tolerance to Ground Combat in World War II*. Washington, D.C., National Academy of Sciences—National Research Council, 1958.

Brill, Norman Q. and Gilbert W. Beebe. *A Follow-Up Study of War Neuroses*, VA Medical Monograph Series. Washington, D.C., Government Printing Office, 1955.

Cooke, Elliot D. *All But Thee and Me*. Washington, D.C., Infantry Journal Press, 1946.

Dollard, John. *Criteria for the Life History*. New Haven, Yale University Press, 1935.

Dornbusch, C. E. (comp.). *Histories of American Army Units: World Wars I and II and Korean Conflict, with Some Earlier Histories*. Washington, D.C., Department of the Army, Office of the Adjutant General, 1956.

Drayer, Calvin S. "Psychological Factors and Problems, Emergency and Long-Term," *The Annals of the American Academy of Political and Social Science*, CCCIX (1957), 151–59.

Fritz, Charles E. and Harry B. Williams. "The Human Being in Disasters: A Research Perspective," *The Annals of the American Academy of Political and Social Science*, CCCIX (1957), 42–51.

Ginsburg, Sol W. *Psychiatric Needs in Rehabilitation*. New York, New York City Committee on Mental Hygiene of the State Charities Aid Association, 1948.

——. "Values and the Psychiatrist," *American Journal of Orthopsychiatry*, XX (1950), 466–78.

Ginsburg, Sol W. and John L. Herma. "Values and their Relationship to Psychiatric Principles and Practice," *American Journal of Psychotherapy*, VII (1953), 546–73.

Ginzberg, Eli. *Grass on the Slag Heaps.* New York, Harper & Brothers, 1942.

——. *The Labor Leader.* New York, Macmillan, 1948.

Ginzberg, Eli and Associates. *Occupational Choice.* New York, Columbia University Press, 1951.

——. *The Unemployed.* New York, Harper & Brothers, 1943.

Ginzberg, Eli and Douglas W. Bray. *The Uneducated.* New York, Columbia University Press, 1953.

Gouldner, Alvin W. (ed.). *Studies in Leadership.* New York, Harper & Brothers, 1950.

Grinker, Roy R. and John P. Spiegel. *Men Under Stress.* Philadelphia, Blakiston, 1945.

——. *War Neuroses.* Philadelphia, Blakiston, 1945.

Hanson, Frederick R. (ed.). *Combat Psychiatry.* Washington, D.C., Government Printing Office, 1949.

Huie, William Bradford. *The Execution of Private Slovik.* New York, Duell, Sloan & Pearce—Little, Brown, 1954.

Kardiner, Abram and Herbert Spiegel. *War Stress and Neurotic Illness.* New York, Paul B. Hoeber, 1947.

Lewin, Kurt. *Resolving Social Conflicts.* New York, Harper & Brothers, 1948.

Lewis, Nolan D. C. and Bernice Engle (ed.). *Wartime Psychiatry: A Compendium of the International Literature.* New York, Oxford University Press, 1954.

Mead, Margaret. *And Keep Your Powder Dry.* New York, Morrow, 1942.

Menninger, William C. *Psychiatry in a Troubled World.* New York, Macmillan, 1948.

Merton, Robert K. and Paul F. Lazarsfeld (ed.). *Continuities in Social Research: Studies in the Scope and Method of "The American Soldier."* Glencoe, Ill., The Free Press, 1950.

Miner, John B. and James K. Anderson. "The Postwar Occupational Adjustment of Emotionally Disturbed Soldiers," *Journal of Applied Psychology,* XLII (1958), 317–22.

Murray, H. A. and C. D. Morgan. "A Clinical Study of Sentiments," *Genetic Psychology Monographs,* XXXII (1945), 3–149; 153–311.

Rees, John R. *The Shaping of Psychiatry by War.* New York, Norton, 1945.

Stouffer, Samuel A. and Associates. *The American Soldier: Adjustment during Army Life; The American Soldier: Combat and its*

Aftermath, Vols. I and II of Studies in Social Psychology in World War II. Princeton, N.J., Princeton University Press, 1949.

U.S. Selective Service System. *Reemployment and Selective Service*, Special Monograph No. 13. Washington, D.C., Government Printing Office, 1949.

Waller, Willard. *The Veteran Comes Back*. New York, Dryden Press, 1944.

Waller, Willard and Reuben Hill. *The Family: A Dynamic Interpretation*. New York, Dryden Press, 1951.

White, Robert W. *Lives in Progress*. New York, Dryden Press, 1952.

Woodward, Luther E. and Thomas A. C. Rennie. *Jobs and the Man*. Springfield, Ill., C. C. Thomas, 1945.

INDEX OF CASES

GENERAL INDEX